FEEDING INDIA

Food security is one of the twenty-first century's key global challenges, and lessons learned from India have particular significance worldwide. Not only does India account for approximately one quarter of the world's undernourished persons, it also provides a worrying case of how rapid economic growth may not provide an assumed panacea to food security.

This book takes on this challenge. It explains how India's chronic food security problem is a function of a distinctive interaction of economic, political and environmental processes. It contends that under-nutrition and hunger are lagging components of human development in India precisely because the interfaces between these aspects of the food security problem have not been adequately understood in policymaking communities. Only through an integrative approach spanning the social and environmental sciences are the fuller dimensions of this problem revealed. A well-rounded appreciation of the problem is required, informed by the FAO's conception of food security as encompassing availability (production), access (distribution) and utilisation (nutritional content), as well as by Amartya Sen's notions of entitlements and capabilities.

Bill Pritchard is Associate Professor of Human Geography in the School of Geosciences, University of Sydney.

Anu Rammohan is Professor of Economics in the School of Business, University of Western Australia.

Madhushree Sekher is Professor and Chairperson of the Centre for Social Exclusion and Inclusive Policies, Tata Institute of Social Sciences, Mumbai.

S. Parasuraman is Director, Tata Institute of Social Sciences, Mumbai.

Chetan Choithani is a doctoral candidate in Human Geography in the School of Geosciences, University of Sydney, and a holder of the Prime Minister's Australia–Asia Endeavour Fellowship.

"The intriguing and immensely important question that motivates this book is: 'How can a fast growing country like India have such a large part of its population that is still malnourished?' The scope of the book goes way beyond food and nutrition; it goes to the heart of the development process underway in India and introduces us to the key debates on some crucial policy issues in a lucid and open-minded way. It is a must-read for any serious student of Indian development."

– *Ashok Kotwal, Professor of Economics, The University of British Columbia, Canada*

"This important book shows how and why rapid economic growth in India has not been translated into food security for large numbers of the country's most vulnerable households. The authors convincingly show how food insecurity is not a problem of food production, or even one of food distribution; it is a problem of livelihood insecurity which, in turn, is bound up in the wider social and political structures and fissures that characterise the contemporary Indian political economy. It is thus a sobering book: addressing under-nutrition is proving to be a lot harder than promoting economic growth."

– *Jonathan Rigg, National University of Singapore*

FEEDING INDIA

Livelihoods, entitlements and capabilities

Bill Pritchard, Anu Rammohan,
Madhushree Sekher, S. Parasuraman
and Chetan Choithani

LONDON AND NEW YORK

from Routledge

First published 2014
by Routledge
2 Park Square, Milton Park, Abingdon, Oxon OX14 4RN

Simultaneously published in the USA and Canada
by Routledge
711 Third Avenue, New York, NY 10017

Routledge is an imprint of the Taylor & Francis Group, an informa business

British Library Cataloguing-in-Publication Data
A catalogue record for this book is available from the British Library

Library of Congress Cataloging-in-Publication Data
    Pritchard, Bill.
    Feeding India: livelihoods, entitlements and capabilities / Bill Pritchard,
    Anu Rammohan, Madhushree Sekher, S. Parasuraman and Chetan Choithani.
        pages cm.
    Includes bibliographical references and index.
    1. Food security–India. 2. Food supply–India.
    3. Poverty–India. 4. Agriculture–India. I. Title.
    HD9016.I42P73 2013
    338.1954–dc23
    2013007885

ISBN: 978-0-415-52966-2 (hbk)
ISBN: 978-0-415-52967-9 (pbk)
ISBN: 978-0-203-11762-0 (ebk)

Typeset in Bembo
by Swales & Willis Ltd, Exeter, Devon

Printed and bound by CPI Group (UK) Ltd, Croydon, CR0 4YY

CONTENTS

LIST OF ILLUSTRATIONS

Figures

Tables

Boxes

LIST OF ABBREVIATIONS

AAY	*Antodaya Anna Yojana* (household income classification category in PDS)
ABC Index	Achievements of Babies and Children Index
APL	Above Poverty Line (household income classification category in PDS)
BJP	Bharatiya Janata Party
BMI	Body Mass Index
BPL	Below Poverty Line (household income classification category in PDS)
CCT	Conditional Cash Transfer
CIFI	Composite Index of Food Insecurity
CIMMYT	*Centro Internacional de Mejoramiento de Maiz y Trigo*
CT	Cash Transfer
DCT	Direct Cash Transfer
DfID	Department for International Development (UK)
FAO	Food and Agriculture Organisation (of the United Nations)
FSR	Farm Systems Research (methodology)
ha	hectare
HDI	Human Development Index
HVH	High-Value Horticulture
HYV	High-Yield Variety
ICDS	Integrated Child Development Scheme
IFPRI	International Food Policy Research Institute
IHD	Institute for Human Development
ILO	International Labour Organisation
kj	kilojoule
MDER	Minimum Dietary Energy Requirements

MDG	Millennium Development Goal
MDMS	Midday Meal Scheme
MESA	Portuguese acronym for the Government of Brazil's "Extraordinary Ministry of Food Security and Fight Against Hunger"
MGNREGA	Mahatma Gandhi National Rural Employment Guarantee Act
MGNREGS	Mahatma Gandhi National Rural Employment Guarantee Scheme
MSP	Minimum Support Price
NAC	National Advisory Council (Government of India)
NCEUS	National Commission for Enterprises in the Unorganised Sector
NFHS	National Family Health Survey
NFSB	National Food Security Bill
NGO	Non-Government Organisation
NRLM	National Rural Livelihood Mission
NSS	National Sample Survey
NSSO	National Sample Survey Organisation
OBC	Other Backward Caste
OECD	Organisation for Economic Cooperation and Development
PDS	Public Distribution System
PER	Purchase-Entitlement Ratio
PoU	Prevalence of Undernourishment
PUCL	People's Union for Civil Liberties
SC	Scheduled Caste
SHI	State Hunger Index
SLA	Sustainable Livelihoods Approach
SMR	Suicide Mortality Rate
SoFI	*State of Food Insecurity* (FAO annual report)
SRI	System of Rice Intensification
ST	Scheduled Tribe
TANDI	Tackling the Agriculture-Nutrition Disconnect in India (research project)
TPDS	Targeted Public Distribution System
UK	United Kingdom
UNCESCR	United Nations Committee on Economic, Social and Cultural Rights
UNDP	United Nations Development Program
UNICEF	United Nations Children's Fund
UPA	United Progressive Alliance
US	United States
WFP	World Food Programme
WHO	World Health Organisation
WPI	Wholesale Price Index
WTO	World Trade Organisation
ZH	Zero Hunger (Brazilian food security program)

ACKNOWLEDGEMENTS

The origins of this book lie in a series of long car trips in rural India. During 2011, three of the authors (Pritchard, Rammohan and Sekher) were involved in administering and supervising village-level surveys of food security in field sites stretching across nine Indian states. In the hours spent together driving along dusty Indian roads, we agreed that our collective insights into the "big picture" of food insecurity in India should be brought together in a single publication. We would like to thank Earthscan (and Tim Hardwick and Ashley Wright, specifically) for enabling this idea to become a reality.

The surveys mentioned above, and the background research for this book, were funded through the Australian Research Council, Project 1094112 ("Institutions for Food Security: Global Insights from Rural India").

1

INTRODUCTION

The Indian food security enigma

Raju (not his real name) is a married man in his late fifties who lives in a rural village in the state of Haryana, approximately 200 km north of New Delhi. Along with his wife, he was born in the village to a family without economic status or social privilege, and, through his entire life, has barely travelled out of his immediate surrounds. As he was the youngest of five children and without a mother (who died when he was an infant), Raju's childhood was defined by hard-scrabble existence. His father had six hectares on which he grew traditional cereal crops, but, without any access to irrigation, he was held to the mercy of the annual monsoon. Raju remembers that in the mud ("kacha") house of his childhood his regular meal would be chapattis with chutney. Fresh fruits and vegetables were eaten only when he and his brothers were able to steal some from the fields of local landowners. He recalls "almost never" eating dal. The only source of protein he would receive was the milk from the one family buffalo. Sometimes, for two or three days, the family would eat only one meal a day, which would be chapatti with salt. He has never attended a day of school in his life and is completely illiterate.

While in his twenties, Raju's father passed away and left a mountain of debt. Family squabbles over inheritance ensued, and the family's land was lost. Raju then worked as a field labourer, but now is too frail for heavy duties and so does only the occasional unpaid odd job for a local landowner (in exchange for which he is given grazing rights for his sole buffalo). His single daughter is married and lives in another village. Of his two sons, the elder has a regular job in a local store, and the other has been bonded to a local landowner for field labouring duties. When his second son has completed a year of work for the local landowner, Raju's family will receive Rs 40,000 (approximately US$800). Some aspects of Raju's life have improved. He now lives with his wife in a brick ("pucca") house, and, for about half the day, has electricity to run a fan and lightbulbs. But their nutritional circumstances remain dire. The couple survives on a daily diet of chapatti, chutney, milk from the family buffalo, tea and sugar. They consume potatoes occasionally (usually provided as gifts from local landowners), and eat fresh vegetables and dal only rarely.

Raju's story was told to us in 2011 during a visit to his village in Haryana. By no means is it unusual. Indeed, it is emblematic of the life circumstances of millions of people across rural India. Two decades of dizzying economic transformation in India seem to have barely touched an enormous proportion of India's population. To walk through many of India's villages is to witness both the hope and betrayal of economic change. Trickle-down consumerism has led to small stores being swaddled in advertising banners for cell phone offers. Look upwards and every second house, it seems, has a satellite dish. New-model motorbikes dodge cows in crowded laneways. Chat with locals, and talk turns quickly to relatives in Delhi, Mumbai, Bangalore, Dubai or Frankfurt. But behind so many of the closed doors in those same villages live households barely surviving. Many people's existences remain bound by social relations that inscribe lives of drudgery, poverty and undernourishment.

To such observations, optimists would counter that India's contemporary "growth spurt" is barely two decades old, and the development challenge for a country as large as India should not be underestimated. These are fair points. Certainly it is not our intention to decry the very considerable economic achievements attained by India since the early 1990s. But yet, the recent Indian experience of growth remains troubling. Seen in international terms, India's GDP growth is contributing too anaemically to the reduction of poverty and food security. This failure has been labelled the Indian "enigma" (Ramalingaswami *et al.*, 1996; Headey *et al.*, 2011; Gillespie and Kadiyala, 2011; Walton, 2009).

The arithmetic of the Indian enigma is as follows. For most developing countries, the prevalence of children underweight for age (a good measure of under-nutrition) falls by roughly half the rate of GDP growth. Thus, if an economy's annual growth averages 4 per cent over a decade, the prevalence of children underweight for age would be expected to fall by 2 per cent annually (Haddad *et al.*, 2003). India, however, has not followed this model. Had international trends applied to India, the nation's average annual GDP growth of 4.2 per cent between 1990 and 2005 should have reduced the prevalence of underweight children by 2.1 per cent annually, or 27 per cent in total over this 15-year period. In fact, this measure of food insecurity fell by just a meagre 10 per cent between 1990 and 2005 (Gillespie and Kadiyala, 2011). Thus, in India, booming economic growth has not reduced under-nutrition at the rate that might have been expected, had international experience applied. India is growing richer, but the spoils of that wealth are not fattening as many pockets and stomachs as comparative international expectations anticipate.

This problem contextualises this book. The notion of India as a food security enigma – a country whose recent experiences with regards to economic progress and hunger alleviation are seemingly at odds – suggests that the Indian case has international significance. For if booming India can make only weak progress in combating food insecurity, what hope is there for developing countries with more modest economic performances? What does the apparent intractability of India's food security problem tell us about the specifics of the Indian condition that may resonate (positively or negatively) elsewhere?

The contribution we make to this problem is to argue that the cause of food insecurity in India is not fundamentally about food *per se*, but about the extent to which the country's marginalised populations are empowered with the rights, freedoms and capabilities that enable them to attain healthy and nourished lives. Through this approach, the discourse on India's food insecurity enigma is recast as a problem of livelihoods. As suggested by Ramalingaswami *et al.* (1996), we see the roots of malnutrition in India running "deep into social soils". Thus, what has been described as a food security problem in India requiring *food policy* solutions actually reflects the manifestations of a socially lop-sided development trajectory which requires broad-ranging, *livelihood policy* responses.

Interpreting the Indian food security enigma (i): rights, freedoms and capabilities

It is an important moment in time to address the problem of food insecurity in India. Since the late 1990s, the concept of the *right to food* has gained heightened political and ideological significance, both in India and globally. The right to food is a concept in international treaties and humanitarian law that asserts individuals' rights to live in dignity, free from hunger and under-nutrition. In 1999, the United Nations Committee on Economic, Social and Cultural Rights specified three core principles for governments, in order that these rights be adhered to. These are *the obligation to respect* (not to take any measures that arbitrarily deprive people of their right to food), *the obligation to protect* (enforce appropriate laws and take other relevant measures to prevent third parties, including individuals and corporations, from violating the right to food of others) and *the obligation to fulfil* (that govern-ments must proactively engage in activities intended to strengthen people's access to and utilisation of resources so as to facilitate their ability to feed themselves) (UNCESCR, 1999: 5; Ziegler, 2012). The following year, a Special Rapporteur on the Right to Food was appointed by the United Nations with responsibilities to monitor compliance and progress on these obligations. Then, in 2004, the Food and Agricultural Organisation (FAO) Council gave further substance to this issue by adopting a set of 19 *Voluntary Guidelines* which specified how member states should ensure their right to food obligations are met (FAO, 2005).

From an Indian perspective, the appointment of the Special Rapporteur and the formulation of the FAO *Voluntary Guidelines* occurred contemporaneously with intensified domestic debate over these issues. This debate was triggered by the submission of a Writ Petition to the Supreme Court of India in April 2001 by People's Union for Civil Liberties (PUCL), an umbrella civil society organisation. The writ – *PUCL vs. Union of India and Others (Writ Petition [Civil] No. 196 of 2001)* – argued that because Article 21 of the Indian Constitution enshrined the right to life, it followed that the Government of India had a constitutional responsibility to ensure all citizens had adequate food. Subsequent to the writ being lodged, the Supreme Court handed down a large number of Interim Orders which compelled the central and state Governments of India to take various actions in support of the right to food. These included such requirements as widening the eligibility criteria for public food distribution, ensuring people's awareness of their entitlement rights and the provisioning of midday meals in schools and child nutrition and health services provided through the Integrated Child Development Scheme (ICDS) (Jaishankar and Dreze, 2005). For compliance with these Orders, the Supreme Court appointed two commissioners, who were supported by a network of advisors across most states.

The combination of "top-down" considerations from the international (FAO) arena and "bottom-up" pressure from public interest litigation provided the catalyst for action from the Government of India. After the 2009 General Elections, the Congress-Party-led United Progressive Alliance (UPA) Government announced an intention to give national legislative backing to the right to food. In 2010, work commenced on drafting a *Food Security Bill*. Although the precise dimensions of the Government of India's food security legislation have not been resolved at the time of writing, the overarching premise of this legislative response is manifest: it makes protection against hunger a justiciable right, enabling legal action to be taken against the Government of India for shortcomings in the provisioning of people with food.

These rights-based perspectives on food are complemented by conceptualising food security through the notions of freedoms and capabilities. The right to food is a hollow concept unless it is linked to the question of whether people are able to exercise, agitate and act to ensure this right is met. This brings into the frame the need for a *human-centred* focus. The issue of food security is understood not in terms of how much food is produced, but, rather, whether and how those in need gain access to that food.

This general premise might appear beguilingly simple, but the application of a theoretical framework based around the concepts of freedoms and capabilities raises substantial and difficult economic, philosophical and moral concerns. As explored and developed in the career-long work of Amartya Sen (inter alia, Sen, 1981; 1985; 1987; 1988; 1992; 1999; 2009), deployment of these concepts requires review of core notions which are at the heart of how individuals are connected to society. These considerations begin with the issue of entitlements. Sen (1981) contends that the ownership and possession of goods are social acts which reflect ownership rights legitimised through reference to other ownership rights. Hence, in his famous example:

I own this loaf of bread. Why is this ownership accepted? Because I got it by exchange through paying some money I owned. Why is my ownership of that money accepted? Because I got it by selling a bamboo umbrella owned by me. Why is my ownership of the bamboo umbrella accepted? Because I made it with my own labour using some bamboo from my land. Why is my ownership of the land accepted? Because I inherited it from my father. Why is his ownership of that land accepted? And so on. Each link in this chain of entitlement relations 'legitimizes' one set of ownership by reference to another, or to some basic entitlement in the form of enjoying the fruits of one's own labour.

(Sen, 1981, pp. 1–2)

Based on this set of principles, Sen theorises how individuals possess particular endowed "ownership bundles" (their land, the financial resources, rights under law, their ability to be employed, their positions within networks of mutual obligation and responsibility, etc.), which enable the acquisition and exchange of goods and services, including food (Devereux, 2001: 246). Sen asserts that an appreciation of "exchange entitlement mapping" (the abilities or restrictions on individuals to create differently composed ownership bundles – exchanging their labour for cash, for example) is central to an understanding of individuals' access to food resources.

The entitlements approach provides an analytical tool to help explain the social topography of food deprivation. But however useful this framework might promise, applied in isolation it contributes little in the way of normative assessment. It does not necessarily answer questions about how these outcomes might be evaluated. For this, it is necessary to move onto the concept of *capabilities* and the connected debate on freedoms and justice.

Through the capabilities approach, the entitlements with which individuals are endowed are interpreted in light of how they enable aspirations to be met. Hence, what matters is not the quantity of material possessions or abstract rights an individual has, but the extent to which this facilitates an enlargement of their *capability space* – "the extent of freedom people have to promote or achieve objectives they value" (Alkire, 2002: 4). This perspective places people at the analytical centre of research (Clark, 2009: 21). As Sen writes: "If a traditional way of life has to be sacrificed to escape grinding poverty or minuscule longevity, then it is the people directly involved who must have the opportunity to participate in deciding what should be chosen" (Sen, 1999: 31; see also Deneulin, 2006: 2).

Taking this a step further, development is consequently understood in terms of the removal of *unfreedoms* which otherwise constrain people's abilities to lead the lives they reasonably wish. In this sense, Sen articulates a classically liberalist philosophy. The object of inquiry is the question of how societal norms, customs, institutions and behaviour act to create the preconditions for a "good life" (Deneulin, 2002; Robeyn, 2005: 101). From these foundations, development is equated in terms of an expansion of people's *substantive freedoms*: "Viewing development in terms of expanding substantive freedoms directs attention to the ends that make development important, rather than merely to some of the means that, inter alia, play a prominent part of the process" (Sen 1999: 3).

Sen (1999: 17) continues:

> [T]he view of freedom that is being taken here involves both the "processes" that allow freedom of actions and decisions, and the actual "opportunities" that people have, given their personal and social circumstances. Unfreedom can arise either through inadequate processes (such as the violation of voting privileges or other political or civil rights) or through inadequate opportunities that some people have for achieving what they minimally would like to achieve (including the absence of such elementary opportunities as the capability to escape premature mortality or preventable morbidity or involuntary starvation).

Ingrid Robeyns (2005: 96) has referred specifically to the role of social and cultural practices in achieving capability:

> For some of these capabilities, the main input will be financial resources and economic production, but for others it can also be political practices and institutions, such as the effective guaranteeing and protection of freedom of thought, political participation, social or cultural practices, social structures, social institutions, public goods, social norms, traditions and habits. The capability approach thus covers all dimensions of human well-being.

The logic of this perspective hinges on the way that a person's *functionings* connect to her/his capabilities. In their most straightforward sense, functionings are "what individuals may value doing or being" (Schischka *et al.*, 2008: 231). They are "distinct aspects of living conditions or different achievements in living a certain type of life" (Deneulin, 2006: 4). Capabilities are then the extent to which functionings can be met (Smith and Seward, 2009: 218; Corbridge, 2002: 188). A person's capabilities are established through their possession of various *conversion factors*, including their personal attributes (metabolism, health, intelligence, etc.), their social contexts (their position with regards to public amenities, gender and social norms, societal hierarchies, etc.) and their situation with regards to environmental goods (their access to land, natural resources, etc.) (Sen, 1992; Robeyn, 2005: 99; Zheng, 2009: 70). Hence, as an example, if an individual's functionings include enjoyment from reading, the extent to which she or he is literate defines her/his capabilities, which in turn are shaped by the conversion factors at her/his disposal. The accumulation of an individual's functioning-capability relationships then defines their capability space (Sen, 1987: 36).

The nuanced terminology of the capabilities approach may appear somewhat aloof to the practical problems at the heart of this book. However, establishing these principles provides a fundamental plank for the strategy we use to address the debate on food insecurity in India. This occurs through four ways.

Firstly, the capability approach frames the issue of food security within a broader conceptualisation of people's lives. Therefore, it is the conduct of those lives, not the particularities of the food system, which should be the focal point of inquiry. This is an important point to make in light of the direction of much research literature on food security. The spike in global food prices in 2007–08 also prompted a spike of researcher attention on issues relating to food security (Rosin *et al.*, 2012). But in our view, much of this literature presented the issue in terms that were somewhat detached from ongoing problems of development and poverty. It was as if food insecurity was suddenly discovered as a problem, without due regard to the longstanding livelihood contexts which defined vulnerable people's worlds. The iteration of substantial freedoms in the capabilities literature provides a palliative to such tendencies. As Deneulin (2006: 1) suggests, "The end of development is multidimensional". Perceived this way, under-nutrition and hunger are important to understand because of their implications in creating unfreedoms in terms of people's social and economic and civic participation. As Sen (1999: 4) argues: "Sometimes the lack of substantial freedoms relates directly to economic poverty, which robs people of the freedom to satisfy hunger, or to achieve sufficient nutrition." As discussed later in this book, under-nutrition (especially in children) is a catalyst that unleashes a much wider array of unfreedoms through people's lives, including poorer health, reduced workforce participation and lesser educational outcomes. Moreover, the highly gendered character of under-nutrition can entrench patterns of gender inequality. The capability approach alerts us to these flow-through implications, ensuring that the issue of food insecurity is referenced by way of its broader relevance for livelihoods.

Secondly, the capability approach throws down a challenge to discourses which channel the portrayal of food security problems narrowly via the prisms of national GDP and economic growth. As an example of this discourse, the WTO has argued that the imperative to raise income levels through economic growth needs to be at the heart of a global food security agenda (WTO, 2005). Such perspectives, of course, hold an important element of truth; poor countries are more likely to suffer from higher rates of under-nutrition than (financially) richer ones. Moreover, as discussed at the outset of this chapter, international development researchers have documented a cross-national relationship between GDP growth rates on the one hand, and declining under-nutrition on the other. But at the same time, the incidence and patterning of food insecurity cannot be explained solely within the lens of macroeconomic national performance (Pritchard, 2012). This, in fact, is the principal argument pursued in the FAO's *State of Food Insecurity* report (SoFI) for 2012. The report draws attention to the need for public policies which make economic growth inclusive, and which help enable poor and vulnerable populations to break the cycle of hunger (FAO, 2012). The capability approach helps navigate this complexity because of its dialogue with welfare economics. The traditional route in welfare economics is to use the concepts of utility-maximisation and Pareto efficiency to measure social good. This approach suggests that the structuring of society is optimal when no-one's utility can be improved without reducing someone else's utility. For Sen and other researchers using the capability approach, the principle of Pareto efficiency measured through utility (otherwise analogous to happiness or desire-fulfilment: Robeyn, 2005: 94) is wrong-headed because it doesn't convey social good in terms of firstly ensuring the needs of the most vulnerable are met. Sen (1993) contends that the welfarist conception of utility gives insufficient recognition to the prioritisation of meeting what he labels basic capabilities: "the freedom to do some basic things that are necessary for survival and to avoid or escape poverty" (Robeyn, 2005: 101). Nussbaum (2001; 2003) goes further, developing a list of the "definite set of capabilities as the most important ones to protect" (2003: 33). This normative premise within the capability approach (*vis-à-vis* the agnosticism of consumer preference assumptions in traditional welfare economics) has key relevance to the subject matter of this book. It stresses the importance of understanding economic growth as grounded in the lives of the poor, rather than generically assuming that economic growth is a process which will "lift all boats".

Thirdly, the conception of *substantive freedoms* in the capability approach has important implications for rights-based policy responses to food security. As noted above, rights-based approaches are currently highly influential in food security debates, both in India and across the world. The application of these approaches, however, is often accompanied by considerable tension and policy dispute. At issue is the extent to which rights expressed as legal obligations translate into manifest changes in individuals' circumstances. Legal rights require monitoring and enforcement if they are to be meaningful. The concept of substantive freedoms gets around this problem by focusing on the enacted reality of how rights are delivered to individuals, rather than rights as abstract obligations. As Sen (2005: 155) argues, "the freedom to have any particular thing can be substantially distinguished from actually having that thing. What a person is free to have – not just what he actually has – is relevant, I have argued, to a theory of justice."

With specific relevance to food security and legal rights, the concept of substantive freedoms implies a human-centric frame of reference. It suggests an analytical approach which commences from the position of identifying the gap between people's capabilities and their functionings, and then asks how the provision of rights to food would address this. The effect is to assess rights-based initiatives by looking outwards from the lived realities of people, so that analytical efforts are anchored to their substantiation, not their promise.

Finally, the capability approach calls to attention the moral dimension of food security issues. By constructing a conceptual architecture about food security in the context of individuals' *unfreedoms*, the default orientation of the capability approach is to question why people's functionings (what they value doing and being) are *not* met. As Sen (2009: 22) explains:

> The perspective of social realisations, including the actual capabilities that people can have, takes us inescapably to a large variety of further issues that

turn out to be quite central to the analysis of justice and injustice in the world.

Interpreting the Indian food security enigma (ii): sustainable livelihoods

The second main conceptual framework deployed in this book is the sustainable livelihoods approach, or SLA. This approach helps give concrete expression to concepts that otherwise may appear abstract. Thus, instead of examining people's right to food in isolation, SLA provides a framework to assess the livelihood strategies people use to bring this into reality.

The SLA approach has its origins in actor-oriented development research in the 1980s. In 1984, Robert Chambers conceptualised post-Green-Revolution agrarian challenges in terms of a need for "pluralist reasoning" (Chambers, 1984: 366). A few years later, Chambers *et al.* (1989) articulated these emergent themes through the Farm Systems Research (FSR). Then, in 1991, the SLA approach was formally laid out by Chambers and Gordon R. Conway in a Discussion Paper published by the Institute of Development Studies (IDS). Their seminal definition specified:

> A livelihood comprises people, their capabilities and their means of living, including food, income and assets. Tangible assets are resources and stores, and intangible assets are claims and access. A livelihood is environmentally sustainable when it maintains or enhances the local and global assets on which livelihoods depend, and has net beneficial effects on other livelihoods. A livelihood is socially sustainable which can cope with and recover from stress and shocks, and provide for future generations.
>
> *(Chambers and Conway, 1991: 6)*

SLA gained immediate traction in development studies. Thematically, it appeared to hold greater integrative and flexible possibilities over the reductionist "production thinking", "employment thinking" and "poverty-line thinking", based around the gathering of data to "fit within pre-set boxes", which had come to dominate rural development research (Chambers and Conway, 1991: 2). In terms of research practice, it emphasised qualitative and grounded methods which drew the concrete life experiences of the rural poor into centre stage. Focussing on the assets (tangible and intangible) of people and households (a framework which morphed over time into what became known as the "five capitals" perspective) implied that researchers had to *get to know* the detail of their research subjects/participants. This frame of reference dovetailed with the "turn to the local" in 1990s social science under the influence of postmodern and post-structuralist ontology. In terms of foci, it deployed a heightened consideration of environmental concerns and intergenerational perspectives. This meshed with elevated political concerns for sustainability in the closing decades of the twentieth century, with particular reference to the concepts of coping strategies, adaptation and resilience. And finally, but perhaps most importantly, the approach garnered rapid support from leading global NGOs (Oxfam in 1993; CARE International in 1994) and then policy sponsorship from the UK Department for International Development (DfID) (from 1996) (Solesbury, 2003). Hence, the approach was quickly established on the front line of donor practice, building a buzz around the concept which encouraged wider emulation.

Although the approach was not doctrinaire in proposing a single *way of doing* sustainable livelihood analysis, most researchers and practitioners tended to follow a standard path, asking a similar range of questions. This involved a fourfold research procedure: (i) outlining the particular context (of policy setting, politics, history, agro-ecology and socioeconomic conditions) which prefigures peoples' lives; (ii) assessment of the combination of livelihood resources (different types of "capital": physical, social, financial, natural and human) which shape livelihood possibilities; (iii) interpretation of how these livelihood possibilities translate into livelihood strategies; and (iv) consideration of the ways in which the institutional environment (encompassing formal and informal practices and organisations: Neilson and Pritchard, 2009: 48–55) can be mediated to construct more advantageous and sustainable livelihood circumstances (Scoones, 2005: 3)

For the purposes of the current discussion, item (iii) above holds particular relevance. Sustainable livelihoods researchers identified livelihood possibilities (embodied in people's "capitals") as being translated into three broad types of strategy: agricultural intensification and/or extensification, livelihood diversification and migration. Thus:

> Either you gain more of your livelihood from agriculture (including livestock rearing, aquaculture, forestry, etc.) through processes of intensification (more output per unit area through capital investment or increases in labour inputs) or extensification (more land under cultivation), or you diversify to a range of off-farm income earning activities, or you move away and seek a livelihood, either temporarily or permanently, elsewhere. Or, more commonly, you pursue a combination of strategies together or in sequence.
>
> *(Scoones, 2005: 9)*

This tripartite framework for categorising livelihood strategies parallels the arguments of Kuznets (1971) who observed that social and economic transformations take place through intersections of scalar processes (increasing the size of agricultural units), sectoral processes (shifts from agricultural to non-agricultural activities) and spatial processes (movements from rural to urban environments) (see Deshingkar and Farrington, 2009: 7). Of specific interest to this book, decisions by individuals and households to go down any of these livelihood strategy pathways are shaped by, and have implications for, food insecurity. Lack of food can be both a constraint to the pursuit of livelihood strategies (because of its effect in weakening people's human capital through under-nutrition and poor health) and an inspiration or incentive for people to follow particular livelihood pathways (the need to gain improved access to food may trigger specific strategies).

From calories to capabilities: the concept of food security defined

With the conceptual framework of this book set forth, the next step is to present a pathway for defining and analysing the problem. Evidently, the quest to understand food security issues in India necessarily requires that we establish the terms of the problem (Box 1.1). Beginning with a nutritional perspective, a single person suffers from undernourishment when they are consuming "too few essential nutrients or using or excreting them more rapidly than they can be replaced" in order to "maintain healthy tissues and organ function" (Farlex, 2012). Nutritional requirements for a healthy life differ among individuals in terms of age, gender and levels of physical activity. The FAO has calculated Minimum Dietary Energy Requirements (MDER) as typically ranging "from as low as 1,600 to 2,000 kilocalories [6,700 to 8,370 kilojoules] per person per day" (FAO, 2008: 8). Using these yardsticks, national estimations of the proportion of populations

---

BOX 1.1 NUTRITIONAL CONCEPTS IN THE FOOD SECURITY DEBATE

Under-nutrition or undernourishment signifies intake deficiencies in energy, protein and vitamins and/or low levels of conversion efficiency of food consumed, resulting in weak physical status.

Micronutrients are the essential dietary substances needed in small quantities which enable the body to produce several enzymes and hormones required for proper growth and development. The lack or absence of micronutrients in the body could significantly hamper the physical and mental development and a weakened immune system also increases the risk of disease and death.

Basal Metabolic Rate denotes the amount of energy (measured in calories/ kilojoules) the body burns at rest in order to maintain its normal functioning. While this depends on individual physical characteristics such as age, sex and body mass, it typically accounts for more than half of energy used.

Hunger refers to uneasiness and discomfort associated with lack of food. The Food and Agriculture Organisation stipulates that the average MDER per capita is 1,800 calories (7,560 kilojoules) per day. Thus, those persons whose food intake is lower than this minimum dietary threshold are considered to suffer from hunger. It must be noted, however, that energy needs vary from one individual to another and are contingent on a person's age, body size and weight and activity level, and exogenous factors such as prevalence of infection and disease.

not obtaining MDERs have been calculated through a series of complicated statistical procedures which connect demographic information on age, gender and physical activity (different kinds of work) with Body Mass Index (BMI) reference tables, national food balance sheets and household budget surveys (FAO Statistics Division, 2008), expressed as "prevalence of undernourishment" (PoU). In the FAO's most recent hunger prevalence estimates (published in 2012), food losses at retail level have also been accounted for (FAO-SoFI, 2012). By these means, the FAO calculated that there were 868 million hungry people in the world during 2010–12 (FAO-SoFI, 2012). Compared with the published estimate of 925 million undernourished people in FAO-SoFI (2011), the most recent data would seem on the surface to represent an estimated decline of 60 million hungry people; however, to a great extent, this shift is reflective of methodological changes.[1] As repeatedly noted by the FAO in its annual reports, these levels of hunger still remain unacceptably high.

Notwithstanding the recent revision in the PoU, the existing gaps in the availability and quality of the data used to quantify the magnitude of hunger imply that the methodological debate on the subject matter continues (FAO-SoFI, 2012: 13). Efforts are constantly underway, therefore, to devise a methodology that not only provides more precise cross-country estimates of prevalence of food deprivation, but one that also captures various facets of hunger. Because of the ongoing methodological debate about how to measure global levels of under-nutrition, this book does not focus extensively on these numerical issues. However, two related issues are worth mentioning briefly. The first of these concerns the relationship between *food* security and *nutrition* security. As noted above, the FAO's methodology focuses on MDERs rather than a more broadly based conceptualisation of nutrition. Yet in addition to obtaining a minimum amount of kilojoules for daily life, an individual's longer-term health also requires an adequate intake of essential micronutrients (vitamins, minerals and trace elements). Food security is a bigger issue than just quantity of food. Specifically, the consumption/availability of adequate micronutrients is critical, especially for infants and young children. Ensuring that sufficient quality and quantity of food is given to individuals, especially at earlier stages, can pave the way for healthy development that will be critical as they grow older and as adults. This deficiency is labelled hidden hunger, and is deemed to afflict "a far greater swath of humanity than insufficient calorie intake" (Cohen *et al.*, 2008: 14). Hence, from a nutrition security perspective, it could be argued that the FAO methodology understates the full extent of under-nutrition in the world today.

Coming from an altogether different perspective, the economists Banerjee and Duflo (2011) contend that the FAO's methodology does not capture a comprehensive picture of the relationship between poor people and under-nutrition. Their argument is quite complex, but boils down to the need to reconcile a series of apparent contradictions between different sources of evidence about the food security status of poor people. The crux of the problem is that whereas many people in the world do not eat enough to attain full dietary and nutrition needs over the longer term, survey data from an array of countries (including India) indicates the seemingly perverse conclusion that these same people often perceive themselves as "having enough food", and that over time, the proportion of their household budgets devoted to food seems to be falling (Banerjee and Duflo, 2011: 23–25). Drawing from these findings, one of the key messages of the 2012 FAO *State of Food Insecurity* report is "the need for poor people to spend their additional spending for improving the quantity and quality of their diets and for availing better health and sanitation services" (FAO-SoFI, 2012: 15). In India, the apparent contradictions between the high measured incidence of under-nutrition and the fact that the poor people "do not seem to want to eat much more even when they can" (Banerjee and Duflo, 2011: 25) will be revisited in the latter section of Chapter Two. For the current purposes in this chapter, however, these arguments are important because of the cautionary note they invoke. Just because an individual or household is measured as being undernourished does not necessarily imply that they do not have the financial or productive resources to redress this circumstance. And nor does it imply that if they obtain additional income, they will spend it on food. Notwithstanding the obviously constrained life opportunities and dire livelihood circumstances of the world's poor, their agency needs to be acknowledged. In contexts of grinding poverty, people may choose to constrain their food consumption in exchange for expenditure that enhances their social status (spending on weddings, for instance) or personal well-being (alcohol or television). As suggested by Banerjee and Duflo: "The basic need for a pleasant life might explain why food spending has been declining in India" (2011: 37). Whilst recognition of this point does not abrogate the importance of food and nutritional security for all, it alerts researchers to the need to ensure they interpret these issues from the perspective of the poor.

The nutritional perspective addressed above focuses at the individual level on the relationship between food intake and bodily functions. These issues provide the vital foundational context for analysing these issues but, in terms of the ambitions of this book, take us only so far. Whilst providing the basis for calculating the prevalence of under-nutrition, they provide little basis for asking how and why these outcomes occur. For this, the metabolic notion of under-nutrition needs expanding into the social scientific concept of *food security*.

This concept was defined at the 1974 World Food Conference as: "Availability at all times of adequate world food supplies of basic foodstuffs to sustain a steady expansion of food consumption and to offset fluctuations in production and prices" (FAO, 2006: 1). However, it became apparent through the second half of the 1970s and the 1980s that this definition was inappropriate. Profound shifts in researchers' understandings of these issues, pioneered through the entitlements approach of Sen (1981), explained above, conceived hunger not simply through the prism of food availability, but through the political arrangements connecting people to food. This perspective radically reshaped official notions of how food security should be conceptualised. By the time of the 1996 World Food Summit, food security was redefined away from its previous, production-centric, emphasis. The new definition of food security held that: "Food security exists when all people, at all times, have physical, social and economic access to sufficient, safe and nutritious food that meets their dietary needs and food preferences for an active and healthy life" (FAO, 1996).

The new definition of food security framed the concept in terms of the ability of a food system to meet the nutritional needs of a population – not its ability to reach a particular production threshold *per se*. In order to animate this perspective into a policy-relevant framework, the FAO held that the attainment of food security required attention to the interplay of three processes:

- food availability: the supply-side factors which shape the availability of sufficient quantities of food of appropriate quality;
- food access: the political, social, cultural and economic processes that connect supply-side processes to individuals; and
- food utilisation: the elements of clean water, sanitation and health care that ensure that food generates nutritional well-being for consumers.

This evolution of food security from a production-centred to a social-centred perspective progressed hand-in-glove with the shift to the capability approach and rights-based perspectives. In an institutional sense, the reorientation of development theory along these lines was influentially carried forward by Sen and his colleague Mahbub ul Huq via the United Nations Development Program's (UNDP's) Human Development Index (HDI) and annual *Human Development Report* (the first of which was published in 1990). These interventions challenged pre-existing top-down paradigms of development, which held that the "getting prices right" logics of liberal market deregulation would serve pre-eminently to assist the global poor (UNDP, 2010). Although not critical a priori of market liberalisation, adherents to these human-centred approaches critiqued policy in terms of how it responded to the "bottom-up" needs of the poor. Vulnerable people were seen not as "objects" in development agendas, but subjects with agency whose needs, wants and aspirations (their functionings, as discussed above) framed the dimensions of the development problem. Thus, in the paradigms which carried forward the Human Development project, the crucible of purpose was whether particular sets of changes (to policies, or economic conditions, etc.) led to the enlargement of peoples' choices.

The way forward: navigating the remainder of this book

The chapters which follow seek to build an expansive understanding of why food insecurity in India persists the way it does. By grounding the definition of food security in terms of people's entitlements, and then framing their deprivations by way of capabilities and functionings, we tell the story of under-nutrition in India through the social and economic circumstances of vulnerable people.

The order and structure of the remaining chapters reflects these logics. Chapter Two establishes the dimensions of the food security problem in India. The chapter investigates trends in the extent and character of under-nutrition, and probes the geographical, gendered and social manifestations of current patterns. Chapter Three then sets out the dynamics of agricultural production which provide the grounded context for *feeding India*. This chapter addresses the dilemma of why India has progressively and successfully increased its production of food grains, thus becoming food self-sufficient at a national level, yet been less successful in terms of addressing its number of undernourished. To investigate this question, the history of the Green Revolution and its aftermath is scrutinised. The chapter concludes by returning to the need for a holistic approach to food security that looks beyond issues of production.

The scene-setting discussion of Chapters Two and Three then leads into consideration of the food security problem of India as seen through the concepts of livelihoods, capabilities and entitlements. The presentation of material is designed to connect the two seminal frameworks in this topic area discussed above: the classification of food entitlement regimes developed by Sen (1981), and the classification of sustainable livelihood strategies developed by Chambers and Conway (1991). As discussed above, Sen's entitlements approach specifies that a person's access to food is defined by the ownership bundles (of land, financial assets, rights, physical and intellectual abilities, etc.) at their disposal, and the "exchange-entitlement mapping" which allows them to change one type of asset for another. For the purposes of analysing food insecurity in modern India, this approach leads to the identification of three crucial entitlement forms: *own-production and natural resource entitlements* (the ability to satisfy food needs through growing food, tending livestock, hunting and collecting), *wage-labour and income-based entitlements* (the ability to satisfy food needs through generating income – in cash or in kind – via waged work, petty or artisanal business, or other productive activities), and *exchange-system entitlements* (the ability to satisfy food needs through access to safety net food policy programs). In its purest sense, the question of how India is fed can be said to come down to the dynamic of how these three forms of entitlement relation combine with one another (also see Pritchard *et al.*, 2013).

Elaboration of these issues is undertaken in accordance with the schema presented in Figure 1.1. In Chapter Four, we ask: *what determines how much food is produced in India, by whom it is produced, and how it helps address food security?* This question invokes consideration of a wealth of interacting issues pertaining to agricultural production, farm systems and the ways in which farming is incorporated into households' livelihood strategies. Acquiring food through the direct cultivation of land, the possession of farm animals and the use of environmental assets – what we may characterise as "growing, tending, catching, hunting and gathering" – has been the traditional recourse used by millions of Indians over millennia for satisfying their nutritional requirements, and continues to this day to have crucial importance for the country. As noted in an influential FAO report in 2002, the challenge of feeding India resides inevitably "with its cohort of small-holder farmers who constitute the overwhelming majority of the country's farmers" (Singh *et al.*, 2002: 2). Although agriculture currently contributes only 17 per cent of Indian GDP, employment in agriculture, mostly through smallholder farming,

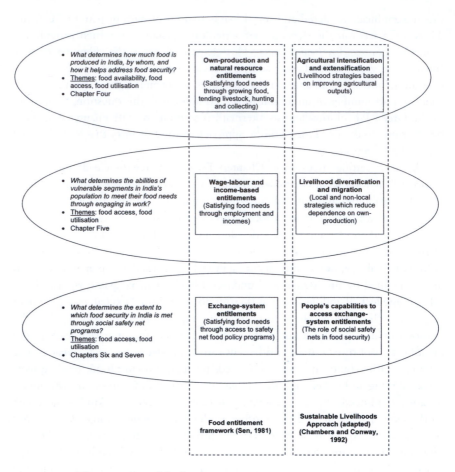

FIGURE 1.1 The structure of the book

is estimated to comprise some 52 per cent of the Indian workforce (Ministry of Finance, Government of India, 2010). However, as we discuss in this chapter, the contemporary context throws down new challenges for the sustainability of these methods for acquiring food.

Then, in Chapter Five, we ask *what determines the abilities of vulnerable segments in India's population to meet their food needs through engaging in work?* There is a wide range of potential activities in this realm including paid work in the formal and informal sectors, reciprocal labour arrangements, artisanal production, trading and hawking and, even, "begging and theft" (Chambers and Conway, 1992: 8). Evidently, these activities can be undertaken either locally, or non-locally; the latter implying various forms of migration (rural-to-rural; rural-to-urban; permanent; circular; seasonal). Although India's booming economy over recent years has been associated with substantial jobs growth, for marginalised populations this has generally been manifested in low-paying, insecure employment, mainly in the informal sector. The precarious nature of much of this employment raises substantial problems for India's problem of food insecurity to be addressed through this avenue.

The final two major thematic chapters of the book, Chapters Six and Seven, ask: *what determines the extent to which food security in India is met through social safety net programs?* This is an issue of considerable public policy concern and represents, for many participants, the tangible manifestations of what has passed for the most part as the food policy debate in contemporary India. In Chapter Six, the current operation of these arrangements is analysed and scrutinised in the terms of the Right to Food principles which are currently forming the central part of the Government of India's policy response to under-nutrition. Then, in Chapter Seven, we enter into what we have dubbed India's "brave new world" of food policy; namely, debate on the introduction of e-Governance and cash transfer mechanisms as strategies to better meet the nation's food security obligations. In light of the profound influence of Brazil in steering the recent Indian policy imagination, we cast a critical eye over the way that lessons from Brazil are translated into the Indian context.

Finally, Chapter Eight sets out the book's main conclusions. Returning to the question of India as an international food security enigma, it synthesises the key arguments from earlier chapters and places these within the contexts of research and policy. Looking forward, it then charts the key issues which need to be central elements of strategies to improve Indian food security, especially in the context of the nation's need to brace for climate change.

The take-home message from this book is this: the inadequate level of food security in India has its roots in many causes, and is manifested across many dimensions. To understand the problem of food insecurity in India therefore requires a holistic frame of reference that gives analytical emphasis to the challenge of understanding nutritional outcomes as the product of a complex interplay of economic, social, political, environmental and cultural processes. These interactions serve either to restrict or empower the capabilities of different segments of India's population to be nourished by safe, nutritionally adequate and culturally appropriate food. Seen this way, the problem of under-nutrition in India therefore represents the inability of an existing ensemble of social, economic and political institutions to deliver to individuals the resources they require to adequately feed themselves. As such, the question of how to feed India is fundamentally about the security of livelihoods and provision of an expanded notion of justice for the most vulnerable of its population.

Note

1   Since 2010, the FAO has reviewed its methodology for estimating PoU. An Expert Round Table confirmed the general validity of the FAO's existing methodology and statistical procedures, but, however, suggested the use of improved sources of data. The FAO's new hunger prevalence estimates, thus, account for average per capita food losses

and incorporate updated food balance sheets, latest household survey data on anthro-pometric measures, living standards surveys on food consumption patterns and revised population projections. In order to ensure time consistency of data that allows the comparison over the period of time, these changes have been applied to generate trends from 1990–92 to 2010–12 (FAO, 2012: 50–56). In general, these methodological and data revisions have led to a reduction in published levels of undernourishment (FAO, 2012:8).

2

THE DYNAMICS OF
UNDER-NUTRITION IN INDIA

Introduction

India has more undernourished persons than any other country in the world. In 2010–12 India had 217 million undernourished people, representing 17.5 per cent of the country's population. By comparison, the country with the next largest number of undernourished people – China – had 158 million undernourished people, representing 11.5 per cent of her population (FAO-SoFI, 2012: 48). On these statistics, if the undernourished people in India constituted a single country, it would be the fifth most populous country in the world. When compared to the situation elsewhere on the planet, the sheer scale of undernourishment in India beggars the imagination.

Beneath these headline statistics, however, lies a complex geographical and social pattern of under-nutrition and a weltering debate about how data should be interpreted. In this chapter, we get inside these issues. To establish the problem in the global context, the chapter firstly frames India's level of under-nutrition in terms of progress in meeting the Millennium Development Goals on hunger. As time has passed, India's MDG targets for hunger have become increasingly elusive. The poor record on this front has repositioned India within debates on global hunger. Then, in the second major section of the chapter, we set out key attributes and arguments about under-nutrition within India's population. In India, under-nutrition is distributed unevenly across geography and social categories. We use the concept of "corrosive disadvantage" (Wolff and de-Shalit, 2007: 133) to capture this process. Hence, nutritional deprivations attributable to one socio-spatial category (for example, tribal status) accumulate and reinforce one another through other categories (thus, tribal populations are also more likely to be located in geographical areas with less developed social and economic infrastructures). Being a woman in a tribal community in a remote, less developed area, for example, implies scraping an existence despite multiple sources of nutritional deprivation. This is especially pertinent in discussion of under-nutrition, because of its catalytic effects in reducing a person's capabilities more generally. As Nussbaum (2011: 44) suggests, lack of food "is a deprivation that has particularly large effects in other areas of life". Finally, in the third major section of the chapter, we ask what this data means for a broader understanding of food insecurity in India. Whilst few would dispute that India has a serious problem of under-nutrition, there remains contention over the background trends. This has been highlighted in recent years following a provocative article by Utsa Patnaik (2004), titled "The Republic of Hunger", and an influential response by Angus Deaton and Jean Drèze (2009). The *Patnaik vs. Deaton and Drèze debate* goes to the heart of India's food security enigma, introduced in Chapter One. We discuss this debate as a means of drawing together key themes about the extent and character of under-nutrition in contemporary India, and what wider significance we attribute to prevailing patterns.

India and the Millennium Development Goals on Hunger

In September 2000, at the United Nations in New York, countries of the world signed onto the Millennium Development Goal commitments. "Goal 1" of the MDGs was *Eradication of Extreme Poverty and Hunger*, and "Target 2" within this was to: *halve, between 1990 and 2015, the proportion of people who suffer from hunger.* The Government of India signed onto these commitments with confidence. The economic take-off of the 1990s seemed to be engendering rapid and fundamental changes to the social condition of the country. Whereas in the second half of the 1970s, over 50 per cent of adult Indians had a Body Mass Index (BMI) of <18.5, this had fallen to around 35 per cent by the early years of the millennium (Ramach-andran, 2007: 259). On the back of India's economic boom, international analysts were clumping the country together with China as being the engine for global progress in reducing hunger. Hence, in 2000, the FAO's *State of Food Insecurity* report bullishly forecasted:

> The [forecast] figures for 2015 indicate that the overall proportion of the developing countries' population that is undernourished will be half what it was in 1990–92, the base period for the World Food Summit target . . . If the goal were applied regionally, South and East Asia would be on track to approach it by 2015 . . . these outcomes would reflect the continuation of long-term declines in the prevalence of undernourishment in Asia, which began in 1969–71 in East Asia and a decade later in South Asia. In the world's two largest countries – China and India – slowing population growth and strong economic growth would bring significant increases in per capita food availability between 1996–98 and 2015.
>
> *(FAO, 2000: 3)*

In 2000, the proposition that economic growth in India would inevitably follow "the China path" seemed uncontentious. A month after the MDG announcements, the highly respected agricultural scientist and policy expert M.S. Swaminathan used an address on World Food Day (16 October) to state that: "What we should work for is a hunger-free India by August 2007, which marks the 60th anniversary of our independence" (Swaminathan, 2000a).

Within a few short years, however, the optimistic discursive tenor about India and hunger had changed markedly. A bellwether for this shift was the 2005 visit to India by the United Nation's Special Rapporteur on the Right to Food. This visit marked a particular moment in the recent history of food security in India. The report from the mission galvanised an emergent scepticism about the country's nutritional condition. It synthesised various pieces of evidence from official and non-official sources into a damning narrative in which the country's shortcomings, rather than the progress it was making, became the focal story:

> Starvation deaths have not been fully eradicated, nor has discrimination against women and against lower castes. Corruption and a wide range of violations including forced labour, debt bondage and forced displacement (destroying people's access to productive resources) remain serious obstacles to the realisation of the right to food. In the current transition to a more liberalised, market-oriented economy, the poorest are disproportionately bearing the costs.
>
> *(Special Rapporteur on the Right to Food, 2006: 2)*

And profoundly:

> Despite the progress made in the progressive realisation of the right to food in India since independence, the Special Rapporteur is concerned that there are signs of regression, particularly amongst the poorest. In monitoring progress towards the Millennium Development Goals (MDGs), the Planning Commission has noted that India was not currently on track to achieve the goals set in relation to malnutrition and undernourishment.
>
> *(Special Rapporteur on the Right to Food, 2006: 15)*

This critique marked a sharp fall in the international representation of India's circumstances. It raises the obvious question: why did India transform from a poster child to a problem child in the quest for a world without hunger?

To understand this transformation, we need to begin with the metrics by which MDG progress has been assessed. The MDGs on hunger are specified in terms of two indicators:

- the prevalence of underweight children, calculated in terms of the proportion of children whose weight-for-age was more than two standard deviations below the median of the international reference population; and
- the proportion of population below minimum level of dietary energy consumption.

Focusing on the first of these indicators, the Government of India initially assessed progress using the benchmark of children *under five years of age*. In 1990 it was estimated that 54.8 per cent of Indian children under five were undernourished. Thus, if the MDG target was to be met, the rate of child under-nutrition needed to be brought down to 27.4 per cent by the year 2015. This ambition was set out in the Government of India's initial MDG commitment, and restated in its first MDG Progress Report, published in 2005 (Central Statistical Organisation, 2005: 109). However, by the time of the 2009 MDG Progress Report, the Government of India had redefined this goal to ensure consistency with data sets collected through the National Family Health Survey (NFHS), which used the proportion of undernourished children *under three years of age* as the statistical benchmark (Central Statistical Organisation, 2007: 2). This recalibrated the goal from an estimated 52 per cent of undernourished children in 1990, to a target rate of 26 per cent in 2015. Figure 2.1 displays progress against this goal. To measure progress in meeting this target, the Government of India used data collected from successive National Health and Family Surveys (NHFS) (in 1992–93, 1998–99 and 2005–06). Whilst India's progress in reducing child under-nutrition closely followed its MDG target until 1998–99, the 2005–06 survey results saw a dramatic slowdown. The "Forecast" line in the graph represents the estimated level of child under-nutrition in 2015 which was published in the 2011 MDG Progress Report (Central Statistical Organisation, 2011: A4). By this reckoning, India would have missed its MDG for child under-nutrition by 6.85 percentage points. Given that India has approximately 110 million children under three years of age (UNPP, 2012), the failure to meet this target represents the equivalent of around seven million additional children being undernourished.

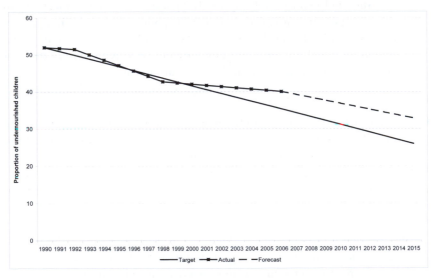

FIGURE 2.1   India's progress in meeting its MDG for child under-nutrition

Source: Central Statistical Organisation (2011: A4)

The human and economic costs of this shortfall are profound. Children growing up undernourished tend to have lesser opportunities later in life. As the FAO has argued, the cycle of deprivation starts at birth:

> From the moment of birth, the scales are tipped against [low birth weight babies] . . . [They] face increased risk of dying in infancy, of stunted physical and cognitive growth during childhood, of reduced working capacity and earnings as adults and, if female, of giving birth to low birth weight babies themselves.
>
> *(FAO-SoFI, 2004: 8)*

More immediately, under–nutrition and infectious diseases interact in ways that inhibit growth among young children and cause damage that may eventually lead to death. Under-nutrition is considered to be a major risk factor in increasing the likelihood of child mortality. International research by Murray and Lopez (1997), Tomkins and Watson (1989) and Pelletier *et al.* (1994) have shown that eliminating under-nutrition would cut child mortality by over 50 per cent and reduce the burden of diseases by about 20 per cent. In India, poor nutrition amongst children was a direct contributor to 54 per cent of all childhood deaths (Arnold *et al.*, 2009: 14). The vast majority of these deaths (44 per cent) are connected to "mild to moderate" under-nutrition, which has the effect of making children considerably more vulnerable to mortality from a range of health problems including measles, malaria, diarrhoea and annual risk of infection (Pelletier *et al.*, 1994). Acute under–nutrition, in which the absence of food is linked in a direct way to the cause of death, was estimated as the cause of 11 per cent of childhood mortality in India (Box 2.1).

BOX 2.1 CHILDREN AND STARVATION DEATHS IN INDIA

In April 2012, the *Wall Street Journal* ran a series of articles under the title "Starving in India" (Parulkar, 2012). A journalist (Parulkar) travelled across the states of Bihar, Jharkand and Madhya Pradesh and interviewed 30 families that had lost family members through lack of food. He was accompanied by Ankita Aggarwal from the Centre for Equity Studies, a New Delhi think tank.

One of the families they interviewed was in the village of Banwara, in rural Bihar. This family was a member of the Bhuyia community, a low-caste group. The story told by Parulkar and Aggarwal is one of a slide into desperation and, eventually, starvation. The family relied on meagre wages earned from casual farm labour. In good times, this was barely sufficient on which to exist:

> Family meals consisted of a small ration of rice and salt. Sometimes, they'd make a dish out of local flora, mixing ninua (a local, wild spinach), jinghi (tree leaves), and mungha, a green sickle-shaped fruit that grows on the trees outside their hut.

Then, after a poor monsoon (July–September) in 2006, family members were unable to gain employment and, with no ration card, were unable to gain provisions from the Public Distribution System. Without access to food, and no cash reserves on which to draw, their situation deteriorated quickly. In early October, three family members died from starvation-related causes: an elderly mother, her malnourished and pregnant daughter-in-law and the girl-child that was born, who lasted just eight days.

The story of this family is by no means unique. But it highlights key signifiers of the social contexts of starvation, especially for children. Starvation deaths in contemporary India are commonly attributable to an amalgam of circumstances involving family status (scheduled-caste or scheduled-tribe households), seasonal and annual particularities (drought, or heavy monsoon), and government failures in safety net provisions. Moreover, they are clustered within household and community contexts. In the case of childhood deaths from starvation, this case reminds us that children are often the most vulnerable members of vulnerable families. Child mortality from under-nutrition reflects both on the status of children and on the status of the households in which they live.

The second indicator used to assess progress against MDGs on hunger is the proportion of the population below the minimum level of dietary energy consumption. The tracking of this indicator in India has an intriguing history. Firstly, there has been considerable dispute over the selection of an appropriate baseline against which to benchmark progress. In 2000 when the MDGs were established, it was determined that 62.2 per cent of India's population was defined as being undernourished in the baseline year of 1990, indicating a target of 31.1 per cent (50 per cent reduction by 2015) (Central Statistical Organisation, 2005: 20). In the 2007 Progress Report, no statistical measurement of progress was offered (Central Statistical Organisation, 2007: 2–3, 20–21). Then, in later MDG Progress Reports, entire reference to this indicator was dropped without explanation. Yet, confusingly, the FAO (in its annual *The State of Food Insecurity* (FAO-SoFI) reports) and the UN, in its flagship MDG annual reports (e.g., UN, 2010) continues to make reference to this indicator. In these international reports, this indicator is assessed in terms of strict FAO definitions of dietary energy consumption, harmonised across countries and time periods (FAO-SoFI, 2011: 51). On these criteria, the baseline measurement of India's level of under-nutrition in 1990 was 26.9 per cent of the population,[1] with the most recent data (for 2010–12) indicating only a modest reduction, to 17.5 per cent (FAO-SoFI, 2012: 48). These results suggest India will fail to meet this MDG target by a wide margin (Figure 2.2).

The emergent gap between targets and actual progress for India's MDG hunger indicators are contextualised at a global level through successive editions of FAO-SoFI. Examination of the text used to describe India over time recounts the

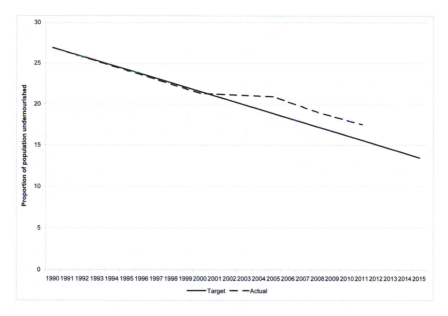

FIGURE 2.2 India's progress in meeting its MDG for proportion of population undernourished

Source: FAO-SoFI (2012: 48)

increasingly fraught tracking of India's MDG hunger targets. In SoFI 2001 (p. 5) and 2002 (p. 8), India was presented as a paradoxical case: in relative terms under-nutrition was falling but, because of population growth, the absolute number of under-nourished persons was increasing. In both these reports, India merited passing reference only, with the major focus being on the fate of sub-Saharan Africa. In SoFI 2003, the tone of discussion about India shifted subtly, with the authors cautioning that whereas China was still making progress in reducing under-nutrition, "India has shifted into reverse" (p. 6). No longer was India grouped with China: it was in a category of countries (including Pakistan, Sudan, Colombia, Indonesia,[2] and Nigeria) where progress for most of the 1990s was followed by a turnaround. By SoFI 2005 (p. 7) and SoFI 2006 (p. 11), India was situated as an "amber" country (designating "little change") within a traffic light colour coding taxonomy (red/amber/green).

SoFI 2008 articulated a new narrative about India. Written in the midst of the global food and financial crises, it presented a more sceptical interpretation of the country's food security situation: "After registering impressive gains between 1990–92 and the mid-1990s, progress in reducing hunger in India has stalled since about 1995–97" (FAO-SoFI, 2008: 15–17).

SoFI 2009 and SoFI 2010 continued this broad narrative, but in the post-crisis context of higher rates of under-nutrition across the entire world. Between 2005–07 and 2009, estimates used by the FAO indicated that the number of undernourished people across the world rose from approximately 850 million to slightly more than a billion (FAO–SoFI, 2010: 9). In this environment, the fates of sub-Saharan Africa and South Asia were aligned as being the regions under severe stress. This reflected a sharp change from the situation, less than a decade earlier, when India was clumped with China as a country with a large population whose rapid economic growth would address problems of hunger.

In any case, in the wake of the Global Food Crisis of 2007–08 the aspiration of meeting MDGs for hunger for many countries had become a pipe dream. The shock of the 2007–08 Global Food Crisis blew countries' food strategies off course, and so the question of MDG targets as a whole has become something of an embarrassing footnote to the high ideals of the new century. Discussion of under-nutrition became progressively detached from the discourse of MDGs. Thus, in the 2011 SoFI, the problem of global hunger was framed mainly in terms of the adaptation and resilience of countries following the 2007–08 shock, rather than around MDG progress. Positioned in these terms, India was understood to have fared not too badly. Because India is not reliant on imports for its food staples, and has comprehensive safety net measures which protect the poor against market-based food inflation (albeit imperfectly), the effects of the 2007–08 Global Food Crisis were modelled as having a relatively muted effect on levels of under-nutrition – especially when compared with what was happening in smaller, import-dependent countries in Africa such as Uganda, Senegal, Malawi, Mozambique and Kenya (FAO–SoFI, 2011: 9).

Who is hungry and where? The social, economic and spatial manifestations of under-nutrition in India

India's faltering ability to meet its MDG goals for hunger is intimately linked to the country's highly differentiated social and spatial landscapes of under-nutrition. The clustering of under-nutrition by geography, gender and social category means that India's hunger challenge requires a complicated task involving the need to address the situated contexts of discrimination and disadvantage that leave groups of people in need of food. We discuss this in terms of the three scales of (i) states, (ii) districts and (iii) villages, and the two social categories of (iv) gender and (v) childhood status.

(i) State-scale geographies of deprivation and under-nutrition

State-wise differences in under-nutrition provide the "big picture" of hunger in India. There are two major state-based indices for measuring this. The State Hunger Index (SHI) constructed by Menon *et al.* (2009) uses data from the National Family Health Survey (2005–06) (NFHS-III) and the 2004–05 61st round of the National Sample Survey (NSS) to capture three interlinked dimensions of hunger—inadequate food consumption, child underweight and child mortality. This Index (which is calibrated to international indices) shows that although India's overall national hunger performance ranks it akin to Burkina Faso and Zimbabwe (66th in a list of developing countries), the best-performing state (Punjab) is equivalent to the 33rd-ranked developing country (Nicaragua) and the worst-performing state (Madhya Pradesh) is equivalent to the 81st-ranked developing country (Chad).

The considerable diversity in Menon *et al.*'s State Hunger Index is mirrored in the parallel calculation of the Composite Index of Food Insecurity (CIFI) by the M.S. Swaminathan Research Foundation (MSSRF) (Athreya *et al.*, 2008). The CIFI uses seven relevant indicators: percentage of women with anaemia, percentage of women with Chronic Energy Deficiency (CED), percentage of children with anaemia, percentage of stunted children, percentage of population daily consuming less than 7,940 kilojoules, percentage of households without access to safe drinking water, and percentage of households without toilets on premises (Athreya *et al.*, 2008: 47). Data for the first five of these indicators was derived from the 2005–06 NFHS, while the last two (drinking water and toilets) were obtained from the 2001 Indian Census.

The results from these two indices are displayed in Figure 2.3 and Figure 2.4. Both indices cover only the 17 major Indian states. Although some differences

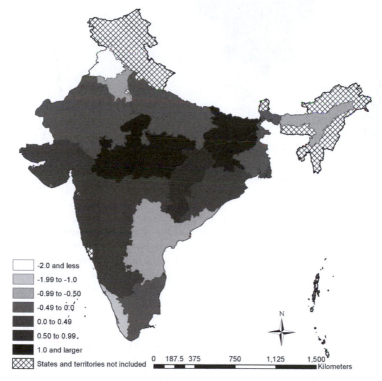

FIGURE 2.3   State-wise incidence of under-nutrition according to State Hunger Index data

Source: Menon *et al.* (2009: 15)

The map shows the z-score for each state, calculated in terms of the number of standard deviations above or below the unweighted 17-state average (hence, the lower the figure, the lower the prevalence of under-nutrition). Note that the borders of this map do not purport to be the official borders of India.

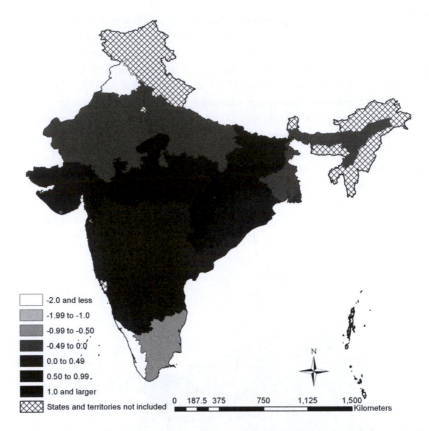

FIGURE 2.4 State-wise incidence of under-nutrition according to the Composite Index of Food Insecurity

Source: Athreya *et al.* (2008: 47)
The map shows the z-score for each state, calculated in terms of the number of standard deviations above or below the unweighted 17-state average (hence, the lower the figure, the lower the prevalence of under-nutrition). Note that the borders of this map do not purport to be the official borders of India.

exist between the maps, the overall pattern in both highlights a band of states – from Gujarat in the west, and then, especially, Madhya Pradesh and Chhattisgarh in the centre and Jharkhand, Orissa and Bihar in the east – which contain the worst food security outcomes in the nation. The latter five states are the epicentre of India's hunger belt. Madhya Pradesh, Chhattisgarh, Orissa and Jharkhand are all characterised by relatively substantial proportions of Scheduled Tribe populations, large forested areas and historically low levels of infrastructure. (Bihar's historical narrative is somewhat different, being characterised in terms of highly unequal resource access (especially land), and proneness to natural disasters (especially floods).

(ii) District-scale geographies of deprivation and under-nutrition

State-level perspectives, however, provide only one geographical dimension of this issue. Spatial unevenness in under-nutrition in India exists not simply at the scale of different states, but also at district scales. During recent years there has been intensified focus on district-scale analyses of food-related deprivation. A crucial prompt to this agenda was provided through the series of state-wise *Food Security Atlases* which the World Food Program funded for the larger and more vulnerable states of India in 2008. Each of these atlases computed a Food Insecurity Outcome Index (FSOI) based on two reliable data sources at the district level: the under-five child mortality rate and the ratio of under-five children underweight for age. *Food Security Atlases* for the five "hunger belt" states mentioned above (Bihar, Jharkhand, Orissa, Madhya Pradesh and Chhattisgarh) showcase the high incidence of intra-state variability in under-nutrition (Figure 2.5). In each state, the FSOI was calculated as a figure between zero and one, and each district was classified as being food

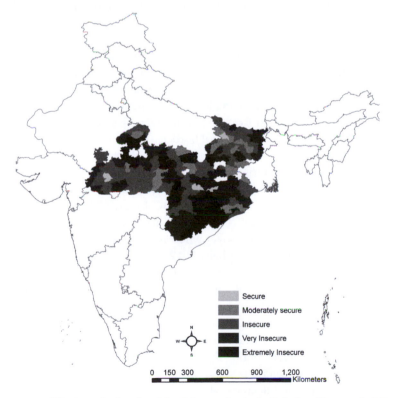

FIGURE 2.5 District-wise levels of food insecurity in India's five "hunger belt" states (Bihar, Orissa, Chhattisgarh, Jharkhand and Madhya Pradesh)

Source: Own work using data from WFP & IHD (2008a; b; c; d; e)

secure (S), moderately secure (MS), insecure (I), very insecure (VI) and extremely insecure (EI).[3] Details of these calculations are provided in WFP & IHD (2008a: 27) [Bihar], WFP & IHD (2008b: 276) [Chhattisgarh], WFP & IHD (2008c: 26) [Jharkhand], WFP & IHD (2008d: 30) [Orissa] and WFP & IHD (2008e: 27) [Madhya Pradesh].

More recently, Drèze and Khera (2012) have constructed a Human Development Index (HDI) and "Achievements of Babies and Children" (ABC) Index at the district scale using an amalgam of data from different sources. Although their analysis relies on data which was were quite dated at the time of publication, they charted a new and highly useful approach to this issue. By comparing these two indexes, perspective is gained on how the cumulative impact of living conditions over a long period of time (measured through the HDI) impacts upon child-related deprivation (the ABC Index). Tellingly, this approach confirmed that the geography of the ABC Index was starker than that for the HDI, suggesting that pre-existing patterns of spatial inequality in India are operating to magnify unequal life opportunities for the next generation (Drèze and Khera, 2012).

The concrete expression of this inequality is revealed in the clustering of inequality in the "problem areas" of northern and eastern India. Drèze and Khera (2012: 43) identify these regions as follows:

> southern Chhattisgarh (the former Bastar region), southern Orissa, northern and eastern Madhya Pradesh, the north–eastern part of Bihar, and the southern and western tips of Rajasthan. Less well understood perhaps is the fact that many districts of Uttar Pradesh, stretching across the entire state, also belong to this group. In fact, the whole "terai" belt stretching across Uttar Pradesh and Bihar along the Nepal border.

Comparative assessment of Orissa and Chhattisgarh provides a set of interesting insights. At the national scale, both states are highly disadvantaged, as evidenced in HDI measurement. But in terms of the ABC Index, Chhattisgarh in general performs better than Orissa. This is significant, inasmuch as the ABC Index is an indicator of the future (as noted above) whereas the HDI reflects past patterns of education, health, etc. (Drèze and Khera, 2012: 45).

At the district level, only two districts in Chhattisgarh (the southernmost districts of Bastar and Dantewada) fall into the two bottom quintiles of child-related deprivation, whereas in neighbouring Orissa, this is true for eight districts in the southern part of the state. These Orissan districts are known as the "KBK region", named after the three districts to which they were previously comprised (Kalahandi, Bolangir and Koraput: during the past decade these three districts have been carved into eight). Kalahandi is in the centre of this belt, both geographically and in terms of Indian political discourse about hunger and starvation. In his study of starvation in India, Banik (2007) observes that "Kalahandi has become synonymous with drought and starvation" (p. 5) and that, as recently as 1996–97, a drought saw 94 people officially recorded as having died from starvation (unofficially, the estimate was more than 300) (p. 6). Subsequent years saw more reported deaths from starvation (in addition to high levels of undernourishment and distress migration) leading to "the projection of Kalahandi as India's starvation capital" with "almost all Prime Ministers of India" over recent years visiting there (p. 6). In his attempt to unpack why Kalahandi is so prone to starvation deaths, Banik contends that it is a particular combination of features embedded at the district level – a history of maladministration, land ownership patterns, high proportions of Scheduled Caste and Scheduled Tribe populations – which determines these effects. The instance of Kalahandi, thus, demonstrates the importance of a district-scale perspective on the spatial patterning of hunger in India.

(iii) Village-scale geographies of deprivation and under-nutrition

Spatial differences in the incidence of under–nutrition occur not only between districts, but *within* districts as well. The individual towns and villages which make up the social landscape of rural India each have their own distinctive characteristics with respect to such matters as the composition and productivity of local agriculture, the natural resource base, the availability of local non-agricultural employment, the extent of internal and international migration among village households (and, thus, the strength of remittance flows) and the adequacy of local governance, such as that enshrined in Panchayat Raj institutions.

Recognition of the importance of the local scale as a hearth for perpetuating inequality and poverty in rural India is well established. It is at the local scale where behaviour such as discrimination on the basis of caste is practised and manifested (for example, prohibitions in access to communal wells or to Public Distribution System rations). Hence, at the local scale, spatial and social forms of inequality collide. It is not infrequently the case that populations from Scheduled Caste communities reside in less amenable quarters of a village (say, low-lying areas in village outskirts, demonstrating a form of spatial inequality) and this reinforces the manifestations of their social and economic disadvantage. Recently published research by Sekhri (2012) based on analysis of the ownership of land parcels in two rural villages from Uttar Pradesh finds statistically significant levels of clustering based on caste. These manifestations of geographical segregation at the local scale concretise unequal access to economic opportunities, with implications for food insecurity.

(iv) The gendered composition of deprivation and under-nutrition

The strong incidence of gendered under–nutrition is a core characteristic of food insecurity in India (Bhutta *et al.*, 2004). Von Grebmer *et al.* (2009) attribute the poor showing of South Asia in the Global Hunger Index to the low nutritional, educational and social status of women which, in turn, contributes to a high prevalence of underweight in children below five years of age. In India, one of the clearest signs of inadequate nutrition within the female population is the high levels of anaemia prevalence among women in the child-bearing age group. This is classified as a severe public health problem, with the World Health Organisation (WHO) estimating that 52 per cent of non-pregnant women of reproductive age are anaemic (WHO, 2008). Moderate to severe anaemia is associated with up to 30 per cent reduction in economic productivity (WHO, 2000), adverse pregnancy outcomes including maternal mortality and neonatal iron deficiency (Geelhoed *et al.*, 2006). The slow decline in the proportion of underweight (severe and moderate) children below three years of age over the period 1998–99 to 2005–06 (from about 47 per cent to 46 per cent) is possibly one symptom of anaemia within child-bearing women (UN, 2010; UNESCO, 2010; WHO, 2009). Chatterjee (2007) argues that the proportion of low birth weight babies has risen in the last ten years even in affluent states such as Haryana.

The strong connections between gendered inequality in nutrition and other aspects of food security is evident in Table 2.1, which uses the 2005–06 NFHS dataset and the MSSRF classification of states into "food secure" and "food insecure". The table compares the demographic characteristics of women in food-secure and food-insecure states using a Body Mass Index (BMI) of 18.5 and below as a threshold for poor nutrition. This level of BMI is significantly associated with decreased productivity, increased morbidity and mortality, low birth weight infants and infant mortality (Nair, 2010). Thirty-nine per cent of women in food-insecure states fall within this category, and 17 per cent within the more severe measure of having a BMI less than 17. With respect to anaemia, the table indicates high levels of anaemia among women in their child-bearing age. Fifty-nine per cent of the women in the food-insecure states of Jharkhand, Bihar and Madhya Pradesh have anaemia. The differences in levels of anaemia between food-secure and food-insecure states are statistically significant; however, it is noteworthy that the prevalence of *severe* anaemia between the two groups of states is not statistically different. Therefore, the data in Table 2.1 highlights an important interpretive aspect of state-wise nutritional inequality in India: that the states defined as "food insecure" by the MSSRF attain this unwanted tag largely on account of the inadequate nutritional status of women. The classification of particular states as "food insecure" is, in reality, a comment on position of women as the bearers of hunger in these states.

Of course, the gendering of food insecurity is connected also to wider contextual circumstances relating to women's educational and wealth status. These correlates are brought to attention in the bottom half of Table 2.1. In each of these measures, women from the food-insecure states fare significantly worse. While 48 per cent of the women in the food-insecure states have no education, the figure is just 17 per cent in the food-secure states. Moreover, while 70 per cent of the women in the food-secure states have secondary and higher levels of education, only 40 per cent of the females in the food-insecure states have education levels higher than secondary schooling. These disparities between women's educational status are also evident in terms of wealth. In the food-insecure states, 26 per cent of

TABLE 2.1 Comparison of nutritional and economic characteristics among women in food-secure and food-insecure states

	Food-secure states (N = 9632	Food-insecure states (N = 11923)	T. test (p-value)
Nutritional characteristics			
Body mass index: less than 18.5	0.21	0.39	0.00
Body mass index: less than 17	0.09	0.17	0.00
Anaemia level: severe	0.01	0.01	0.89
Anaemia level: moderate	0.09	0.14	0.00
Anaemia level: mild	0.28	0.44	0.00
Anaemia level: no	0.62	0.41	0.00
Economic characteristics			
Education: none	0.17	0.48	0.00
Education: primary	0.13	0.13	0.36
Education: secondary	0.57	0.32	0.00
Education: more than secondary	0.13	0.08	0.00
Wealth index 1st (poorest)	0.01	0.26	0.00
Wealth index 2nd	0.05	0.18	0.00
Wealth index 3rd	0.15	0.13	0.00
Wealth index 4th	0.32	0.18	0.00
Wealth index 5th (richest)	0.47	0.25	0.00

Source: NFHS (2005–06), Author's calculations

the women in the sample belong to the poorest wealth quintile, whereas the figure is 1 per cent in the case of the food-secure states. On the other hand, nearly half the women in the sample from the food-secure states belong to the richest wealth quintile. As noted by Jose (2011: 101), the "gender gap in nutrition is likely to be more complex than generally assumed" because of intersections between gendered inequality on the one hand (with negative proportionate effects on women) and high levels of inequality (which equally implicate men and women).

(v) Childhood under-nutrition

The significance of these issues gains traction when connected to childhood under-nutrition. As discussed above in relation to the MDGs, the incidence of stunting and wasting among children in India remains high.[4] As a subset of this issue, there is a robust debate in India about the extent to which gendered discrimination and inequality flows into poorer outcomes for childhood nutrition. Tarozzi and Mahajan (2007) argue that there were worsening gender differentials in under-nutrition during the 1990s, as a result of aggravated discrimination in intra-household resource allocations of food and medical care. A common pattern flowing through a number of studies is the claim that a strong son preference in Indian society manifests itself in the form of discrimination against girls in the household (Bardhan, 1988; Behrman, 1988; Harriss, 1999). The Hunger and Malnutrition (HUNGaMA) survey conducted across 3,360 villages in 112 rural districts during 2010–11 concluded that girls appeared to have a nutritional advantage over boys in their first few months of life, but in higher childhood age cohorts this was reversed, potentially indicating "feeding and care neglect" (Naandi Foundation, 2011: 9). Nevertheless, not all researchers have accepted these arguments (Basu, 1989; 1993; Pelletier, 1998; Mishra *et al.*,1999). Yet, as Udry (1997), Rose (1999) and Maitra and Rammohan (2011) have argued, failures to statistically uncover a gendered basis of differentiated outcomes in childhood nutrition could be due to the fact that gender-based discrimination is manifested in higher mortality rates amongst girls (especially as infants), and that, for surviving girls, there are no substantive gender differences.

Separate to these highly contentious issues about intra-household discrimination against girls, there is, in any case, substantial evidence about the strong connections in India between child nutritional outcomes and various manifestations of inequality and deprivation on account of caste and community status, household assets and wealth (Lokshin *et al.*, 2005; Tarozzi and Mahajan, 2007; Pathak and Singh, 2012; Nandy *et al.*, 2005). Disaggregation of these different components of deprivation and disadvantage is made difficult by their mutually reinforcing attributes; thus, low caste status tends to manifest in low income, etc. Moreover, with specific reference to caste, the classifications used in the major statistical datasets (notably NFHS) are quite broad, and therefore do not capture much of the subtlety in the ways that caste is expressed in the day-to-day rural social landscape of India.

How worried should we be about under-nutrition in India?

This chapter so far has demonstrated the scale and manifestations of under-nutrition in India. Firstly, it told the story of how, during the past decade or so, optimism about the country's progress in reducing hunger has been replaced by a more critical perspective. Then, it focused on the spatial and social elements of Indian under-nutrition. Hunger in India is highly differentiated across place, social category and gender, in a way that highlights a multiple layering of deprivations. These points made, this final major section of the chapter asks what, at first flush, might appear to be a perverse and paradoxical question: how concerned should researchers and policymakers be about the problem of under-nutrition in contemporary India?

We ask this question not as a provocation, but as an entry point into a contentious debate which has roiled across this field of research and policymaking in India over recent years. For convenience we label this the *Patnaik vs. Deaton and Drèze debate*, after the names of the chief protagonists. Utsa Patnaik, a Marxist economist from the Centre for Economic Studies and Planning at Jawaharlal Nehru University (until her retirement in 2010) kick-started the debate with a Public Lecture in 2004 titled "The Republic of Hunger" (Patnaik, 2004). In that lecture, she argued that per capita availability of food grains in India was the lowest recorded since the Second World War. She contended that the onset of the market liberalisation reforms of the early 1990s in India caused the average annual per capita availability of food grains to fall dramatically, and that the mainstream policy and academic elite were in "denial mode" (2004: 10) about this. This was the case, she asserted, because of the elite's enthral with the advent of market rule; a process in which the "ruling class . . . [sought] to sanitise and justify the deeply anti-humanist and negative trend of increasing hunger" (Patnaik, 2004: 10). Over the next few years, Patnaik's "Republic of Hunger" paper was cited extensively (inter alia, Ray and Lancaster, 2005; Dev, 2005; Popli *et al.*, 2005; Qadeer and Priyadarshi, 2005; Patel, 2007), and its influence was cemented further when it provided the lead chapter and title for a collection of essays by the author (Patnaik, 2007).

Whilst not all researchers citing Patnaik's work wholly agreed with her interpretation of the reasons for declining per capita food grains availability in India, a comprehensive alternative explanation did not exist until 2009, when an extensive critique was published by Angus Deaton and Jean Drèze. These two researchers approached this issue from a quite different standpoint to Patnaik. Deaton (a microeconomist at Princeton University) and Drèze (a development economist and frequent collaborator with Amartya Sen) rejected key aspects of Patnaik's explanation of trends. Instead, they proposed that per capita decline in Indian food grains consumption was better understood through an eclectic model that attributed this phenomenon to a range of different causal processes including nutritional shifts, changes in mean daily dietary requirements, and better health within the Indian population. This research intervention reframed debate on this issue. It emphasised the contradictions between nutritional and economic data in India, yet without subscribing these processes within a meta-narrative of neo-liberalisation of the Indian economy, intensification of class relations and agrarian impoverishment (*à la* Patnaik). Through their more nuanced, partial and open analytical approach, Deaton and Drèze brought the nutritional contradictions of contemporary India more fully within the mainstream of the nation's bureaucratic and scholarly communities.

Key aspects of Deaton and Drèze's interpretation (especially with regards to income and poverty data, discussed below) ruffled the feathers of Patnaik, who re-entered the debate to defend the credentials of her case (Patnaik, 2010). This, in turn, elicited further responses from Deaton and Drèze (2010a; 2010b). Other researchers have also joined the fray (inter alia, Basu and Basole, 2012; Imai *et al.*, 2012) such that, at the time of writing, this debate is marked by considerable intellectual energy and contention.

At the heart of this back-and-forth debate is the attempt by all contributors to make sense of the statistical contradictions which define what we labelled India's "food security enigma". Deaton and Drèze (2009: 43–44) lay out the statistical basis of the enigma as follows:

- In the 21 years from 1983 to 2004–05, mean per capita household expenditure as measured through the NSS increased in real terms by 26.7 per cent for rural populations and 32.3 per cent for urban populations. These increases are broadly consistent with other national economic data and the perceived wisdom about India's economic transformations over this period.

• Yet, over this same period, mean per capita real expenditure *on food* rose by only 9.9 per cent for rural populations and 2.3 per cent for urban populations. Moreover, this increase in spending on food occurred almost wholly in the period 1983–87. In the 17 years between 1987 and 2004–05, mean per capita real expenditure on food remained virtually stagnant for rural populations and actually declined for urban populations.

• The energy content of food consumed by the Indian population during this period fell markedly. Between 1983 and 2004–05, mean per capita consumption of calories fell by 8.6 per cent for rural people (from 9,372 kj to 8,565 kj) and 2.4 per cent for urban residents (from 8,661 kj to 8,456 kj).

• Reduced apparent consumption of cereals (rice, wheat, coarse grains) was the major contributor to measured reductions in calories consumed. Between 1983 and 2004–05, mean per capita consumption of calories from cereals fell by 17.5 per cent for rural populations and 12 per cent for urban populations.

Hence, to simplify the message, Deaton and Drèze argue that in the period from 1983 to 2004–05, (i) Indians became wealthier, (ii) but did not use their increased incomes to buy more food and, (iii) of the food they acquired, they received fewer calories, (iv) particularly as a result of consuming much lower quantities of cereals. Therefore, the consuming question (no pun intended) is why apparent improvements in the material conditions of the Indian population coincided with reduced nutrition intake. Four broad arguments can be identified in the research literature to explain this conundrum.

The first of these, advanced most passionately by Utsa Patnaik (2004: 10; 2010; 2011), is to reject the contention of rising per capita household expenditure in India. For Patnaik, measured falls in per capita calorie consumption simply reflect the progressively worsening economic status of India's masses that has followed the liberalisation of the economy. This argument broadly invokes the immiseration thesis in classical Marxism (that is, the logic of capitalism requires over time ever greater reductions in real wages to maintain accumulation).

To assert this case, Patnaik engages in a technical critique of the methodologies used to calculate official poverty lines in India (Patnaik, 2010). She argues that in 1973–74, the Planning Commission of India created a set of calculations which established the poverty line in terms of calorie equivalence: in other words, how much income did it take to procure the necessary 10,042 kj [2,400 calories] (rural) or 8,786 kj [2,100 calories] (urban) for livelihood sustenance? Patnaik argues that the failure to update the basket of goods and services used to make these calculations caused poverty rates to be underestimated. Deaton and Drèze (2010a; 2010b) endorse some technical parts of this argument but reject its overall logic. At the end of the day, they conclude that the claim of *absolute reductions* in mean household expenditure across India during the reform period do not stand up to intuitive or technical critique. They argue:

we do find it difficult to believe that . . . average real spending declined in both rural and urban areas in that period [1993–94 to 2004–05], as if the economy's entire income growth had been stashed away in Swiss bank accounts. Yet this is the sort of cataclysmic picture that emerges from Utsa Patnaik's work; fortunately, it is a picture based on conviction rather than on evidence.

(Deaton and Drèze, 2010b: 91)

The second argument used to explain the calorie consumption puzzle relates to the shifts in the calorie norms assumed to be required by the Indian population (Sen, P., 2005). There are two overlapping dimensions to this argument. On the one hand, Deaton and Drèze (2009) argue that the proportion of India's adult population that has been engaged in hard physical work has declined, and the intensity of physical effort amongst those in this category has also tended to fall, due to technological advancements. Reduced physical activity, in turn, has encouraged reduced food consumption. This is then augmented by the way that overall improvements to health, especially in terms of hygiene, have tended to increase the absorptive capacity of food (the extent to which the human body makes use of consumed calories). Deaton and Drèze (2009: 43) invoke the historical experiences of Britain (during the Industrial Revolution) and China (in the 1980s) to conclude that: "just as there is no tight link between incomes and calorie consumption, there is no tight link between the number of calories consumed and nutritional or health status" (Deaton and Drèze, 2009: 43).

The third argument suggests that reduced calorie consumption reflects voluntary decisions by householders. Householders either reduce calorie staples (i.e., cereals) in a "flight to quality" for more expensive and "more interesting" foods, or they reduce food consumption overall in exchange for increased expenditure on non-food items. Either way, these processes reflect Engels' Law: the principle that when people's income rises, the proportion of income they spend on food falls (especially staple foods such as food grains), even if their actual expenditure on food rises. Banerjee and Duflo (2011: 22–40) advance this argument within a global context, drawing specifically on the Indian case. Starting from the position that "the poor must know what they're doing" (Banerjee and Duflo, 2011: 25), the authors state:

If most people are at the point where they are not starving, it is possible that the productivity gains from consuming more calories are relatively modest for them. It would then be understandable if people chose to do something else with their money, or move away from eggs and bananas toward a more exciting diet.

(Banerjee and Duflo, 2011: 27)

Generally, it is clear that things that make life less boring are a priority for the poor. This may be a television, or a little bit of something special to eat—or just a cup of sugary tea. . . . Where televisions or radios are not available, it is easy to see why the poor often seek out the distraction of a special family celebration of some kind, a religious observance, or a daughter's wedding. In our eighteen-country data set, it is clear that the poor spend more on festivals when they are less likely to have a radio or a television.

(Banerjee and Duflo, 2011: 37)

Banerjee and Duflo's arguments contain an important set of perspectives which often go missing in accounts of food insecurity. By focusing on how food fits within peoples' lives, the poor are animated as having (at least some degree of) agency over their destiny. That said, the notion that India's calorie consumption puzzle wholly reflects voluntary choices by the poor seems to treat the structural circumstances of food insecurity too lightly. A complex piece of this puzzle is the fact that there has been a per capita decline not only in food grains consumption (which might be expected in line with Engels' Law) but in protein levels as well (Deaton and Drèze, 2009: 43). Furthermore, per capita calorie declines have occurred across all income segments in rural areas (Deaton and Drèze, 2009: 46). If the "voluntary" thesis of Banerjee and Duflo is accepted, it would seem more likely that calorie consumption would be reduced to a larger extent in wealthier households. As Deaton and Drèze (2009: 47) ponder: "It is puzzling that a country as poor and malnourished as India should react to growing prosperity without increasing real food consumption and by actually cutting back on its calorie consumption."

Finally, the fourth broad argument relates to the effects of a food budget squeeze. As summarised by Basu and Basole (2012: 10), "the entire increase in real monthly per capita [household] expenditure in the past two decades has taken the form of increased spending on education, health, transportation, etc., while food budgets have remained stagnant in real terms". This line of argument holds that poor rural households have been buffeted by an array of new, runaway expenditure items which have required savings elsewhere in household budgets. Further aggravating this problem is the fragmentation of rural holdings over time and the increased non-agricultural component of the rural population, which have reduced the capacity for rural households to provision their food needs from own-production (discussed in more detail in Chapter Four). Less ability by households to grow their own food has placed increased reliance on purchased food, thus straining household budgets. Hence, although rural incomes have grown in India during recent decades (c.f. Patnaik), in the opinion of Basu and Basole (2012: 25) they have "not increased enough" to accommodate both the increased non-food expenditure needs on household budgets, as well as the need to sustain nutritional intakes.

The discussion above has separated out four broad arguments that have been used to help explain India's calorie consumption puzzle. Each of these arguments denotes different degrees of concern about the implications of these trends (Table 2.2). Practically, however, with the exception of "Argument 1" (Patnaik's claims of reduced household expenditure in India), the other three arguments probably operate in some form of combination. In a general sense, this seems to be a central

TABLE 2.2 Different explanations for India's calorie consumption puzzle: a summary

	A cause for concern?
Argument 1: Statistical errors in the calculation of household expenditure levels suggest that there is no "calorie consumption puzzle". Reductions in per capita calorie intake in India reflect the injustices of the current economic regime (see Patnaik, 2004; 2007; 2010).	If this line of argumentation is accepted, this is a major cause of concern and requires a fundamental restructuring of the Indian economy, involving widespread re-regulation of markets.
Argument 2: Reduced physical effort and improved hygiene in India have reduced the population's metabolic need for calories (Deaton and Drèze, 2009).	This argument suggests there is little cause for concern about the calorie consumption puzzle.
Argument 3: Falls in per capita calorie consumption represent voluntary shifts by people to redirect their expenditure (see Banerjee and Duflo, 2011)	If accepted, this argument suggests there is little cause for concern about the calorie consumption puzzle. However, dispute remains about the extent to which the Indian data is consistent with this line of argument.
Argument 4: Falls in per capita calorie consumption represent a food budget squeeze caused by new household expenses and reduced self-sufficient production.	This argument suggests a major cause for concern, as peoples' nutrition is being reduced against their wishes due to microeconomic forces.

proposition of Deaton and Drèze (2009), who suggest the need for an eclectic account which takes on board a multi-pronged set of contextual reasons.

Conclusion

The discussion above makes clear that India is a food security enigma. This chapter has mapped India's faltering progress against the MDG hunger goals, and then considered the key spatial and social elements of this problem. In the last major section of the chapter, the puzzle of why per capita calorie consumption is declining, in contexts of widespread under-nutrition and economic growth, has been explored. As the discussion has indicated, the full answer to this issue is still not fully explained. The heat and energy attached to the *Patnaik vs. Deaton and Drèze debate* underlines the relevance of this debate within public discourse in India. Across the board, it is now widely accepted that India's nutritional outcomes are contradictory. The questions of what is causing this, and what it implies for public policy, are the pertinent problems at hand.

In terms of the wider themes developed in this book, this chapter has placed India's food security position in international and domestic contexts. Following on from this material, the next chapter asks questions about how food is produced in India, and whether it is sufficient to feed the nation.

Notes

1 It is important to note that while FAO's baseline year of 1990–92 remains in alignment with the MDG declarations, the published estimates of "prevalence of undernourishment" for the baseline year (and for subsequent reference periods) have varied in annual SoFI reports. This is attributed to the use of revised data on population age–sex structure, household consumption expenditure on food, food demand and supply sheets, etc. For example, in 2009, FAO-SoFI reported a baseline level of 24 per cent of the Indian population being undernourished. This was revised downwards to 20 per cent, which was used in the 2010 and 2011 SoFI reports. Then, for the 2012 SoFI report, the FAO revised the baseline estimate once more (this time upwards) and estimated that 26.1 per cent of the Indian population fell below the minimum-dietary-energy-requirement threshold during 1990–92. Clearly, monitoring MDG attainability is a movable feast.

2 The inclusion of Indonesia in this list reflects the massive disruption to living standards in that country following the economic and political turmoil of the East Asian financial crisis of 1997–98.

3 Note that the exact terminology and definitions of these categories differ slightly between the reports. For consistency, the terminology used for Jharkhand is adopted in this book.

4 The trend rate of progress in addressing childhood under-nutrition remains unclear. The main body of evidence cited in this book suggests relatively slow gains in this area; however, in December 2012 survey data from Maharashtra was released which suggests a quickening rate of decline in the incidence of stunting for children under the age of two (UNICEF, 2012).

3

HOLDING OUT THE BEGGING BOWL NO MORE: INDIA AS FOOD SELF-SUFFICIENT BUT FOOD INSECURE

Introduction

> Between one half to two-thirds of India's people do not get food of the right type, and between one quarter to one third do not get even enough quantity to eat in order to sustain a healthy active life. Add to this the staggering magnitude of malnutrition and actual hunger, the accelerating growth of population which even on a conservative assumption is expected to reach 625 million by 1980 and the one billion mark by 2000, and one has the colossal dimension of India's food problem.
>
> *(Sukhatme, 1965: 90)*

The quote above was written in 1965 by the Director of the FAO's Statistics Division, and encapsulates the seeming impossibility at the time of feeding India's population. In the 1960s, India's food security dilemma was framed as a problem of production. There were too many mouths, and not enough food. Four decades on, the nature of this problem has changed profoundly. Gone are the Malthusian undertones of the issue. In Chapter Two we documented the scale and dimensions of under-nutrition in India. In this chapter, we put to rest the hypothesis that this is because of the *unavailability* of food. Under-nutrition in modern India exists in contexts where domestic food grain storage facilities bulge, and export markets beckon. In 2012, India became the world's largest rice exporter (Chandrasekhar, 2012).

This change is bound up in issues connected to the advent and aftermath of the Green Revolution – the interlinked series of agro-technological innovations in the 1960s and 1970s that saw the widespread introduction of High-Yield Varieties (HYVs) of cereal crops. The Green Revolution transformed the supply/demand balance of food grains in India, placing the nation as a whole in a much better position to feed itself. However, at the same time, it dramatically altered the social relations between the production and consumption of food. By encouraging a concentration of production into fewer places and farmers, the Green Revolution created new economic and environmental dependencies, on which the nation's food security has hinged.

The Green Revolution

Seen in wider significance, the Green Revolution provided the basis for a set of optimistic perspectives on progress against global hunger which were dominant for much of the latter decades of the twentieth century. Between the 1960s and the mid-1990s, the proportion of the world's population that was undernourished fell substantially. FAO data published in successive *The State of Food Insecurity* annual reports suggests that in 1969–71 there were 880 million undernourished people in the world. Approximately 25 years later, in the mid-1990s, this had fallen to approximately 780 million people. While a reduction in the hunger prevalence by 100 million people over nearly a quarter of century may appear modest, this fall occurred against the backdrop of a sharp rise in the world's population during this period (from 3.7 billion to 6 billion). Seen in percentage terms, the prevalence of under-nutrition declined from 23.8 per cent to 14.1 per cent of the world's population. Never before had such a high proportion of the planet's population gone to bed nightly with adequate nutrition.

These bottom-line measures of progress were built on social applications of new agro-technologies within a specific global politics of food. Research by Norman Borlaug on wheat varieties in the *Centro Internacional de Mejoramiento de Maíz y Trigo* (CIMMYT) in Mexico during the 1940s was then internationalised in the following decade through the Rockefeller Foundation and, along with parallel developments in rice, became the basis of the Green Revolution. The hallmark of these innovations was to produce staple cereal crops which matured quickly, were less sensitive to local climatic factors, and which generated higher yields. The new high yield varieties (HYVs) radically and rapidly altered the global demand/supply ratio of food stocks globally. As Michael Lipton and Richard Longhurst wrote in the late 1980s:

> food production (per acre per season) has doubled or tripled in 20–30 years, outpacing population growth; short-duration [modern crop] varieties have permitted many farmers to take two crops a year; and more land has been put into cereals, because modern varieties made them more profitable or safer. History records no increase in food production that was remotely comparable in scale, speed, spread and duration.
>
> *(1989: 1)*

In a very real sense, the boost to world food production coming from the Green Revolution mitigated the immediate spectre of famine for many vulnerable segments of the global population. It dramatically increased the holdings of food grain buffer stocks by many developing countries, including India, thus removing the need for these countries to use precious foreign reserves for food purchases, or to rely on food aid. Nevertheless, as a swathe of researchers have documented over the years, the distribution of benefits from the Green Revolution was socially and geographically uneven, and the longevity and environmental externalities problematic.

De Janvry and Sadoulet (2002) provide a conceptual framework for understanding the uneven distribution of benefits and costs from the Green Revolution. Its first and primary impact was to transmit lower prices into markets, to the benefit of consumers. The price fall in food staples during the Green Revolution years was dramatic (Pinstrup-Andersen, 1979). Between 1960 and 1990 the real price of wheat halved (von Braun, 2008: 3). Moreover, the absolute increase in production volumes assisted the abilities of governments to divert supplies to public food programs for redistribution to the poor at discounted prices, such as what happened in India through the Public Distribution System (PDS). The second impact of the Green Revolution was on farm incomes. As elaborated below, different types of farmers were able to extract different levels of advantage from the potential of HYVs. The "package" nature of the technology (in which the adoption of varieties was optimised through accompanied combinations of weedicides, fungicides and fertilisers) also created new credit relations within the farm sector, which linked the economic outcomes from HYVs to social and political decisions about the allocation of credit. Thirdly, the Green Revolution technologies had the potential to create new forms of economic exclusion. De Janvry and Sadoulet note that: "There were also losers among the poor. Small farmers were sometimes displaced by large farmers, tenants by owners, workers by labour-saving innovations, and producers in marginal areas by those in better endowed environments" (2002: 2). Thus, the Green Revolution produced a diverse range of *direct effects* (increases to the welfare of poor farmers who adopted these innovations) and *indirect effects* (reduced food prices; changes in employment arrangements in agriculture; and employment and income effects in non-agricultural sectors). These direct and indirect impacts cross-cut one another in complex ways.

In India, the advent of the Green Revolution is generally dated to 1962, when Government of India wheat-breeding scientists received HYVs sent from Mexico. The following year, the Government of India invited Norman Borlaug to visit. Trials of HYV wheat were undertaken in 1963–64 under the watchful eyes of the Director of the Indian Agricultural Research Institute, M.S. Swaminathan. The Government of India then purchased 250 tonnes of HYV wheat seeds (from CIMMYT in Mexico) for 1965–66 and, following their initial success, another 20,000 tonnes of seed during 1966–67. Further field trials by Swaminathan and his colleagues generated a series of Indian dwarf wheat varieties germinated from the CIMMYT stock, and by 1969–70, these had become dominant within India, being grown on an estimated 10 million hectares out of 17 million hectares of wheat-cropping land across the country (Johnson, 1972: 167–68).

The dramatic expansion of HYVs in India needs contextualisation. In the 1950s and early 1960s, India was a major recipient of food aid from the US (Mujumdar, 2006: 21). These disbursements were integral elements of the Cold War politics of the time (Perkins, 1997). They aimed to enshrine a set of bonds between India and the capitalist West, as part of a broader fabric in the global food system which connected the domestic politics of providing subsidies to American farmers with the global geopolitical interests of American commerce (Friedmann and McMichael, 1989). However, in 1965, widespread harvest failures due to the late and weak arrival of the Monsoon coincided with the Second India–Pakistan War and a decision by the US to place trade sanctions on India. The non-availability of American wheat in 1965 caused a national food crisis (Gupta, 2008: 5). Although US sanctions were removed the following year (and 8 million tonnes of US emergency food grains imported: Landy, 2009: 86), this shock heightened policy imperatives in India to increase national self-sufficiency in food staples. The substantial investment by the Government of India in the purchase of CIMMYT-produced seeds, along with financial support for Indian wheat-breeders, therefore represented a desperate attempt to escape trade and aid dependence.

These geopolitical contexts then dovetailed with an institutional environment in the key target areas for HYVs that was highly conducive to rapid dispersal and adoption. These regional aspects of the Green Revolution in India warrant close attention. The CIMMYT wheat HYVs had their primary effects on a relatively small area of India's geography – the lush Gangetic Plains of the north-west states of Punjab, Haryana (which split from Punjab in 1966) and western Uttar Pradesh. In these areas, introduction of HYVs in wheat and then rice fostered a high-input-high-output rotational cropping regime which radically transformed the region's agricultural system. In Punjab, the epicentre of these developments, wheat production grew from 1.9 to 5.6 million tonnes in the short seven-year period from 1965 to 1972 (Singh and Kohli, 2005: 285). This explosion in productive capacity was constructed on the combination of pre-existing infrastructure (especially roads and canals) of which HYV farmers could take advantage, informational strategies about HYVs which were easily understood by Punjabi farmers, and supportive policy incentives (relaxation of agricultural credit enabled HYV-related investments by Punjab's farmers) (Dantwala, 1996). The latter of these contexts is witnessed most readily in the boom in tractor ownership around this time – which Sidhu (1972, cited in Singh and Kohli, 2005) documented as being linked to the position of tractors as prestige goods from which Punjabi male owners derived considerable social status. The HYV production regime in north-west India was connected, furthermore, with fundamental shifts in agro-technological systems. To support HYV production, in 1971–72 each hectare of food grain production in Punjab was subjected to 73 kg of fertilisers (the all-India average was 10.2 kg) and 1.12 kg of pesticides (the all-India average was 0.4 kg) (Singh and Kohli, 2005: 288).

The effects of the Green Revolution on poverty and inequality

Impressive statistics on food production do not necessarily equate to improved food security within a population. The complex intersections between the direct and indirect effects of Green Revolution innovations served in different contexts to connect or estrange needy people from food. In India, the Green Revolution's hunger-alleviating capacity needs to be understood as being circumscribed by the social arenas in which it was inserted, and which it thereby acted to reproduce. Lipton and Longhurst's book *New Seeds and Poor People* (1989) sets out a definitive account of these processes. Decrying the use of the word "revolution" to describe these changes, they argue that the poor "are neither much rarer nor much stronger, absolutely or relatively, to the groups that held power before [HYVs] arrived" (1989: 3). The new varieties were seen to represent an *evolutionary* (not *revolutionary*) technique, "used first by richer, less risk-averse farmers, with better access to information and inputs" and they would, "when introduced into an entrenched power structure, . . . be used so as to benefit the powerful" (Lipton and Longhurst, 1989: 401). As established by Lipton (1978) in an earlier research contribution, evidence from a wealth of different empirical studies showed that: "The poorest consumers reaped a share of benefit from HYVs, by not dying; but the poorest *producers* – small farmers and landless labourers – got poorer relatively, and in some non-HYV areas absolutely" (1978: 335). Corroborating this general theme, a meta-study of 300 research papers investigating the distributional effects of the Green Revolution between 1970 and 1989 across the international context found that "80% of those studies which had conclusions on the distributional effects of the new technology found that inequality increased, both inter-farm and inter-regional" (Freebairn, 1995: 265).

These dynamics, however, played out very differently across different production sites. Within rural Punjab, it was certainly the case that the Green Revolution years were coincident with relatively rapid changes in land ownership. The Gini coefficient of rural land ownership in Punjab rose from 0.38 in 1961 to 0.63 in 1971 (Nicholson, 1984: 573), which would seem to indicate (i) substantial consolidation of holdings by wealthy landowners and (ii) the fragmentation of smaller holdings by other rural classes. However, this simple narrative of heightened inequality is somewhat complicated when trends in land ownership are contextualised against other processes of social change. Chaudhri and Dasgupta (1984: 118) argue that rural inequality in Punjab, when measured in terms of household consumption, actually fell. Their analysis suggests a reduction in the Gini coefficient from 0.38 in 1960 to 0.30 in 1971. How, then, should these apparently anomalous results be reconciled?

Two factors seemed to be at play in producing a concentration in land ownership on the one hand, but a relative drop in household inequality on the other. Firstly, the "class bias" nature of the Green Revolution (that is, the assertion that technologies were more suited to larger than smaller farms) didn't come into effect so much in Punjab. This was because of the high take-up rate of these technologies by small farmers, aided and abetted by easier credit rules, as noted above. Indeed, the high propensity of adoption gave rise to the so-called "miniaturisation thesis"; higher yields from HYVs enabled farm holdings to remain economically viable at smaller sizes than previously possible. Thus, although the Green Revolution in Punjab was associated with an overall concentration of land, farmers at the "small end" of the inequality spectrum were still able to generate incomes from their holdings, notwithstanding the pressures of inter-generational fragmentation. Parallel research from western Uttar Pradesh comes up with similar set of conclusions, noting that land size was not closely related to HYV uptake, with caste status being the most important factor shaping rates of adoption (Baker, 1975; cited in Jewitt and Baker, 2007: 77).

Secondly, the advent of HYVs gave rise to labour market churning that enabled agricultural households to be inserted into the rural economy in new ways. According to Singh Gill (1988), during the 1960s there was a movement off the land by many tenant-tillers from the Jat (agricultural) castes, because large landowners reorganised tenant relations in the context of higher yield and profit opportunities. Members of the land-owning communities tended to use additional income to move into the industrial and urban sectors of Punjab, which were also expanded rapidly on the back of the agricultural boom. Research by Jodhka (2012) in rural Haryana speaks of similar processes. Prior to the Green Revolution, landowner castes maintained local political control through patronage systems based around credit relations and labour bondage. In the period afterwards, bonded tenant relations have been replaced by cash-based, casualised and (sometimes) reverse tenancy relations (where the tenant wields more economic power than the landowner).

The increased fluidity of community relations and power structures was facilitated by an accelerating trend of migratory labour inflows to Punjab and Haryana of Dalit and low-caste community members from the poorer northern states. The effect of these migratory flows on Punjabi labour markets remains in dispute. Singh Gill (1988) argues that their entry led to lower wages because of their poor bargaining positions as restless and desperate people in need of work. However, in contrast, Nicholson (1984: 572) argues that agricultural wages in Punjab rose 23 per cent in real terms from 1961–1971, which was considerably higher than in most other states. He contends that wages rose notwithstanding a flood of itinerant migrants because of the robust demand for labour caused by the shift into double-cropping of grains made possible by HVYs. Other studies have also confirmed that the combination of increased production volumes and more intensive use of land made HYVs *labour-using* rather than *labour-saving* innovations (Pinstrup-Andersen and Hazell, 1985; Hossain, 1988). Moreover, increases in agricultural productivity generated increased non-farm local employment. According to a study by the Asian Development Bank, approximately 40 per cent of income increases derived from agricultural productivity gains "is spent on locally produced, labour-intensive nonfarm goods and services" (Bolt, 2004: 2). Therefore, although the Green Revolution encouraged greater inequality *in land ownership* in rural Punjab, its broader effects in recomposing the Punjabi rural economy meant that these patterns did not translate directly into greater inequality among households.

Research from western Uttar Pradesh (Jewitt and Baker, 2007; Baker and Jewitt, 2007) supports these interpretations. Tendencies for wealth gaps to widen were cushioned by the propensity for larger land owners to use their larger incomes to secure non-farming careers for their children, and as these families' incomes became progressively more connected to the urban, rather than rural, economy, they sold or leased land to smallholder, landless and Scheduled Caste community members (Jewitt and Baker, 2007: 80–81). These dynamics at the village level strongly support the notion that the most important social effect of the Green Revolution was to destabilise pre-existing social arrangements, which opened opportunities for improved livelihoods across the board. When Jewitt and Baker (2007) asked their representative sample of community members in western Uttar Pradesh about these issues: "85% of our respondents disagreed with the idea that the Green Revolution had made poor villagers poorer" (p. 81), and, in the words of one respondent, "before the Green Revolution, poor people had only enough food for 3–4 months of the year . . . Nobody sleeps with an empty stomach nowadays" (p. 78). Exploring these issues further with a group of villagers in the Uttar Pradesh community of Sabdalpur, they posited a tripartite explanation of change in which (i) the largest landowners had increased their holdings; (ii) smaller landowners had reduced the size of their holdings because of intergenerational land fragmentation, but preserved their household incomes through non-farm work; and (iii) a significant proportion of previously landless people had become land owners for the first time, by recycling money earned from the non-farming sector into land (Baker and Jewitt, 2007: 331–32).

Therefore, it is fair to conclude that the Green Revolution produced muted and somewhat complex implications for economic inequality within rural north India. As observed by Mollinger (2010: 416), changes associated with the Green Revolution "did not exhibit patterns such as accumulation of irrigated land by the rich peasantry/capitalist farmers and full-scale dispossession of the poor peasantry", but contributed to more nuanced socioeconomic shifts involving the appropriation of environmental commons and implications for gender relations (see below). Nevertheless, what was true of north–west India did not necessarily translate into other parts of the country. As early as 1984, Chambers was qualifying wheat in north–west India as a "special case", because of:

> A generally uniform environment and fertile soil, good groundwater, good infrastructure, land consolidation and commercially-minded farmers provided the preconditions for rapid adoption of the HYV package once it was available. But elsewhere, and with other crops, conditions were not as favourable.
>
> *(Chambers, 1984: 363)*

Nevertheless, the importance of the Green Revolution for modern India does not stop with assessment of the social and economic changes it brought forth. Two further important dimensions require consideration. Firstly, its effects in catalysing spatial transformations to the Indian food system, and secondly, its mobilisation of a set of new agro-ecological relations within Indian farming that have had problematic implications for sustainability.

The Green Revolution and the spatial reorganisation of India's food economy

The Green Revolution had profound effects on the spatial organisation of the Indian food system. Close on the heels of the first field trials of HYVs in the early 1960s was a series of policy shifts that established new institutional configurations for food policy. In 1965, the Government of India created two important institutions: the state-operated Food Corporation of India (FCI), set up to manage and redistribute national food stocks, and the Agricultural Prices Commission (APC), charged with the task of setting floor prices for market procurement from farmers. The twinned actions of these two institutions established the channels for procuring large surpluses of food grains from the north-west, storing these in a nationwide system of godowns (warehouses), and then distributing them to state governments across India. Thus, the motor of the Green Revolution in the north-west states fuelled an institutional apparatus for the national redistribution of food staples. The task of "feeding India" depended no longer on the "begging bowl" of foreign food aid, but government purchases from the "food bowl" of modern agriculture in the north-west. From 1969–70 onwards, state procurement systems accounted for the purchase of more than 75 per cent of Punjab's rice, and more than 50 per cent of its wheat (Landy, 2009: 154).

Writing in 1970, Dantwala described this principle as a kind of "benevolent dualism": "If, as a result [of the Green Revolution, spatial] disparities are widened, it will at least be a consequence of a forward thrust" (cited in Landy, 2009: 90). Over time, however, this flipside of India's attainment of self-sufficiency in food grains became an increasingly apparent policy irritant. India was meeting her food grain needs, but the related financial benefits were being captured by farmers in a small number of food surplus states. Moreover, the wheat-based nature of the initial productive boost from the Green Revolution did not serve equally well the diverse dietary preferences across India. Dietary cultures based around traditional coarse cereals (millets, sorghum, maize) received fewer direct benefits from Green Revolution initiatives. Evidently, the next challenge for policymakers was to widen the spatial range of the Green Revolution.

Landy (2009: 89) dates the transition to a "second stage" of Green Revolution policies in India to approximately 1976–77. At this time, the prior single-minded focus on the need to increase food grain production gave way to a focus on strategies which would spread Green Revolution approaches to other parts of the country. This "second Green Revolution" (Fujita, 2010) involved the development, disbursement and adoption of modern varieties of rice, jowar (sorghum) and bajra (pearl millet). The efforts with regards to rice productivity are noteworthy.

Although the Indian population as a whole eats substantially more rice than wheat, national food grains policy favoured wheat over rice distribution during the early Green Revolution (Landy, 2009: 134–35). It was only in the 1980s that HYVs of dwarf rice generated major boosts to overall production. Compound annual growth in rice productivity in the 1970s was just 1.05 per cent, but in the 1980s it was 3.62 per cent (Barah, 2005: 14). This trend was broadly similar in coarse grains, where substantial growth in total factor productivity was correlated to the dates of when HYVs for these coarse grains were introduced in each state, mostly in the late 1970s and 1980s (Janaiah et al., 2005). Close on the heels of these developments was the so-called "White Revolution" in dairy enacted through "Operation Flood" of the Government of India (Cunningham, 2009). For vegetarians in India, milk is a crucial part of nutrition security. The boost to dairy production in the 1980s made a substantial contribution to helping address the "protein gap" that the original Green Revolution left unresolved (Johnson, 1972).

Taken altogether, these "second wave" initiatives bolstered the productive capacity of Indian agriculture, extending the social and geographical reach of modern cropping and livestock systems. It is important to note, however, that these developments evolved with considerable temporal and spatial diversity. Hence, while a generalised story of the Green Revolution in India begins with wheat cultivation in the north-west states and then fans out to other agricultural systems, in actual fact the Green Revolution was composed of myriads of place-based transformations to the social and economic basis of agriculture, which created intricate spatial arrangements of benefits and costs. Hence, at the global level, the Green Revolution altered the international relations connecting India to world food production and trade. At the national level, it executed a set of spatial dependencies between food exporting and food importing states. At district and local levels, it catalysed changes to the patterning of land ownership, which prefigured new processes of class development. In brief, the Green Revolution needs to be understood as a complex, but systemic, process of change.

The Green Revolution and the environment

Appreciation of the spatial and social complexity of the Green Revolution leads the way into a further set of critiques about its environmental sustainability. As earlier noted, the Green Revolution mobilised a set of new agro-ecological relations within Indian agriculture which in overall terms have deepened farmers' dependences on capital expenditures and synthetic inputs.

The environmental critique of the Green Revolution has been distilled with greatest vigour by the environmental researcher and activist Vandana Shiva, especially in her landmark books *Staying Alive: Women, Ecology and Survival in India* (1988) and *The Violence of the Green Revolution* (1989). Shiva's environmental argument is that the technologies which underpinned the Green Revolution have created a form of agriculture with "reduced genetic diversity, increased vulnerability to pests, soil erosion, water shortages, reduced soil fertility, micronutrient deficiencies, soil contamination, [and] reduced availability of nutritious food crops for the local population" (Shiva, 1991: 57). For Shiva, the success of Green Revolution agriculture rests on the unwillingness of its proponents to recognise its associated localised ecological losses. Shiva disputes descriptions of Green Revolution varieties as being "high yield". She argues, alternately, that they are "high responsive" (1988: 116). Their ability to produce increased yields hinges on their capacity to benefit from synthetic fertiliser additions to ecosystems. Moreover, when placed in "whole-of-farm" perspectives, the benefits of HYVs are seen as partial:

> [in] India, crops have traditionally been bred to produce not just food for humans, but fodder for animals and organic fertilizer for soils. In the breeding strategy for the Green Revolution, multiple uses of plant biomass seem to have been consciously sacrificed for a single use. An increase in the marketable output of grain has been achieved at the cost of a decrease in the biomass available for animals and soils from, for example, stems and leaves, and a decrease in ecosystem productivity due to the over-use of resources.
>
> *(Shiva, 1991: 58)*

Shiva brings an alternative, holistic philosophy to the debate about the Green Revolution. For her, the promotion of industrialised seed and food systems is part of an epic myth, founded in the Enlightenment view of science and progress, which denies the essence of these ecological systems as "the source of life and nourishment" (Navdanya, 2012). The Green Revolution is premised on the creation of surpluses through destruction of systems:

> The strategy for creating a fictitious abundance has become a means for creating real scarcity by destroying the quiet ways of nature's work, peasants' work and women's work. The sorghum–pulse intercrop, which the new seeds displaced, is simultaneously a means of maintaining soil fertility, controlling pests and disease and reducing vulnerability to rainfall failure. The dramatic visibility of a large sorghum grain manufactured in the lab and research stations, the drama of killing pests by spraying poisons, the obvious flow of water in large irrigation channels create a mind-set which fails to see the few kilograms of nutritious pulses which invisibly fix nitrogen and provide it to their fellow sorghum plants, or the habitat in mixed crops for predators which keep pests under control, or the fodder for the cow and bullock and the organic matter from crops and animals which give back food to the soil, conserve moisture and keep soil alive.
>
> *(Shiva, 1988: 120)*

At the epicentre of these changes is a profound re-gendering of society–nature relations. Shiva argues that the Green Revolution embodies not only the disruption of nature's ecological cycles, but of the role of women in maintaining those cycles (Shiva, 1988: 93). This cosmology is the expression of an ecofeminist perspective that sees the subjugation of nature by industrial systems as a process of disempowering the world that Indian women inhabit (Shiva, 1988: xvi). These observations on the Green Revolution through the lens of gender highlight the interconnections between the economic basis of agriculture, household divisions of labour and gendered social status. Citing an ethnographic study by Kelkar (1981) in Etawah District, in the Green Revolution cradle of south-western Uttar Pradesh, she argues that the shift of farming to a high-input model of production for sale to the market correlates to a commensurate shift in household power structures. Under traditional subsistence and semi-subsistence systems, women's positions as decision-makers about the management of food grains for household consumption provided an important source of power. However, with the shift to high-input-high-output cultivation for the market, the management of cash becomes the most important vector of household power. In the Indian experience, this was socially constructed entirely within the domain of men. As a result, the status of women within households suffered relative disempowerment with the advent of the Green Revolution. Thus: "As women carry more burdens *for* society, they are increasingly seen as becoming a burden *on* society" (Shiva, 1988: 112) (italics in original). This general line of argument has been corroborated in a series of studies including Agarwal (1984), Basu and Scholten (2012b), Ramamurthy (2011) and Srivastava and Srivastava (2010). Shiva connects the processes of female disempowerment to the heightened importance of male succession within the Green Revolution heartland (especially Punjab) as witnessed in female foeticide and infanticide and dowry-related violence (see also Agarwal, 1990). She argues it is not coincidental that gender inequality in contemporary India is exhibited in greatest degree in exactly the same areas of the country where there is the greatest rupturing of ecological cycles within agriculture.

Finally, Shiva argues that the disruptions to ecological systems and their implications for gender relations have important nutritional dimensions. This argument has three broad manifestations. Firstly, consumption of wheat and rice increased at the relative expense of other cereal crops and, in particular, traditional coarse grains such as jowar (sorghum), ragi (finger millet) and bajra (pearl millet). The dramatic shift in production within India's cereal grains sector is captured in Figure 3.1 and Figure 3.2. These charts illustrate the sharp increase in production and yields for wheat and rice, *vis-à-vis* jowar and bajra over a 60-year period. The increased consumption of wheat and rice has important nutritional effects because of the generally higher levels of iron and calcium (and, to a lesser extent, protein) within traditional crops (Table 3.1). Secondly, increased production of wheat and rice through Green Revolution systems has come at the expense of pulse production. This relative trend is also apparent in Figure 3.1 and Figure 3.2. As a general rule, intensive, high-input rotation cropping of rice and wheat displaced previous mixed cropping systems involving pulse (and also oilseed) cultivation (Shiva, 1988: 123; Bhalla and Singh, 2009). The nitrogen-fixing properties of pulses in traditional cropping regimes were replaced by synthetic inputs in the Green Revolution. Third, high-input wheat and rice cultivation displaced many complementary crops which had particular and strategic niches within localised diets. Shiva (1988: 122) tells the story of bathua (*Chenopodium album*) which is a fast-growing leafy plant found widely across northern India. In traditional cropping systems, this plant would often grow untended alongside wheat. Women would weed out this plant, and use it as an essential ingredient in the cooking of *sarson da saag* (a North Indian dish made predominantly from mustard leaves). Nutritionally, bathua has high levels of calcium and potassium. In the fields, it also has the property of attracting insects away from wheat, thus serving a role in ecological pest control. With high-input wheat cultivation, however, bathua is killed with herbicides and weedicides, thus eliminating households' prospects of making use of this plant.

Shiva's critique of the Green Revolution throws down important but difficult-to-resolve questions within the policy debates of contemporary India that form the

TABLE 3.1 Nutrition content of common Indian cereal grains (per 100 grams)

	Bajra	Ragi	Jowar	Rice (milled)	Wheat (refined flour)
Energy (calories)	361	328	349	345	348
Protein (grams)	12	7	10	7	11
Calcium (mg)	42	344	25	10	23
Iron (mg)	8	4	4	1	3

Source: MedIndia (2012)

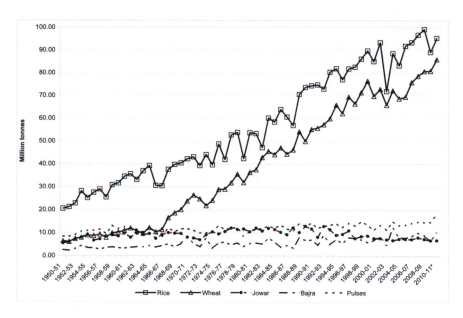

FIGURE 3.1 Production of selected agricultural commodities, India, 1950–51 to 2010–11

Source: Government of India – Ministry of Agriculture (2012)

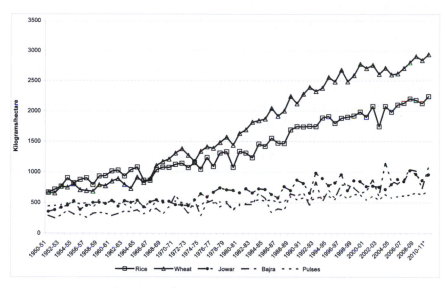

FIGURE 3.2   Yield of selected agricultural commodities, India, 1950–51 to 2010–11

Source: Government of India – Ministry of Agriculture (2012)

mainstay of this book. At the conceptual level, her arguments represent a robust damnation of the negative social and ecological implications of the Green Revolution. The ecological limits of high-input cultivation have gained credence in recent years given concerns about the increasingly apparent biophysical contradictions of the industrialised mode of agriculture (Weiss, 2010). This includes, inter alia, groundwater depletion in north-west India (Vaidyanathan, 2006; Rodell *et al.*, 2009), the effects of peak oil on agro-chemical supply (World Bank, 2008b), the loss of soil micronutrients from intensive cropping (Baker and Jewitt, 2007: 330) and the unsustainable situation whereby global agriculture contributes one-third of world greenhouse gas emissions (Harvey and Pilgrim, 2010). Indeed, in their recent food and nutritional security stocktaking exercise for the Government of India, Gulati *et al.* (2011: 23) call for "out-of-the-box" thinking to help resolve the agricultural problems facing India, a seemingly tacit acknowledgement of the limitations, if not failings, of the prevailing paradigm. Paralleling this at the global level, Pretty *et al.* (2010: 221) specify "100 questions" about agriculture which need urgent answers if the sector is to be sustained "across a far more complex landscape of production, rural development, environmental and social justice outcomes". There is little doubt that the agro-technological model set in train by the Green Revolution appears ill-suited to the challenges of the twenty-first century.

Yet at the operational level, Shiva's critique is immersed within an oppositional philosophy which posits a differently ordered world. She "looks to the past for solutions", according to one critical perspective (Jewitt and Baker, 2007: 74).

Nevertheless, Shiva certainly practises what she preaches, running her Navdanya seed-saving network and an organic farm in Uttarakhand. Moreover, across India and the world, Shiva's critique of modern agriculture has provided the inspiration for a large number of initiatives based around the principle of a re-localised food system set within ecological cycles. These models form part of a broader network attached to the concept of food sovereignty, which is a discourse and strategy about food that prioritises local over non-local, biologically diverse agro-ecologies over monocropping systems, and local control over agricultural rhythms over systems attached to corporate interests and intellectual property. Evidently, the accelerating and multifaceted nature of challenges which face industrialised modes of agriculture give credence to the need to "think about food" in ways advanced by Shiva. At the very least, promotion of food security strategies rooted in the local mitigate external dependence and foster resilience. But to cut to the chase, are the documented contradictions of the Green Revolution so ecologically damaging and socially dire that they demand a thorough rejection of modern agriculture, and its replacement by arrangements which revert to pre-Green-Revolution ecological systems?

Any attempt at providing an answer to this question is conditional to normative assumptions about what humanity's relationship to nature should be. Shiva's understanding of this relationship is embedded within an ecofeminist philosophy derived from key aspects of Hindu cosmology. Alternative stances, however, potentially allow for the contradictions of the Green Revolution to be recognised, yet without advocating a totalising, oppositional model. Thus, for instance, in Akhil Gupta's (1998) anthropological research on a Green Revolution agrarian community in western Uttar Pradesh, relationships between traditional ways and modern technologies are cast more flexibly and fluidly. The question at the heart of Gupta's research is why farmers were outwardly critical of Green Revolution technologies, arguing that their indigenous methods and knowledge were superior, yet at the same time took up the Green Revolution enthusiastically. He explains this apparent contradiction through the argument that farmers inhabited "hybrid zones" that mutually incorporate different knowledge systems. Thus, "farmers switched codes, speaking of the 'system' of indigenous agronomy in one instance and the 'system' of bioscience in the next" (Gupta, 1998: 5), and "while being fundamentally shaped by colonial modernities, many of the everyday practices of the farmers I met . . . displayed a distinct lack of fit with the dichotomy of 'modern' and 'traditional'" (Gupta, 1998: 9). In other words, understandings of agricultural change that are premised on reified dualisms (traditional versus modern; outsider versus indigenous; global versus local) represent simplifying categories that do not reflect the agency held by farmers as they navigate through rapidly changing social and economic landscapes.

Research by Kathleen Baker and Sarah Jewitt (Baker and Jewitt, 2007; Jewitt and Baker, 2007) broadly complement this framing of the "lived effects" of the Green Revolution. Village participants in their studies were acutely aware of a host of ecological problems attached to Green Revolution cropping systems, but saw the way forward in terms of the need to ground introduced technologies within local contexts and knowledge systems, not to revert wholesale to traditional methods (Jewitt and Baker, 2007: 87). This theme is captured in research into the expansion from cropping into livestock – mainly dairying – which has been labelled the "first-level diversification opportunity" for the bulk of Indian smallholders (Datta and Sahai, 2008: 98). According to Basu and Scholten (2012a, b), communities have connected the requirements of new (high-yield hybrid) crops with the management responsibilities associated with new (cross-bred) dairy cattle to chart new livelihood strategies. Their analysis points to a set of ongoing intersections between cropping and livestock systems that were not prefigured by government plans, but evolved out of farmer and community agency. Furthermore, contrary to Shiva's assertion that the Green Revolution wholly ruptured the connections between cropping and livestock, Basu and Scholten identify new arenas for interactivity between these systems. They cite the example of how the creation of dairy cooperatives has enabled large quantities of dung to be pooled at the village level, with landless community members being involved in selling this dung for application to agricultural lands. Thus:

> the success of the Green Revolution cannot be considered in isolation from the inputs provided by the White Revolution and vice versa . . . crop–livestock interactions demonstrate an ethos of self-sufficiency, as locally available human and environmental resources combine to mitigate excessive dependence on market-based inputs.
>
> *(Basu and Scholten, 2012b: 176)*

After the Green Revolution: the tapering of productivity growth and agro-technological choices

A final important issue about the Green Revolution relates to its endurance. Dramatic boosts to cereal crop yields in the early Green Revolution period have given way, over time, to slower rates of improvement. Figure 3.3 shows average annual decadal changes in yield for wheat and rice since their respective Green Revolution take-offs (1960s for wheat, 1980s for rice). In both cases, yields fell significantly after the initial Green Revolution boost. This trend can also be seen, though in a less visibly obvious way, in the tapering growth trend in Figure 3.2. Various explanations for these trends have been proffered over the past two decades. As discussed already, one crucially important factor was the fact that early-stage Green Revolution technologies reached their environmental limits. By the 1990s, conventional plant breeding techniques in north-west India had to confront myriad environmental problems including groundwater exhaustion, the depletion of micronutrients in soils, and intensified incursions of pests, diseases and weeds (Atkins and Bowler, 2001: 225). Hazell (2009: 15–16) cites the research of Ali and Byerlee (2002), Murgai *et al.* (2001) and Pingali *et al.* (1997) to argue that deteriorations in soil and water quality, including the build-up of toxins in the soil from extensive pesticide use, have played a key role in reducing yields within north-west India. Data from field trials in the late 1990s and early 2000s found that yields stagnated unless additional agro-chemical inputs were applied (Pingali *et al.*, 1997). Thus: "farmers have had to use increasing amounts of fertilizers to maintain the same yields over time" (Hazell, 2009: 16). This response by many farmers – to lace production with increased quantities of agro-chemicals – highlights the constrained capacity of the Green Revolution as a model for generating further growth in yields in the core cereal cropping sectors of rice and wheat. These explanations are corroborated by total factor productivity modelling by Nin *et al.* (2003: 936), who found that when Indian cropping output growth as a whole over the extended Green Revolution period was deconstructed, there was a net decline in total factor productivity. Further, this was found to be falling markedly over time (Kumar, Kumar and Mittal, 2004). In the early and middle Green Revolution periods (1971–86), growth in total factor productivity accounted for 52 per cent of the increase in rice production, and 43 per cent of the increase in wheat production in northern India. In the latter period of 1986 to 2000, however, total factor productivity contributed just 4 per cent (rice) and 22 per cent (wheat) to increased output (Kumar and Mittal, 2006: 79). In other words, the rice–wheat complex of northern India has become increasingly a technological treadmill, in which farmers have had to add ever larger quantities of inputs just to maintain production levels.

Declining productivity and stagnant yields in India's cereal cropping heartland have triggered a series of debates about the role of technology and research in the post-Green Revolution period. At one level, this has been framed in terms of a

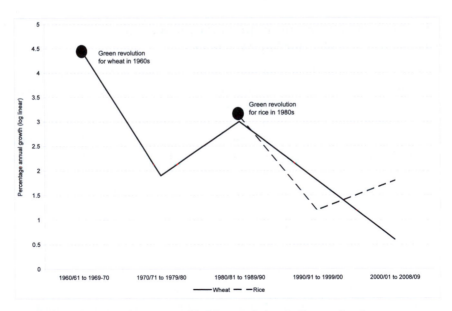

FIGURE 3.3   Average change in yield, wheat and rice, India, per decade

Source: Gulati, Ganguly and Shreedhar (2011: 31)

need to re-prioritise agriculture in R&D funding and international development assistance. Since the 1980s, agriculture lost favour at a global level for public-funded R&D and aid. During the years 1980–85, approximately 16 per cent of global Official Development Assistance (ODA) was directed to agriculture. By 1990–95, this had halved to 8 per cent of global ODA, and by 2005 it had halved again to 4 per cent (Giovannucci *et al.*, 2012: 15). These reductions are now widely considered as having had negative implications for global food production (Lipton, 2001; IFAD, 2001; World Bank, 2008: 156–77; Piesse and Thirtle, 2010). India is not immune to these tendencies, with public investment in agriculture having fallen considerably during recent years and with a level of public-funded R&D (0.5 per cent of agricultural gross product) which is half that recommended by the Indian Council of Agricultural Research (Gillespie *et al.*, 2012: 3).

Yet at the same time, it is not just the quantum of funding that has been problematised, but its character. At the risk of simplifying a complex set of arguments, contemporary discussion on these issues has tended to progress down two discrete paths: attempts to address yield problems through the application of genetic modification, and strategies based around participatory, agro-ecological and context-driven research practices.

Focusing on the first of these, the question of genetic modification raises a host of environmental, ethical and agronomic questions that have been discussed extensively across a number of forums, and are somewhat beyond the direct concerns of this book. However, the fact that this pathway is implicated with the mobilisation of intellectual property owned (mainly) through private companies and distributed via commercial-based licensing arrangements obviously raises important questions about the way these technologies articulate with the food security needs of the hungry and vulnerable (Ramaswami and Pray, 2007). The United Nations Development Program (UNDP) has brought into question the food security ramifications from the use of modern seed varieties which go hand-in-hand with the replacement of traditional farming practices of "saving, selecting, re-sowing, exchanging, sharing and selling seeds" (UNDP, 2012: 2). Clearly, economic benefits from the increased yields and/or reduced pesticide requirements of genetically modified crops needs to be weighed against any adverse social effects arising from losses of agro-biodiversity and culturally embedded, indigenous and informal cultivation practices.

To the time of writing, the only genetically modified crops approved for use in India are Bt cotton and Bt brinjal (eggplant) (Gupta, 2011). So called "golden rice", a genetically modified rice variety with heightened levels of beta-carotene (thus helping to address the dietary problem of vitamin A deficiency among poor people in India) was developed in 1999, with the developers donating the intellectual property rights to a charitable trust hence enabling full "freedom-to-operate" for small farmers without legal or commercial restrictions. To date, however, golden rice has not been approved for use in India (Fuchs and Glaab, 2011). Decisions to delay or deny approvals for genetically modified agricultural products in India have meant that, to date at least, this pathway has not had a significant impact in shaping India's food security problem.

The second broad R&D pathway in the post–Green Revolution period has involved practices which seek to transform the *processes* through which scientific knowledge is produced. The Green Revolution model was premised on outsider experts giving advice to local farmers. This model might have suited the challenge of encouraging farmers to adopt new varieties; however, its top–down logic made it ill–fitting to post–Green Revolution contexts defined by the need to address inter-linked problems of agriculture, landscape management, sustainability, ecological resilience and livelihood maintenance. Such circumstances merited participatory and agro-ecological research practices tailored more intricately to local conditions (Hall *et al.*, 2001) and constructed around the circulation of knowledge among local and non-local stakeholders (Arora, 2012; Uphoff 2002). Geography played a key role in encouraging these shifts in approach. As development agencies and practitioners sought to expand the logics of the Green Revolution into "diverse, risk-prone and resource-poor environments" (Ellis and Briggs, 2001: 443), the specificities of local biophysical and livelihood contexts became increasingly pivotal to rural development agendas.

These approaches took as their starting point the assertion that: "The most direct way to reduce poverty is to raise the productivity of those factors of production controlled by the poor: first of all, their labour, but also their knowledge and skills" (Uphoff, 2007: 218). A cause célèbre in the literature embodying these shifts is the case of SRI [System of Rice Intensification]. SRI refers to a set of changes in cul-tivation practices in rice which deliver increased yields in the context of reduced water use, reduced chemical inputs and ancillary health benefits to local communi-ties. (Because it makes more sparing use of water, it interrupts malarial mosquito breeding cycles.) Crucially for this discussion, it was developed completely outside the institutionalised network of agricultural research activities, being typecast as "a kind of bottom-up innovation in rice farming, an insurgent scientific heterodoxy ranged in more or less explicit opposition to the orthodoxy of the rice science establishment's high-input Best Management Practices" (Glover, 2011: 750). The application of such approaches depends on local adaptive experimentation in part-nership with farmers, rather than being hinged on the introduction of agro-tech-nological silver bullets.

Conclusion

This chapter has sketched out the ways that the Green Revolution has provided the anvil on which the contemporary food economy of India has been shaped. The broad consensus of most social scientists is that it made a major dent on the level of malnutrition both in India and globally, and, hence, its benefits have outweighed its costs (Jewitt and Baker, 2007: 74). As Lipton and Longhurst argued: "Without modern plant science, poverty would have got far worse still" (1989: 3). But, as Chambers adds: "the history of ideas about rural poverty and rural development in the 1960s and 1970s is sobering. So many insights have become available so late; so many professions and professionals have been so wrong so much of the time, and yet so sure they were right" (Chambers, 1984: 366). Rural communities braced by the advent of high-yield crops experienced a raft of differing processes. As a set of concluding observations, we emphasise three key points.

Firstly, against odds, the Green Revolution successfully addressed key food security problems in India during the 1960s and 1970s. Although it had a solely productivist orientation with no food entitlements agenda, it managed to make substantial inroads into poverty and under-nutrition. In an important paper, Lipton (2007) looks backwards and asks why this eventuated. The answer he proposes to this question is remarkably candid. He contends this was "partly luck" because the nature of the Green Revolution innovations just happened to "walk two tight-ropes" between productivity and food availability for the poor:

> In Green Revolution areas, [modern varieties] raised total factor productivity (so poor farmers gained) faster than [they] lowered the price of staples output (so poor consumers gained). And the Green Revolution raised the average and marginal products of labour (so employed workers got more income per hour), but in land- and/or water-scarce areas it raised the average and marginal products of land and/or water faster (so farm unemployment fell).
>
> *(Lipton, 2007: 39)*

Over time, however, productivity growth in the Green Revolution heartlands stagnated and, in the expansion of this model to other parts of the country, development agencies and practitioners were forced to confront local biophysical and livelihood conditions that varied considerably from the amenable circumstances of north-west India. The Green Revolution, therefore, represents a food policy intervention in place and time which holds lessons, but does not create a template for the navigation of these issues in contemporary India.

Secondly, there is an evolution in tensions between relatively narrow interpretations of the Green Revolution (for example, social survey-based research measuring the restructuring of wealth profiles in villages) and broader accounts of its impacts on food cultures, traditions and ecology, typified in the work of Vandana Shiva. For much of the past two decades, differences in the visions of how food should relate to society have created "parallel interpretive universes" in literatures about the Green Revolution. However, to some extent, it is possible to see a softening of the trenchant nature of this debate in recent years. It is notable that mainstream voices in the Indian agricultural policy debate (Gulati, 2011) as well as the global agricultural research elite (Pretty *et al.*, 2010) have called recently for the need for paradigmatic transformations to the agro-technological foundations of food production. Recognition of the magnitude of potential climate change, along with the social and economic limitations attached to "peak oil", has accelerated these debates. Whilst the concern over these issues by mainstream policy and research communities does not equate precisely to the "localism" strategies advocated by Vandana Shiva, the widely held view of current systems as unsustainable provide new room for dialogue.

Finally, it needs to be noted that the history of the Green Revolution occurred commensurate with a broader set of changes in food policy from production-centric to livelihoods perspectives. By the mid-1990s, when the initial boosts from the Green Revolution were lagging, the FAO was redefining food security in line with the tripartite availability–access–utilisation framework, and donor organisations were shifting their budgets towards programs that addressed livelihood concerns, rather than agriculture singularly. These more broadly defined and contextually articulated perspectives reshaped how policymakers saw the food security problem. Food security was progressively redefined and reinterpreted as being manifested in terms of the social dimensions of "access" to food. In the next chapters, we address these issues directly.

4

FOOD SECURITY THROUGH AGRICULTURE-BASED LIVELIHOOD STRATEGIES

Introduction

For millennia, the vast majority of the Indian population has fed itself through the acts of growing crops, tending livestock and catching, hunting and gathering foods. These practices have ensured that the fortunes of Indians have rested close to the soil, water and natural environment of the country.

Such "own-production" systems (in the nomenclature of Sen's theory of entitlements) remain the food security anchor for a considerable swathe of the Indian population. Agriculture continues to be the primary means of livelihood for 58 per cent of people in India (Government of India, 2012), including many of the country's poorest and most vulnerable. Yet whilst this sector is central to the lives of more than half of India's population, its food and nutrition security role appears increasingly vexed. The International Food Policy Research Institute (IFPRI) argues that there is an "agriculture–nutrition disconnect" in India; agriculture in contemporary India seems to be providing a weak engine for vulnerable people to improve their food security. This is an important and powerful claim, because it suggests the Indian experience runs counter to international research affirming a strong general relationship between agricultural growth and improvements to food security (OECD, 2006). Clearly, if the direction of agricultural change in contemporary India is inconsistent with the requirement to provide improved food and nutrition security for those most in need, a large proportion of India's rural population is consigned to a problematic future.

IFPRI's articulation of an *agriculture–nutrition disconnect* provides a launch pad for this chapter. This term is a recent invention, being introduced through the TANDI ("Tackling the Agriculture–Nutrition Disconnect in India") research project which commenced in 2009 through funding provided by the Bill & Melinda Gates Foundation. Phase I (2009–12) of the project was coordinated by IFPRI in New Delhi.

Phase II (which began in 2012) is being coordinated through the Indira Gandhi Institute of Development Research in Mumbai.

TANDI takes as its starting point the observation (also made in Chapter One) that India's progress in reducing key indicators of under-nutrition is slower than its GDP growth rate would suggest, and asks what role agriculture has had to play in this outcome. This approach is innovative because it inverts the way questions about these issues are usually posed. Rather than beginning with an assertion that agricultural production needs to be increased because of a problem of food security, TANDI asks how agriculture should be restructured in order for it to better address food and nutrition security. In doing so, it focuses attention on how different types of agriculture (large-scale, small-scale, specialist, diverse, etc.) and different agriculture–household connections (farm labour, own-production, by women/ men) contribute in different ways to food and nutrition outcomes. The TANDI researchers spell this out via a framework which identifies seven different pathways in the agriculture–food–nutrition relationship (Table 4.1).

TABLE 4.1 IFPRI's seven key pathways linking agriculture to improved food and nutrition security

Pathway 1. **Agriculture as a source of food for households which cultivate crops.** This is the most direct pathway by which household agricultural production translates into consumption. In India, many farmers involved even in the cash cropping sectors nevertheless still devote or retain a portion of their farm production for own-consumption (in the form of kitchen gardens or more substantive undertakings), as a kind of "insurance policy" against-market fluctuations or failures. However, agricultural households with higher proportions of own-production allocated to own-consumption do not always have better nutritional security, as reliance on own-consumption creates dependencies that can be extremely problematic in cases of crop failure or during non-harvest ("hungry season") periods.

Pathway 2. **Agriculture as a source of income, either through wages earned by agricultural workers or through the marketed sales of food produced.** In poor rural households, a considerable share of income is expended on food. Agriculture is usually a major source of wage employment for poor households in rural areas. Hence, growth in agricultural employment and/or agricultural wages would be expected to have robust transmission into improved food and nutrition security for participating workers. This is confirmed in research which indicates high elasticity between income growth and intakes of micro- and macro-nutrients (Gaiha *et al.*, 2010). However, the extent to which children's nutritional status is positively associated with income growth is strongly mediated by intra-household factors, as discussed by De Walt (1993), Kumar (1977), von Braun and Kennedy (1986) and addressed in Chapter Two of this book.

Pathway 3. **The link between agricultural policy, food prices and the incomes and food security of agricultural households.** Further to Pathway 2, fluctuations in the price of food can have important ramifications for household food purchasing and therefore food and nutrition security. Thus, improvements to agricultural production efficiencies can assist in helping reduce food prices, with commensurate positive connections to food and nutrition security. However, these supply–demand dynamics often take place in contexts (i) of imperfect competition within local food economies, meaning that farmers, agents and other middle-actors may capture any gains and not pass these on to poor consumers, and (ii) where prices are determined institutionally (for example, via the PDS), thus detaching the directness of links between agricultural efficiencies and prices.

Pathway 4. ***The extent to which income derived from agriculture is spent on welfare-improving activities (notably, health).*** Health is an important component of food and nutrition security. Higher incomes potentially allow households to increase their health and medical expenditures. However, Gillespie *et al.* (2012) note that there is very limited research on the elasticity of the relationship between rural incomes in India and health expenditure.

Pathway 5. ***The relationship between women's socioeconomic status and their ability to influence household decisions and intra-household allocations of food, health, and care.*** The extent to which agriculture provides income-earning opportunities for women is an important aspect of the agriculture–nutrition relationship, because of the propensity for women to expend income on food and health services for their families. This set of issues brings into focus the relevance of female participation in agricultural employment, and the importance of institutional arrangements (legal and cultural) which empower women in terms of ownership and control of agricultural land.

Pathway 6. ***The connection between women's participation in agriculture and their ability to manage the care, feeding, and health of young children.*** There may be important trade-offs between child nutrition and health on the one hand, and mothers' participation in agricultural income-earning activities on the other. De Walt (1993) speculated that shifts from self-sufficient to commercial agriculture, implying transitions in women's activities from own-production to wage-labouring, may reduce time budgets available to the caring of children; hence, "decreases in the time working mothers have to address child morbidity (especially diarrhoea) may offset any nutritional gains from increased income through commercialization" (Gillespie *et al.* 2012: 14). However, further investigation of this issue by Headley *et al.* (2011) found no appreciable relationship between increased agricultural labour hours by women and reduced child caregiving.

Pathway 7. ***The connection between women's participation in agriculture and their own nutritional status.*** As suggested by Gillespie *et al.* (2012: 15): "Griffiths and Bentley (2001) found that women working in agriculture were 1.52 times more likely to be underweight than those who are not, and Panwar and Punia (1998) found that farming women have significantly lower protein intake."

Source: adapted from Gillespie *et al.* (2012)

Building on the insights provided via TANDI, this chapter uses the notion of agriculture–food–nutrition connections/disconnections to enquire into the ways that contemporary agriculture in India takes place. This discussion explicitly draws on the concept of Sustainable Livelihoods Analysis (SLA), introduced in Chapter One. As seminally developed by Chambers and Conway in 1991, SLA specified that rural households could pursue three broad types of livelihood strategy. Firstly, rural households could improve their livelihood prospects by producing more agricultural output. This could be done either through increasing the productivity of their land (agricultural intensification) or increasing their holdings (agricultural extensification). Secondly, households could diversify their sources of income through new forms of (non-farming) employment. Finally, households (either *in toto* or via individual members) could use migration as a way of improving their life circumstances. This chapter shines a light on the first of these three forms of livelihood strategy; the other two are considered in Chapter Five.

In overall terms, this chapter inclines towards a pessimistic reading of the potential for agriculture, as presently constructed in India, to contribute to improved food and nutrition security. We argue that the legacy of the Green Revolution has given rise to four socioeconomic processes which encourage problematic relationships between agriculture and food and nutrition security. These are: (i) steady reductions in average size of agricultural holdings; (ii) intensified technological treadmills in the context of environmental stresses (which have had their most dire impacts on smaller and more vulnerable farmers); (iii) "class bias" in participation in newly emerging high-value agricultural sectors, (which has tended to bypass smallholders); and (iv) contradictions in the political economy of agricultural support programs in India (which tend often to favour medium and large-sized holdings). Taken together, the interaction of these processes creates substantial hurdles for small farmers, with the overall effect of mitigating agriculture's contribution to India's food security problems. However, the narrative in this chapter is not wholly depressing. In the latter sections of the chapter we point to opportunities for smallholder inclusive agricultural development. The chapter concludes by emphasising the need for such institutional innovations in the contemporary Indian agricultural policy realm, if agriculture is to improve on its promise of helping to alleviate food insecurity.

The effects of a declining size of agricultural holdings

Successive Agricultural Censuses of India have recorded a consistent decline in the average size of operational holdings in Indian agriculture.[1] The first national Agricultural Census, conducted in 1970–71, measured the average size of agricultural holdings at 2.28 ha. By 2000–01 it had fallen to 1.33 ha, and by 2010–11, to 1.16 ha. For Scheduled Castes, it fell from 1.15 ha in 1980–81 (the first Agricultural Census to collect caste-based data) to just 0.8 ha in 2010–11. The proportion of landowners defined as "marginal" (with holdings less than 1 ha) increased from 51 per cent in 1970–71 to 67 per cent by 2010–11. Moreover, the average size of 'marginal' landholdings in this period also fell (from 0.4 ha to 0.38 ha), indicating that landholdings for this most vulnerable cohort were declining (all data, Ministry of Agriculture, Government of India 2012).

These patterns cannot be pinned down to one single cause. Land reform and land ceiling initiatives had a considerable impact in earlier years, in some states. Moreover, as discussed in Chapter Three, the Green Revolution encouraged significant churning of land and labour relations in some places, which dramatically reshaped the size distribution of agricultural holdings. However, across all of India, the most significant overarching engine for these trends was the subdivision of holdings via intergenerational transfers. A persistently high fertility rate amongst poor segments of the rural population has led to progressive carve-ups of holdings between generations. Although the precise dimensions of these arrangements differ from place to place, the overall effect has been to divide a relatively fixed amount of land into a larger number of holders. Apart from the obvious problems this raises in terms of trying to sustain a household's nutritional requirements from ever smaller holdings of land, there are three important corollaries from this process: (i) the effects of subdivision on the gendered division of property, (ii) the way land subdivision can aggravate problems of land fragmentation (i.e., the non-contiguity of farmers' plots) and (iii) the transformation of agricultural households into net food buyers (that is, their inward purchases of food are greater than any surpluses they sell).

(i) The importance of gender

A gendered perspective on these issues is vital because of historical conventions across much of India favouring male inheritance. In rural India, wills are rare, which means that inheritance is structured through social conventions in the overarching legal context of the 1956 *Hindu Succession Act* (Muslim and Christian minority populations are governed through different legislative arrangements). This Act accorded female descendants a lesser stake in inheritance than males (Deininger *et al.*, 2010: 9–10). Reforms to this Act to equalise gender rules of succession occurred in the southern states of Andhra Pradesh, Karnataka, Tamil Nadu and Maharashtra in the 1980s and 1990s, and then in 2005 the Government of India enacted gender-neutral reforms to the Act for the entire country. Yet despite the intent of these reforms, Brulé (2012) finds that gender inequality in inheritance has persisted, because female successors are loathe to press inheritance claims because of potential negative backlash from family members. Hence, the passive resistance of social conventions has seemingly trumped the progressive intents of legislative reform.

This issue takes on key importance for the current discussion because of the increasingly feminised character of Indian agriculture. Just 10 per cent of arable land in India is owned by women (Brulé, 2012: 2) but recent patterns of rural restructuring have meant women often remain engaged in agricultural work even if their husbands find alternative work in the non-agricultural sector (Agarwal, 2003: 192). The reality of modern India is that women are more likely than men to be in the fields, but the fields are far more likely to be in the hands of men than women. In these contexts, intergenerational subdivisions have the effect of burdening women on increasingly sub-economic-sized holdings whilst their male spouses act out greater freedoms to pursue livelihood opportunities in non-agricultural realms (see Chapter Five). If male husbands and sons do not share the cash benefits from their efforts equitably to household members (and there is significant evidence for this: Agarwal, 1984; Ramamurthy, 2011; Srivastava and Srivastava, 2010) the resultant effect is to place intensified pressures on women's efforts in agriculture as a means of feeding households. Gendered inequality in succession and the gendering of agricultural work, therefore, are piled onto intergenerational land subdivision to aggravate the potential scale of the agriculture–nutrition disconnect in rural India.

(ii) Land fragmentation

Land fragmentation is an important corollary of reduced operational holding size because, as individual plots become smaller and demand for land is intensified, it becomes more likely that the holdings of an individual household become non-contiguous. Whereas there is extensive evidence (both in India and elsewhere) that smaller farms tend to be more productive than larger farms (Banerjee, 1999; Ghatak and Roy, 2007: 254), this tendency is weakened if smallholdings are frag-mented. Evidence from Bangladeshi rice farmers points to fragmentation having significant detrimental effects on agricultural productivity and efficiency (Rahman and Rahman, 2008). This is because farmers need to split their efforts across differ-ent plots with potentially differing agro-ecological contexts, and cannot so readily take advantage of economies of scale. Research from Himachal Pradesh has also suggested that land fragmentation reduces possibilities for favourable sharecropping arrangements, another key strategy for agricultural-based improvements to liveli-hoods (FAO, 2007: 29).

(iii) Conversion of rural households into "net food buyers"

The third implication from land subdivision relates to the transformed status of agricultural households into net food buyers. This concept refers to the rela-tionship between cash spent on buying food versus cash earned from producing food (see Table 4.2). Survey-based research by de Janvry and Sadoulet (2012: 21)

TABLE 4.2 The concept of net food buyers and net food sellers

Smallholder household produces only for own-consumption	Meets all its food needs	Food neutral
	Own-production does not meet all its food needs, so needs to buy food	Net food buyer
Smallholder household produces for own-consumption and sells surplus	The cash spent on food purchases is *greater than* the cash earned from the sale of farm products	Net food buyer
	The cash spent on food purchases is *less than* the cash earned from the sale of farm products	Net food seller
Smallholder household sells all of its production	The cash spent on food purchases is *greater than* the cash earned from the sale of farm products	Net food buyer
	The cash spent on food purchases is *less than* the cash earned from the sale of farm products	Net food seller

concluded that 74 per cent of rice smallholders in India are net food buyers, which is a relatively high proportion when compared with evidence from other developing countries (Aksoy and Isik-Dikmelik, 2008). Analysis of data from the 59th Round of the National Sample Survey indicates that, on average, an Indian farm household requires at least 4 ha of cultivated land to meet all their consumption requirements through farming (NSSO, 2006b; cited in Bhalla, 2012: 19). Less than 5 per cent of Indian farmer households have holdings of this size.

The issue of net food purchases is especially pertinent because of its ramifications for smallholders in the post-2007 period of food price inflation. Without an appreciation of the status of agricultural households as net food buyers, it may seem that food price inflation would provide powerful incentives for agricultural intensification and/or extensification. This is because (i) when additional production is diverted into home consumption it helps insulate households from dependence on purchasing food within inflating markets, and (ii) when increased production is sold, it enables households to reap benefits from higher food prices. Yet the realities of net-food-buying smallholder households mitigate and complicate the direct transmission of such price incentives into supply responsiveness. In practice, for net-food-buying households higher food prices have a negative welfare effect, because the additional costs of buying food at local shops and markets exceeds any additional income these households receive from the sale of their agricultural production. Hence, "not only did 100% of non-farm households suffer from this crisis [higher food prices since 2008], but so did the vast majority of smallholder farmers" (de Janvry and Sadoulet, 2012: 22).

Furthermore, even if smallholder net-food-buying households wish to "produce their way out of trouble" there are substantial institutional barriers in their way. Studies have found the supply responsiveness of smallholders to higher agricultural prices to be "typically marginal in their impact" (FAO-SoFI, 2011: 15) because of the institutionally dense contexts facing smallholder farmers with regards to accessing credit and/or the additional land that is required for intensification or extensification (Minot and Goletti, 1998; Zezza et al., 2008; Zezza et al., 2011). And, at least in the post-2008 era, higher food prices have been accompanied by higher input prices (especially fertiliser) which have mitigated the size of any additional net returns to farmers. Hence, there is a relative inelasticity of supply when it comes to the link between higher food prices and smallholder production levels.

Taken together, these arguments point to the fact that the progressive reduction in average sizes of agricultural holdings in India has had important ramifications for the ways farming is incorporated within households' livelihood and food security strategies, especially for those at the small and marginal end of the continuum. On the one hand, smallholding size can generate what can be labelled a "food security trap" for households. This works as follows. Firstly, smallness in size of agricultural holdings inhibits opportunities for households to feed themselves from own-production, which in turn places a heightened onus on households to engage in off-farm and non-farm economic activities (see Chapter Five). Then, secondly, this diverts household labour away from their own plots, which further reduces their capacities to use their land to feed themselves. On the other hand, smallness in holding size can create a barrier to households' potential pathways from self-sufficient to marketable production. Although strategies vary greatly across different contexts, typically a smallholder household would retain enough of their own-production to feed themselves, and then use any surplus for sale. Agricultural-based pathways of livelihood improvement would then occur as households reinvest the proceeds from these sales into farm intensification or extensification (i.e., new plantings, farm improvement or the purchase or leasing of land). But with smaller-sized operating holdings, households have generally lesser (if any) surplus to sell, and so the overall process of reinvesting income into farming is curtailed.

Technological treadmills and environmental stress

Reductions in average holding sizes are aggravated by the way the Green Revolution's legacy has left many farmers on problematic technological treadmills, in contexts of intensified environmental stresses. Yield improvements have been steadily harder to generate; increased insect and disease resistances have required farmers to devote greater volumes and/or more expensive agro-chemicals; and soil nutrient depletion has imposed heightened dependence on synthetic fertilisers. Moreover, these processes have occurred in the context of greater pressures on environmental common property resources, such as water, grazing lands and forests. For the purpose of this chapter, the key importance of these issues rests in the way they encourage an unequal burden-sharing of social and environmental costs in rural India, to the overall disadvantage of small and marginal farmers.

Starting with the issue of agro-technology, small farmers caught up within the mainstream of commodity production have faced a progressively more untenable context from which to sustain livelihoods. The concept of the "technological treadmill" was coined in the 1950s (Cochrane, 1958) to describe the creeping capital intensiveness of American agriculture. In post-Green-Revolution India, this concept has been distilled into the more specific notion of a "pesticide treadmill" and a "fertiliser treadmill", on account of sharply rising pesticide and fertiliser demands.

In Chapter Three, we noted that the advent of High-Yield Varieties (HYVs) of rice and wheat in Punjab was followed closely by rapid increases in pesticide applications (Singh and Kohli, 2005). By the early 2000s, further rounds of increased pesticide uses were a prime strategy for combating the insect threats that were decimating yields. Shetty (2004) identifies "pesticide hot spots" across the country, often associated with large-scale, single-cropped cotton and paddy production, and high levels of pesticide resistance from insect populations. Shetty's analysis reveals a widespread "cowboy mentality" in the use of pesticides, including large volumes of substandard and spurious products, extensive over-application and a large illegal inter-state trade in chemicals to avoid state taxes. Successive increases in pesticide applications added substantial costs to farming budgets. In the early 2000s it was estimated that pesticide use can account for up to 50 per cent of the cost of cultivation in cotton, and up to 25 per cent in paddy, despite the fact that many pesticides are heavily subsidised by Indian state governments (Shetty, 2004). In Uttar Pradesh, the state with the largest number of farmers in the country, the cost to farmers of pesticides has been subsidised by up 50 per cent (*Indian Express*, 2012).

The use of synthetic fertilisers in Indian agriculture has followed a similar path. Use of nitrogen, phosphorus and potassium (the so-called "NPK" group) has grown rapidly during recent decades, and is associated most closely with HYV and irrigated agriculture. Across India, the rate of NPK fertiliser application per hectare of cultivated land increased by 4.57 per cent per year between 1983 and 2006 (Roy *et al.*, 2009: 6). Like pesticides, fertilisers have traditionally been subsidised heavily by the Government of India. Under long-standing arrangements, farmers would pay a fixed price for fertilisers with the Government incurring the difference between this ceiling and the market price. However, the surge in international fertiliser prices during the global food crisis of 2008 caused the quantum of these subsidy payments to balloon, from Rs 403 billion in 2007–08 (US$9.95 billion at prevailing exchange rates) to Rs 966 billion in 2008–09 (US$20.77 billion at prevailing exchange rates) (Mishra and Gopikrishna, 2010). As a result, in 2010 the Government of India restructured these subsidies so that they were linked directly to market prices. Nevertheless, Indian agricultural policy continues to be caught in a bind whereby the nation's farmers are heavily dependent on substantial usage of synthetic fertilisers, which are accessible to most only through the high levels of subsidy.

Pesticides and fertilisers are delivered to farmers through a combination of state-managed and private sector arrangements. Over time, the state was generally withdrawn from this field, leaving greater space for private operators. At the time of writing, the most recent incarnation of this trend has been the commencement of cash transfers (*Indian Express*, 2012). Under pre-existing arrangements, the Department of Agriculture would buy pesticides and fertilisers in bulk and then sell these at a subsidised rate to farmers through its network of distribution centres. Under the new arrangements (which have been adopted by most of the larger states), the Department of Agriculture now makes direct cash transfers into farmers' bank accounts, with farmers being able to choose the (private sector) dealer they wish to purchase from.

If expenditure on pesticides and fertilisers generates production increments that exceed extra costs, this is a win–win for agribusiness providers and farmers (though, perhaps not for the environment – see below). But if these costly applications do not generate the expected financial returns, farmers can be left facing high levels of debt that are not necessarily easily repaid. In rural India, debt traps are magnified because of the ongoing reliance of many farmers, especially those at the small and marginal end of the spectrum, on informal credit providers. High rates of interest charged by informal credit providers can place farm households in unsustainable financial positions and when, for one reason or another, a household is plunged into additional financial obligations due to illness, marriage consequences or natural disasters, it can fall rapidly into poverty. This interpretation of the social effects of agro-technology strongly complements the influential arguments of Krishna (2010) about the roles of risk and circumstance in the production of poverty. Krishna suggests that descents into poverty are often propelled by "ordinary events" (such as ill health, crop diseases, funeral costs, etc.) which may confront households unexpectedly and which they are ill-prepared to face.

The severity of social burdens attached to farm indebtedness is brought into sharpest relief with respect to the highly charged issue of farmer suicides. The actual number of farmer suicides in India remains contested because of poor data collection systems, especially in remoter and backward districts. Nevertheless, according to official data (which probably understate this phenomenon) the Suicide Mortality Rate (SMR) for male farmers rose from 12.3 per 100,000 persons in 1996 to 18.2 per 100,000 persons in 2005. During this same period the rate for male non-farmers increased at a far slower rate (from 11.9 to 13.4) (Mishra, 2008: 41–42). Whilst social scientists must tread cautiously when discussing the incidence of suicide – this is a phenomenon which can be triggered through a complex web of factors including psychological status, family relations and drug and alcohol addiction, etc. – it is widely accepted within India that indebtedness associated with the capital and technological requirements of farming has played a key role in higher SMRs. In a report to UNICEF, the Chairman of the Indian Government's Commission of Agricultural Costs and Prices concludes: "It is known that farmers' suicides . . . have been primarily due to indebtedness" (Dev, 2009: 18). An investigation of the causes of farmer suicide in the district of Western Vidharba, in Maharashtra – where the SMR in 2004 was 140 (more than seven times higher than the national average: Mishra, 2006: 2) – found that the two major suicide risk factors were indebtedness and loss of economic status (cited in Mishra, 2008: 43–44). A key point about Western Vidharba District is that it has an agrarian economy based around cotton, and the rise in suicides was coincidental to the introduction of genetically modified Bt cotton in the district. Not surprisingly, this prompted much debate about the causality between genetic modification in agriculture and farmer distress. Considered assessment of this issue (Gruère and Sengupta, 2011) suggests that whilst Bt cotton cannot be identified in isolation as the chief contributor to higher suicide rates, it was inserted into a pre-existing agrarian economy characterised by high levels of informal credit, seasonal crop dependence and smallholding size, which together created a local institutional context that significantly aggravated financial hardship among farmers.

Stresses to the natural environment provide a further dimension to the uneven social and financial burdens associated with smallholder agriculture in India. Farmers now face severe problems associated with groundwater depletion, over-extraction of surface water, soil contamination, loss of agro-ecological biodiversity, and natural resource depletion among common environmental property resources, including coastal fisheries, timber, non-timber forest products and grazing lands. These issues have particular resonance in terms of their constraining effects on agricultural-based livelihood pathways for marginal rural households.

Firstly, environmental stresses combine with socioeconomic marginality to exacerbate vulnerabilities and to restrict options for adaptation. Environmental vulnerabilities are rarely neutral across class and social strata. In rural India it is often the case that land held by members of marginalised populations (often manifested one-and-the-same as Scheduled Castes and Tribes) is sited in environmentally inferior locations (away from water courses, on land with poorer and/or more rocky soil, more prone to flood, with less groundwater extraction capabilities, etc.). This means that intensified environmental stresses may impact with relatively greater severity on already-marginalised populations, creating vicious cycles of environmental vulnerability that further corrode the socioeconomic wellbeing of poorer population segments. For example, a survey of rice growers supplying 65 mills in Uttar Pradesh revealed a distinct pattern of environmental vulnerability with respect to water, in which two thirds of small farmers bought water from around half of all the larger farmers (Reardon et al., 2012: 60). Hence, at times of scarcity smaller farmers may be left without water, while larger farmers may continue to have reserves on which they can draw.

Secondly, land fragmentation can cause an additional layer of environmental-related problems for smallholders. As we have already discussed, the fragmentation of holdings into non-contiguous plots has negative impacts on agricultural efficiency. However, what is not so widely recognised is that land fragmentation also impairs smallholders' adaptive capabilities when it comes to dealing with environmental stress. Although agricultural and resource economists have sometimes argued that land fragmentation can intersect positively with environmental stress (plots spread across a wider area can ameliorate the vulnerability attached to a single environmental risk) (see Ellis, 2000: 294), recent FAO research in India has come to a different conclusion. In a study of Himachal Pradesh, FAO (2007: 35) observes: "land fragmentation appears to have intensified vulnerability to climatic and market-based shocks" for small and marginal populations, because individual plots are too small in themselves to effectively reduce overall risk. Further, the FAO observes that in these traditional rural populations, common property resources (especially grazing land and forests) provided a key mitigating agent for managing environmental risk, and the shrinkage of these assets over recent years has substantially reduced marginal households' coping capacities in times of environmental stress. As a result, more smallholding households have become reliant on casual employment, and this increase in available labour supply, the FAO (2007: 37) notes, has tended to place downward pressure on wages.

Class bias in high-value, new agricultural opportunities

A crucial aspect of India's contemporary agricultural economy is that the engine of growth has shifted from the commodity and food grains sectors, to high-value commodities, and especially high-value horticulture (HVH) – fruits and vegetables tailored to new middle-class and export markets. Diversification into higher-value agricultural production took off in the 1990s in southern and western India (Joshi et al., 2006). From 1981 to 2009, the high-value portion of the Indian agricultural sector grew on average by 4.1 per cent per annum, whereas the non-high-value sector grew by only 2.3 per cent per annum (Chengappa, 2012: 2). For the purposes of this chapter, this shift has important ramifications for agricultural-based livelihood strategies. At face level, the shift to higher-value production would seem to signify a set of new opportunities for small farmers to improve their incomes and livelihoods. Indeed, national data suggests that small farmers account for 70 per cent of commercial vegetable production and 55 per cent of commercial fruit production (Birthal et al., 2011). As suggested by Singh and Singla (2010: 10), HVH provides a potential good match for smallholder interests because these production systems are "labour intensive, provide recurring income, have high value markets (domestic and export), offer value addition possibilities and are a mechanism of risk management against field crop failure risk". However, not all smallholders are well positioned to take advantage of opportunities, and when the sector is viewed in overall terms, a conglomeration of factors can be seen to exist which give advantage to larger over smaller farmers (Singh and Singla, 2010).

Research into contract farming in India reveals this tale. Contract farming is a supply management mechanism used by downstream buyers (traders, processors, retailers, etc.) to encourage farmers to meet various attribute requirements. The typical way this works is that a buyer seeks to lock in farmer suppliers at the commencement of a growing season by providing various incentives, which could include the supply of seeds, a prearranged price for output or farm credit. These inducements may be attractive to farmers because of their role in reducing the uncertainty of operating in volatile markets. Characteristically, contract farming tends to be prevalent in HVH, because of the need for buyers to ensure exacting product attributes from farmers, such as crops grown from a specific seed variety, assurances about the (non-)use of particular agro-chemicals, or where cultivation and harvest need to occur in line with highly regimented timescales.

In India, there is a live debate about the extent to which contract farming has a class bias. In a number of influential contributions, Birthal et al. (2005), Prabakaran et al. (2006), Ramesh and Gracy (2006) and Dev and Rao (2006) found no bias against smallholders. Notably, however, these studies were all undertaken in South India within "progressive farming" circles in local contexts where contractors had little choice but to engage with smallholders, because of the absence of larger-sized farming entities. A more nuanced analytical approach is provided in Pritchard and Connell's (2011) study of high-value export chilli production in South India, which revealed that, over time, the contracting firm migrated from small to large farmers. The extensive work of Sukhpal Singh on contract farming, largely undertaken in North India, also suggests that when contracting firms have the freedoms to do so, they tend to favour dealing with larger farmers rather than smallholders (Singh, 2002; 2005; 2007; 2008). These findings are consistent with long-standing international research on this topic (Rickson and Burch, 1996).

The politics of agricultural land can add further to these tendencies. As a means of seeking to facilitate the expansion of high-value forms of agriculture, during the past decade the Government of India has embarked on a policy of clustering development ambitions within specially earmarked "Agri-Export Zones" and

"Special Economic Zones". Farmers operating in these zones gain privileged access to research and extension services and are eligible for a range of subsidies. However, the dynamics of agri-export zones as a strategy for rural development are often difficult to isolate from the politics of land grabbing. Singh (2006) documents the intersection of political deal-making with demands for large-scale, value-added agriculture across India. He contends that land transactions are frequently plagued by a lack of clarity in their commercial arrangements, and can also act as a Trojan horse for conversion from farming to non-agricultural uses such as real estate and industry. The loss of farmland through these actions directly contradicts a major recommendation from the Government of India's 2006 National Commission on Farming, chaired by Professor M.S. Swaminathan, which argued for a need to prevent diversion of prime agricultural land and forest to the corporate sector for non-agricultural purposes (PRS Legislative Research, 2006).

Issues relating to land appropriation reflect an important dimension to debate on smallholder agriculture. They suggest a broad trajectory of agricultural development in India dictated by the politics of land. The default position of the contemporary Indian agrarian economy seems to be one in which it slides into a state where larger investors capture the lion's share of benefits from new agricultural markets, hence foreclosing involvement by smallholders.

Nevertheless, this default orientation can be challenged through smallholder-inclusive institutional innovations. During recent years, international research has occurred on the question of what policy settings and organisational structures facilitate smallholder engagement in high-value agricultural chains (Vorley et al., 2012). In India, a widely cited case in point is Mahagrapes, a cooperative-managed exporter of table grapes from Maharashtra. According to Roy and Thorat (2008), the cooperative model pioneered by Mahagrapes enabled small growers to successfully increase their net returns from farming whilst participating in an export market characterised by intense quality safeguards. Mahagrapes collectivised small producers within a strongly regimented convention-setting regime pertaining to quality and standards. Moving outwards from the Mahagrapes case, Singh and Singla (2010) synthesise evidence from a range of case studies from Gujarat, Punjab and Karnataka which point to the unrealised potential for enhanced smallholder participation in high-value agricultural markets. Two critical factors are the role for producer companies, and the need for appropriate investment in post-harvest coordination. Producer companies are a relatively new category of ownership structure in India, deriving from amendments in 2003 to the *Corporations Act*. It provides a means for ten or more primary producers to organise themselves into a collective marketing or producing entity, in a legally more flexible and robust way than possible in a cooperative. Singh and Singla (2010: 261) suggest that recognition of producer companies by state agencies can provide a means for smallholders to deliver coordinated volumes of produce in a way that allows them to compete with larger farmers.

The second key institutional reform to enhance smallholder inclusiveness in high-value agricultural chains relates to the need to reduce post-harvest losses and improve the transaction cost performance of agri-food supply chains. Research by the Government of India's Central Institute for Post-Harvest Engineering and Technology indicates that harvest and post-harvest losses amount to up to 18 per cent of the volume of production of fruits, 12.5 per cent of vegetables, 6.1 per cent of cereals and pulses, and 6 per cent of oilseeds (Chengappa, 2012: 5). Transaction costs have traditionally been high in post-harvest segments of Indian agriculture due the multiple handling of product, poor transport infrastructures and inefficiency and corruption in some market nodes (Pritchard *et al.*, 2010). To take a modest but illustrative example, in early 2011 when retail prices for tomatoes in Delhi spiked to Rs 70–80/kg, they were selling for just Rs 40/kg in Chennai and Rs 35/kg in Kolkata (*Indian Express*, 2011). These differences speak to the inefficiencies in moving product across the nation in response to demand.

Preliminary evidence, however, suggests improvements to this situation. According to Reardon and Minten (2011) and Reardon *et al.* (2012) there is a "quiet revolution" currently taking hold in India's agri-food chains. The authors argue:

> the broad traditional segment of the wholesale sector is . . . transforming; supply chains are *shortening*, as village brokers are reduced to a minor role and as *mandi* (public wholesale markets) wholesalers buy direct from farmers. In addition, cold stores have expanded rapidly and have taken on wholesale functions (even to the extent of supplanting wholesale markets) and provide credit to farmers. This all indicates a ferment of change in supply chains, which in the medium/long run can transform the conditions faced by farmers.
>
> *(Reardon and Minten, 2011: iv; italics in original)*

A core question posed in Reardon and Minten's research concerns the degree to which these transformations exacerbate or diminish the differences in competitive positions of larger and smaller farmers. Although the authors do not provide a simple answer to this question their case study of the potato value chain in northern India suggests that the modernisation of chains does not necessarily disadvantage smallholders (Reardon *et al.*, 2012: 280). The exact reasons for an apparent scale-neutrality in benefits, however, remain unclear. Reardon *et al.* (2012: 284) suggest there is no single "silver bullet" with respect to how and why particular innovations generate specific social outcomes. What is apparent, however, is that the policy environment plays a key factor, and it is to this we now turn.

Contradictions in India's agricultural political economy

Indian agriculture takes place within the context of a considerable web of government programs and policies. Post-Independence "Nehruvian socialism" mandated widespread state monitoring and regulation of agricultural price-formation, marketing and production. In the "new economic policy" era of post-1991 India, much of this regulatory infrastructure has been liberalised, but a considerable swathe of arrangements remain in place. Furthermore, there has been a "two steps forward one step back" dynamic to many aspects of reform, whereby agricultural liberalisation in one dimension has been followed by new programs and policies in another, with the aim of placating and/or capturing electorally important rural vote-banks. The "Indian way" of agricultural liberalisation has occurred in contradictory fashion.

The story of India's contemporary agricultural political economy is too multi-faceted to tell within the confines of this chapter (for a fuller analysis, see Mujumdar and Kapila, 2006). For the specific purposes of the current discussion, the important question is the impact of programs and regulations on small-scale farmers.

Posing this question opens a broad field of political science theory. The state does not exist as a singular entity, but has considerable internal pluralism. Activities undertaken by one of its arms can be contradicted by another. Nevertheless, examination of the broad contours of rural governance and public administration by Birner et al. (2012) provide a useful framework for considering this issue. Through a Karnataka-based study involving interviews with 206 field-level staff officers and 966 rural households receiving services from the agencies they represented, the authors were able to generate a highly detailed picture of the ways that program delivery intersected with the deployment of power in rural India. They argue that small and marginal farmers can face the triple jeopardy of being at the wrong end of market failures, state failures and community failures. Market failures exist through small farmers being exploited through monopoly buying conditions caused by dependence on one buyer, or collusion between different buyers. State failures occur in the guise of the derogation of state functions. In backward districts of India, it is not uncommon for the agricultural policy supports from the state to be defined more in their absence than presence. The concept of community failures points to the way in which weak local institutions become complicit in the capture of community resources by elites.

These processes are in evidence through the inadequate and inequitable provision of agricultural extension in India. Only 5 per cent of small and marginal farmers have access to agricultural extension services (roughly half the level of access enjoyed by medium and large farmers). A crucial reason for these inequities is that 40 per cent of agricultural extension posts in India remain unfilled (Agarwal, 2011: 10), and it would reasonably be expected that unfilled posts are more common in poorer areas more dominated by marginal farmers and tribal communities.

A further set of examples of state failure is provided through the vexed issue of fertiliser and electricity policies. These policy areas highlight a series of anti-poor perversions in policy (Birner et al. 2011). Under the aegis of rural development, a number of states have offered highly subsidised or zero-tariff supply of power to farmers (Deshingkar and Farrington, 2006: 77–79). Benefits from these schemes, however, have tended to flow to larger farms. This is hardly surprising. Their size and higher levels of capital intensiveness make them more voracious consumers of power, implying that they capture the lion's share of subsidies. Furthermore, the rolling out of the power grid in agricultural areas is an act of politics which may respond to and thereby entrench pre-existing geographies of wealth. During field research in Andhra Pradesh, one of the authors observed that a long-distance power line had its terminus at a machinery shed in a rich farmer's field, whilst a tribal village just a few kilometres further away remained off the grid.

Sarkar's (2012) detailed study of the relationship between electricity subsidies and groundwater depletion in Punjab documents the chain of economic, ecological and social impacts attached to electricity subsidisation in agriculture. It was found that the provision of free electricity to farmers in Punjab has dramatically hastened groundwater depletion with the wealthy minority of farmers receiving most of the subsidy benefits and hence being responsible for most of the ecological costs. However, these costs are actually mainly borne by small farmers, who have a lesser capacity to invest in the technologies required for recovering water from ever deeper lower groundwater tables. Their only other option is to make greater use of canal water, "but the irony is that . . . due to lack of maintenance, most of the canals have dried up" (Sarkar, 2011: 189). As such, there has been a tendency for small farmers in Punjab to shift from (water-thirsty) rice to the cultivation of maize, which (in the absence of MSP arrangements) provides a lower financial return. Other options (such as high-value horticulture) are difficult for smallholders to pursue because the state has made virtually no progress on developing a supportive policy environment in this area, despite repeated expert committee recommendations (Johl, 2012). Therefore, Punjab's experience suggests that the net effect of electricity subsidies in the absence of any other smallholder-friendly policies has been to widen social differences in agriculture, and is therefore reflective of the scale bias in favour of large producers that is prevalent in various guises across rural India.

Conclusion

The aim of this chapter has been to assess the role of agriculture-based livelihood strategies as a means of improving food security outcomes in contemporary India. The chapter has covered much ground, but the overall insights are clear: the contemporary social organisation of agriculture in India constrains the capacity of small and marginalised rural households to use these activities as a means of improving their food security status. This pessimistic inclination was elaborated in the context of four key arguments. First, reductions in the average size of agricultural holdings impair opportunities for households to "cultivate their way" out of food insecurity. Second, the burden of the technological treadmill and the increasingly degraded status of India's rural environment act to restrict opportunities for small-scale farmers to improve their social situations. Third, the contemporary growth sectors in the agricultural economy associated with high-value production are not always amenable to smallholder involvement. Successful participation by smallholders in these sectors is conditional on appropriate institutional environments, including policy settings. And finally, despite much of the rhetoric of governments in India, it is not necessarily clear that important facets of agricultural and rural policy operate to the net benefit of small and marginal farmers.

Taken together, the four factors underline the reality that for millions of rural Indians today, agriculture is not seen as a route into better livelihood circumstances. The consequence of these agriculture–food–nutrition disconnections is to funnel poor households into livelihood strategies outside of agriculture. In the following chapter, we assess these livelihood options.

Note

1 Estimation of land ownership patterns in rural India is subject to complexities in definition and measurement. The concept of "operational holdings" provides a catch-all mechanism to aggregate all land which farmers either: (i) own (deemed as a "right of permanent heritable possession with or without the right to transfer the title, e.g., *pattadars*, *bhumidars*, jenmons, bhumi-swamis, rayat sithibans, etc."; (ii) have long-term rights over; (iii) lease-in (including encroached lands to which there is no formal title); and (iv) otherwise possessed land ("all public or institutional land possessed by the household without title of ownership or occupancy right" (NSSOa, 2006: 3–4).

5
FOOD SECURITY THROUGH THE NON-AGRICULTURAL ECONOMY

Introduction

The common pathway of human history is that the share of the population directly dependent on agriculture as a source of livelihoods and sustenance declines over time. However, societies' transitions away from agriculture are rarely painless. In the seminal case of Britain during the Industrial Revolution, de-agrarianisation was associated with widespread socioeconomic and political upheavals, including the forced enclosure of village commons, the creation of an urban-based working class and underclass, and counter-political responses including fights over suffrage and unionisation. Integral to these dynamics was a new politics of food security, framed around the *Corn Laws* debates and the need to furnish urban populations with cheaper food (McMichael, 1997).

Equally, de-agrarianisation in modern India is far from painless, with urban infra-structures and social institutions heaving under the stresses of rapid change. Obviously, these transitions have many aspects cutting across economic, cultural and political realms. From the specific perspective of food security, these processes are best viewed using a livelihoods perspective. De-agrarianisation in contemporary India character-istically takes a form in which one or more members of a household leave farming in pursuit of non-agricultural livelihood opportunities. If these processes operate by way of a virtuous cycle, the diversifier gains sufficient livelihood resources to support a nutritious diet for themselves, and then remits additional income back home to support the food security needs of her/his family. Alternately, a vicious cycle occurs when the diversifier is trapped in conditions of livelihood vulnerability and margin-ality, and thereby unable to support other household members. In too many cases, among India's poor, a vicious cycle has prevailed over a virtuous cycle.

This chapter's focus on these issues corresponds to what Amartya Sen (1981) labels the "wage-labour entitlement" component of food security. However, consistent with Sen's usage of the term, our discussion in this chapter encompasses not just formal wage labour, but the diverse array of activities that characterise the generation of income in developing country contexts, including paid work in the formal and informal sectors, reciprocal labour arrangements, artisanal production, trading and hawking, etc. Moreover, and this is a crucial point, within individual households a variety of such activities can and do coexist. Households engage in diverse combinations of activities to "construct and contrive" a living (Chambers and Conway, 1992: 8). Consistent with the capabilities approach set out in Chapter One, the interest is to build an understanding of how the "ownership bundles" of vulnerable, non-farming households (i.e., their land, money, substantive freedoms under law, ability to undertake wage labour, positions within networks of mutual obligation and responsibility, etc.) interact with the socioeconomic environment of contemporary India, to create or constrain opportunities for addressing their food security.

This chapter develops these ideas through a dual focus which gives attention both to the decision-making matrices which inform livelihood choices from the perspective of households, and to the broad contexts of the Indian economy which frame households' livelihood options. Focusing on the first of these two themes, our discussion is constructed around the varied sectoral and spatial dimensions of how households diversify their livelihoods away from farming. Then, in the second major section of the chapter, attention shifts to the structural composition of the Indian economy; the landscape of jobs and commerce in which poor people seek their chances. This discussion outlines the problematic issues of economic composition and employment which are contributing to a current failure to generate a sufficient volume of decent employment opportunities to soak up the large number of unskilled and semi-skilled persons who are seeking livelihood opportunities outside of agriculture. Finally, the chapter then weaves together these insights in the context of food security. Our discussion of this issue analyses how economic marginality and vulnerability within de-agrarianised, poor segments of India's population are being expressed in a deepening exposure to food price inflation and resultant pressures on food security.

The agency of India's rural poor to construct sustainable non-farm livelihoods

Rural India is alive to myriad livelihood formulations amongst poor households. The issue of how and why certain households travel down particular livelihood pathways is an important one that has generated an intense research effort over decades. Focusing on *non-farm livelihood diversification* (decisions by agricultural landholders to re-orient their sources of livelihood dependence away from farm own-production), complex connections exist between the background circumstances of households, and their livelihood decisions. How these actions impact on the food security of participants (alleviating or aggravating vulnerabilities) is a key question.

A starting point for this discussion is the important (but sometimes overlooked) observation that the non-farm livelihood diversification amongst the rural poor is not novel. Although researchers such as Rigg (2006) rightly emphasise the importance of these processes in recent rural restructuring across the developing world, the rhythms of life for many rural households over generations have involved a range of diversification activities. The seasonality of agriculture means that rural lives progress through annual cycles of busy and lean times, and livelihood diversification has traditionally been employed by many households as a "labour smoothing" vehicle to keep up the flow of income outside of peak farming times (Bryceson, 1999). "Diversification is the norm" (Barrett *et al.*, 2001: 315) when it comes to rural livelihoods.

Posing the question of "why" non-farm livelihood diversification occurs brings in the oft-cited distinction between distress/necessity (when current situations do not sustain the basic expectations of a standard of living any more), and opportunity (tailored decisions by householders to improve their lot). A traditional approach to this issue within development theory tends to emphasise the importance of distress. The classic argument suggests that where "agriculture is unable to provide sufficient employment, rural [informal non-farm employment] picks up a part of the slack" (Kundu and Chakrabarti, 2010: 202). In other words, de-agrarianisation and non-farm livelihood diversification are fundamental symptoms of agricultural crisis. Alternative approaches, however, identify the rural non-farm economy not as a residual destination of distressed would-be farmers, but in terms of a positive symbiosis with agriculture (Hazell and Haggblade, 1990; as discussed by Kundu and Chakrabarti, 2010: 202). Evidence from sub-Saharan Africa suggests the primacy of this latter process. Reardon (1997) finds that there is a greater propensity for diversification into non-farm activities in "better-than-average" agricultural districts, suggesting that opportunity, not distress, is a chief driver for these strategies. Moreover, in the Indian context, the regularly cited exemplar of this dynamic is the way the Green Revolution in Punjab (see Chapter Three) induced significant non-farm rural employment in the tertiary sector (Tripathy, 2009: 117). The evidence on whether diversification is distress-induced or opportunity-pulled is rather mixed, primarily due to the varying social, economic, geographic and cultural contexts under which it occurs.

Although it is conceptually alluring to wrap this debate on non-farm livelihood diversification within the simple framework of distress versus opportunity, the reality is much more complex, with non-farm livelihood diversification existing within a spectrum of household decision-making contexts and motivations. Household members navigate intricate "micro-portfolios" of livelihood activities including agricultural and pastoral production, accessing common property resources, wage work, caring for children, elderly and infirm family members and "a selective, often precarious incorporation into the non-farm trading and service economy" (Harriss-White, 2008: 555). This is evidenced in a survey of livelihood diversification in rural Orissa (Tripathy, 2009) which found that about 40 per cent of adults were engaged in multiple economic activities to earn their livelihood, with slightly more than 30 per cent engaged in three or more activities. Moreover, the basket of activities which comprise household members' livelihood activities was found to be highly volatile – "Most of the households in rural areas diversify their livelihood options frequently" (p. 135) – and shaped heavily by social norms and cultural conventions.

Appreciation of this point returns us to the seminal framework established by Chambers and Conway (1992) which categorises livelihood strategies within two broad vectors (Table 5.1):

- sectoral vectors – whether diversification occurs through engaging in livelihood opportunities off-farm (i.e., still in agriculture but on other people's farms) or non-farm (i.e., entirely outside of the agricultural sector); and
- spatial vectors – whether diversification occurs through new livelihood sources located locally, or non-locally.

The discussion that follows uses the broad logic of this framework to tease out key dimensions of non-farm livelihood diversification in India. The overarching theme we pursue is that these processes are being expressed in increasingly differentiated, fragmented and complex forms. The trajectories of India's national development (discussed later in this chapter) are widening the overall range of livelihood diversification options for rural households. However, of crucial importance, households are positioned very differently in terms of their abilities to engage with these options, leading to new patterns of livelihood and food security. This is manifested in three core ways:

i. Social conventions and cultural norms, based particularly around caste and community in the rural Indian context, continue to generate restrictions for some and enable opportunities for others. In contexts where non-farm diversification is becoming more crucial for the maintenance (and indeed, in some cases, survival) of livelihoods, these factors can perpetuate and even aggravate the social distinctions of food and livelihood insecurity.

TABLE 5.1 A typology of livelihood diversification

		→ Spatial vector	
		Local	Non-local
↓ Sectoral vector	Off-farm	Local agricultural wage-labour	Harvest migration and other seasonal agricultural flows
	Non-farm	Petty business Artisanal activities Employment in non-agricultural rural economy Hunting, gathering	Circular and permanent rural-to-rural migration Circular and permanent rural-to-urban migration

Source: Own work, derived from concepts in Chambers and Conway (1992)

ii. Pre-existing patterns and size distributions of agricultural land holdings stratify dependence on non-farm livelihood diversification, with small landholders generally having more dire needs to access sources of non-farm livelihood. The growing trend towards smaller land holding sizes across India for the bulk of poor and vulnerable households (see Chapter Four), coupled with pressures on common property resources (forests, fisheries, grazing lands) is pushing more households into potential situations of distress-induced needs to diversify their livelihoods. However, these households are not always well placed to participate in the non-farm economy in advantageous ways.

iii. Increased motivations/incentives to participate in non-farm livelihood activities are refracted through intra-household dynamics of gender, age and household position (first-born, unmarried, etc.). These refractions create socially differentiated patterns of participation in the non-farm economy. Different members of a household may receive different degrees of benefit/detriment from the decision by one household member to engage in (particularly non-local) forms of livelihood diversification.

The first of these three factors has important analytical weight in the Indian context. Much of the international literature on livelihood diversification emphasises the economic incentives behind household decisions. Thus, based largely on observations from the sub-Saharan African context, Ellis (2000: 294) characterises livelihood diversification in terms of a set of trade-offs between households concentrating their efforts in fewer activities (enabling "a higher total income involving greater probability of income failure") or spreading their interests (creating "a lower total income involving smaller probability of income failure"). Barrett *et al.* (2001: 320–21) argue that livelihood diversification is more prone to exist in situations where there are diminishing returns to scale from agricultural effort, and where there is time-variance in returns on productive assets (for example, through seasonality, as mentioned above).

In India, however, economic incentives relating to livelihood diversification are enacted within situated contexts deeply saturated by social conventions and cultural norms. Despite their formal disavowal by the Indian State, categories of caste continue to shape the scope of livelihood options for many, thereby tempering the extent to which economistic assumptions about incentives (such as those discussed above by Barrett *et al.* in the context of sub-Saharan Africa) readily translate in Indian settings to behavioural responses.

The persistence of these dimensions of rural social life in modern India means that within individual communities, distress and opportunity can often co-exist as prompts for livelihood diversification This capacity for differentiation was highlighted by Sinha (2007) in a useful study which examines non-farm diversification through a comparative survey of 1,500 households in three districts of Uttar Pradesh (Saharanpur, Jhansi and Kanpur) and two districts of Uttarakhand (Dehradun and Almora). Disaggregation of survey data revealed that different caste and community groups adopted quite varying incidences of non-farm livelihood diversification (which is not particularly surprising) but, significantly, this differed considerably for the same groups across different case study areas. Hence, in one community, Scheduled Caste households exhibited high levels of non-farm livelihood diversification while, in another, this group did not. Adding to these inequities, economic opportunities in village life in India are often orchestrated by livelihood gatekeepers, such as Gram Panchayat presidents/secretaries, large landowners and moneylenders, whose preferences and interests are connected closely to caste and community. Social and cultural capital remain vital ingredients in access to employment in rural India (Jodhka, 2012: 7). A study by Lanjouw and Shariff (2004) on non-farm employment in rural India, based on the 1993–94 survey of 32,000 rural households spread across 1,765 villages, highlights significant differentials in the access to non-farm incomes by wealth, education and social status. It found that while the share of non-farm income from "casual non-farm employment" is higher for populations belonging to poorer wealth quintiles, participation in more remunerative "regular nonfarm employment" is higher among richer wealth groups. As summarised by Tripathy (2009: 137): "The greater mobility of high-caste people due to their influential contacts, helps them in accessing opportunities better, while it is restricted for the lower caste households." Thus, in making decisions about livelihood diversification, households traverse an intricate terrain of social obligations, economic uncertainty and local politics.

One of the key factors that appear to shape the different propensities of caste and community groups to engage in non-farm livelihood diversification is the patterning and size distribution of agricultural land holdings. As an illustrative example of the ongoing pervasiveness of caste and community in structuring rural land, Jodkha (2012: 8) reports that in his case study village in Haryana, 95 per cent of the Dalit community was landless whilst 88 per cent of the dominant caste owned land. Across India, the average holding size for rural Scheduled Caste (SC) households is 0.304 ha, compared with 0.767 ha for Scheduled Tribe (ST) rural households, 0.758 ha for Other Backward Caste (OBC) rural households and 1.003 ha for other groups. Fully 77.1 per cent of SC rural households in rural India have holdings between 0.02 and 0.5 ha, emphasising their marginality (NSSO, 2006).

The importance of land assets as a shaper of the social patterns of livelihood diversification has been demonstrated by Kundu and Chakrabarty (2010) in a study which makes use of data from the NSS 59th round (undertaken in 2003). These authors find that a strong negative relationship exists between the size of a household's landholdings and the relative size of their earnings from non-farm activities (Table 5.2). In other words, households with very small land holdings tend to have their livelihood dependence immersed more deeply in non-agricultural sectors than is the case for households with somewhat larger holdings, on average. These data point to the analytical fallacy of conceptualising small agricultural landholders as simply "farmers". Their agricultural holdings might be a core asset within their livelihoods (and a vitally important source of their food security: see Kundu and Chakrabarty, 2010: 218–19) but sustain households only in combination with (often more economically significant) non-farm activities.

TABLE 5.2 Net receipts (Rs) from non-farm activities, per hectare of land owned, 2003 (major agricultural states only)

State	Size of land holdings				
	0.01–0.4 ha	0.41–1 ha	1.01–2 ha	2.01–4 ha	4.01–10 ha
Andhra Pradesh	595	226	140	21	44
Assam	1,746	275	77	17	229
Bihar	1,039	250	70	56	100
Gujarat	498	214	86	48	23
Haryana	1,595	488	233	73	25
Karnataka	1,473	173	80	51	16
Maharashtra	980	304	43	74	185
Orissa	615	209	56	139	111
Punjab	3,361	238	227	109	18
Tamil Nadu	1,244	194	94	66	12
Uttar Pradesh	1,088	217	78	65	10
West Bengal	1,951	390	380	142	49

Source: Kundu and Chakrabarty (2010: 205), calculated originally from data in NSS 59th round

These relationships have crucial importance in light of the progressive diminution of the average sizes of agricultural land holdings in India (see Chapter Four). A key emergent dynamic is the growth of a cohort of households with increasingly small landholdings and ever more dependence on the non-farm economy. At the extreme, there is some evidence that these forces are encouraging a significant number of small and marginal landholding households to abandon cultivation altogether, either leaving their lands fallow or leasing them out to others. Although the leasing of agricultural land was made illegal "almost everywhere" in post-Independent India (Deshingkar and Farrington, 2006: 81) due to capacity for tenant exploitation within interlocking rent, credit and labour markets controlled by landlords, the persistence of semi-feudal landlordism across many parts of the country has underpinned a continuation of these practices. In any case, whether legal or not, these arrangements are poorly monitored and regulated, and the liberalisation ethos during India's present reform period has encouraged, rather than restrained, their proliferation. One of the few studies of this issue suggests there is strong evidence of an increased propensity for leasing in Indian agriculture (Ramchandran et al., 2010).

Increased leasing arrangements in agriculture have given rise to an apparent new social category in rural India, labelled as "non-cultivating peasant households" (NCPHs). A specific study of these developments argued that the share of NCPHs among India's rural population probably doubled between 1981 and 2002, and may constitute around 20 per cent of all rural households (Vijay, 2012: 40). On the other hand, this shift away from agriculture to non-farm employment by the small and marginal farm households may encourage the participation of traditionally disadvantaged landless poor (often belonging to Scheduled Caste and Scheduled Tribe groups) into farm activities, primarily resulting from the emergence of new sharecropping arrangements. It is unclear how these developments impact on the food security circumstances of vulnerable groups. Some insight is provided by the results of a primary survey of 400 rural households, conducted by one of the authors (Choithani) in the Siwan district of Bihar during February–May 2012. Sharecropping, called *batai* in local parlance, is becoming an increasingly important feature of local agricultural systems in Siwan. Out of the 302 households who reported having been engaged in farming during 2011–12, 48.3 per cent had increased the size of their holdings through leasing. The average landholding size of these farm households, including the land leased in, was however less than 0.25 ha, which inhibited sustained improvements in households' food security status by farm production alone and, thus, supplementary income sources were needed to meet food consumption needs.

In such instances, a crucial question then becomes the relationship between changes in the ownership of agricultural landholdings, and agricultural land use practices. One of the important characteristics of traditional forms of agriculture in rural India is that it has tended to be strongly embedded in local economies, often creating substantial employment opportunities through local stores and public sector agencies provisioning farmers with inputs (seeds and agrichemicals, etc.) and post-farm-gate activities (packing sheds, storage facilities, and crop processing factories for sugar refineries, cotton gins, wheat and rice millers, etc.). However, one of the great unknowns in contemporary Indian agricultural policy is whether and how recent processes of land use change, connected to crop diversification and modernisation, alter these local economic relations. According to Kundu and Chakrabarty (2010), these developments have the potential for radically disrupting these local sources of employment. Following on from arguments made in the previous chapter, a potential implication of the emergence of modern forms of high-value horticulture in India is a fracturing of the local linkages connecting farm production with agricultural input supply and post-farm-gate warehousing and processing. Citing the work of Sukhpal Singh (2008), Kundu and Chakrabarty (2010: 216–17) point to the potential situation where high value crops are:

> siphoned off for "big city" consumption or for exports, and on the other hand, modern inputs and modern farm services are introduced into the agricultural sector. The same channel could even be used to sell "big city" products in rural areas without consideration for the local economy (Singh, 2008). Thus, there could be loss of the local relative autonomy . . . The complementarity between agriculture and the informal, non-farm economy is replaced with a tacit conflict, wherein development of "modern" agriculture displaces rural non-agricultural production.

Finally, it should go without saying that intra-household dynamics play a crucial role in influencing livelihood pathways. Households are not all alike when it comes to size (how many children and elders need to be looked after), the sex ratios of household members and their human capital attributes (health, education, disability, etc.). Focusing on these issues, Nair *et al.* (2007) explore the differences in household livelihood responses to a crash in agricultural prices in a village in Wayanad District,

Kerala, in the early 2000s. Their analysis situates livelihood diversification within household-based permutations of risk and adaptation. The researchers found that smallholder households adapted to lower agricultural prices through a diverse array of responses including: (i) reducing household consumption; (ii) replacing hired labour on their holdings with family labour; (iii) selling family and farm assets; (iv) borrowing money and mortgaging gold; (v) making greater use of traditional labour-sharing practices; (vi) diversifying their farm activities (mainly through an increased role of dairying); (vii) diversifying crops; (viii) leasing land; and (ix) (for women) making increased use of self-help groups (SHGs). How and whether individual households pursued any of these options was determined by their internal characteristics.

The discussion above of how livelihood diversification is shaped by social conventions, cultural norms and landholding patterns has focused primarily on the local "spatial vector", to use the terminology of Table 5.1. However, non-farm diversification is not restricted to only local opportunities, but also involves a wide range of activities in distant locations as well. In the case of India the significance of migration as a rural livelihood strategy is on the rise. Thus, our attention now focuses on enquiring various facets of this *non-localised* dimension of non-farm livelihood diversification in India and its interrelationship with food security outcomes.

For the land-poor and landless rural households of India, earnings from wage labour, however meagre, have traditionally formed an important component of household income. The low levels of economic activity and imperfect nature of rural labour markets, however, imply that more often than not they have to seek wage employment in the distant labour markets. Thus, migration has long been an integral part of rural livelihood strategies. The predominant stream of migration in India has involved rural to rural circulation of labour, for instance the migration from the agriculturally poor regions of eastern Uttar Pradesh and Bihar to the Green Revolution frontiers of Punjab and Haryana. Agrarian crisis – seven million farmers quit agriculture during 1991–2011 (Sainath, 2011) – and the urban-centric nature of India's economic growth, however, are altering the patterns of migration, with rural to urban migration growing at a much faster rate than before. Some 35 per cent of India's urban population is constituted by migrants (NSSO, 2010: 22).[1]

A defining feature of migration among rural dwellers is its seasonal and circular character, constituting a bulk of migratory movements. Consequently, rural out-migrants have been defined variously as "nowhere people" (Breman, 2010: 17) and "unsettled settlers" (de Haan, 1997: 482). Using data from the 64th round of the NSSO survey, Keshri and Bhagat (2010: 83) estimate the number of temporary migrants in India to be around 13 million. Alternative estimates, however, suggest that between 50 million (Breman, 2010: 7) to 100 million (Deshingkar and Akter, 2010: 3) people remain on the move for their livelihoods in any given year. This official failure to capture the true magnitude of seasonal and circular migration has resulted in an "abysmally low" understanding among policymakers of the importance of migration for the rural poor (Deshingkar and Start, 2003: 1).

The apparent recent surge in the mobility levels among the rural poor has been aided by significant improvements in transport and communication infrastructure, reducing both the physical and emotional distance between places of origin and work. Furthermore, new forms of population mobility are fast emerging. For example, as a result of expansion of peri-urban space blurring the boundaries between rural and urban areas, commuting for work is becoming increasingly popular. In 2009–10, 8.05 million non-agriculture rural workers commuted to urban areas for work (Chandrasekhar, 2011: 22). The heightened levels of mobility among the rural poor, thus, beg the question of the potential impacts of migration on rural poverty and livelihood and food security.

The traditionally prevailing view of migration among the rural poor is that it tends to be dominated by distress-induced flows, with very little prospect for their upward social and economic mobility (or that of the household they belong to). To quote Breman (2010: 10–11):

> For a large majority of these people, poorly educated or totally illiterate, labour circulation is not a free choice but a strenuous and tiresome expedition that has to be repeated again and again, rarely rewarded by getting skilled or bringing back savings that can be used for productive investment leading to a more secure economic condition.

However, missing from this thinking is the consideration "what these individuals or households would have done in the absence of the opportunity to migrate" (Deshingkar and Grimm, 2005: 40). As Stark (1991: 19) suggests: "Good policies should employ effective means to minimize or eliminate the few (if any) undesirable consequences of migration, but not eliminate migration itself."

In fact, the research on rural livelihood systems suggests that migration by rural poor may not necessarily be a response to shocks and may actually represent a calculated strategy of allocating household labour more efficiently (Bigsten, 1996) in order to attain a diversified livelihood portfolio to mitigate income risks (Stark, 1991). Furthermore, there is compelling evidence to suggest that, despite its distressed nature, migration can not only provide a *safety valve* for poor populations, but can also contribute to their sustainable human development (UNDP, 2009). The overall gains from migration far outweigh the losses, albeit varying by the skills, resources and social networks of the migrants. Empirical evidence gathered by Deshingkar and Start (2003) in six villages in each of the two Indian states of Andhra Pradesh and Madhya Pradesh suggest that, over time, "distress-induced migration" becomes "accumulative migration" as migrants acquired skills and establish relationships with the employers. They also find that accumulative migration streams assist poor people not only to escape poverty but also break free of caste constraints. Findings of a primary survey conducted on rural–urban migrant households in the slums of Delhi also found that as migrants acquire experience, they are more likely to move from low-income and casual jobs to high-income and regular jobs, thus improving their living standards (Gupta and Mitra, 2002). A study by de Haan (2002) of circular migrants from the Saran District of Bihar to Kolkata also supports this finding. Another study focusing on labour out-migration among rice-farming households in three districts of eastern Uttar Pradesh highlighted that remittances from the migration had a favourable impact on housing investment and consumer durables and goods (Paris *et al.*, 2005).

From the perspective of food security, the most direct impact of migration on food and nutritional outcome of rural households may be felt through the remittance sent by migrant members. Income from migration can not only prevent the food entitlement failures but also significantly enhance access to food by all household members. The predominantly seasonal and circular character of migration in India implies a scope of interaction between rural and urban economy. De Haan's study finds that remittances sent by migrants are used to invest in household-owned agriculture (de Haan, 1997: 486). This, by the means of enhancing farm output, can potentially raise household farm income as well as food availability for its own consumption and, in turn, the overall food security status of the household.

The growing importance of migration in the rural livelihood systems warrants a greater policy attention than it currently receives. A policy environment that acknowledges the increasingly multi-locational forms of rural livelihoods (Deshingkar and Farrington, 2009) can greatly enhance the food and livelihood security outcomes of the people on the move.

The structural constraints of economy and employment in contemporary India

> In the Commission's view, the dualistic nature of the Indian economy has significantly moved away from the textbook division of agriculture and non-agriculture (often referred to as traditional and modern) sectors and has been replaced by the informal and formal dichotomy, cutting across the sectors.
>
> *(National Commission for Enterprises in the Unorganised Sector, 2007: 12)*

Although India's GDP has grown rapidly over recent decades, the characteristics of growth have meant that poor and marginal segments of the population have not necessarily been in a strong position to capture benefits. The bare statistical bones of this argument are as follows. Cross-national comparisons suggest that economic take-off in India since the early 1990s has been associated with a relatively low elasticity of poverty reduction, especially for those in absolute poverty. The number of Indians living in absolute poverty (defined in monetary terms as less than US$1.25 per day, in 2005 Purchasing Power Parity) fell by only 0.7 per cent annually over the years from 1994 to 2005 (from 49.4 per cent to 41.6 per cent of the population). By contrast, other Asian countries tended to exhibit a much stronger elasticity of poverty reduction during their phases of economic take-off. In rural China, the average annual rate of absolute poverty reduction was 4.5 per cent during the period 1992–2005; in rural Indonesia it was 2.8 per cent (1993–2005), and in Vietnam it was 3.6 per cent (1993–2004) (all data, World Bank, 2010). Similarly, in the past decade Brazil has exhibited impressive performance on reducing poverty and inequality despite slower GDP growth than India (we discuss the social policy experience of Brazil in Chapter

Seven). Comparing the growth elasticity of poverty reduction in Brazil, China and India, Ravallion (2011: 78) notes: "If India had Brazil's elasticity; then India's growth rate would have delivered a rate of poverty reduction of 15% per annum."

Not surprisingly, India's relatively weak progress in combating poverty in the context of rapid economic growth has been allied with evidence of increased economic inequality across the country. Between 1994 and 2005 the Gini coefficient (measuring the rate of inequality) rose from 28.6 to 30.5 in rural India and from 34.3 to 37.6 in urban India (World Bank, 2010). And furthermore, in recent years there has been intensified debate in India about the apparent faltering in progress against poverty. The Tendulkar Committee (which inquired into these issues on behalf of the Planning Commission of India) recommended an upward revision of the official measurement of poverty, so that the ratio for 2004–05 was increased from 27.5 per cent to 37.2 per cent of the population. Recent updating of the Tendulkar methodology[2] suggests that India's poverty headcount ratio had fallen to 29.8 per cent in 2009–10, indicating progress, however with an overall incidence of poverty that is higher than what was assumed to be the case half a decade earlier. State-wise analyses of these data, moreover, point to significantly different experiences with regards to poverty reduction (Table 5.3). Between 2004 and 2005 and 2009–10, most states exhibited progress against the incidence of poverty; however,

TABLE 5.3 Percentage of population in poverty, 2004–05 and 2009–10, major states

	2004–05	*2009–10*	*Percentage point change*
Bihar	53.5	54.4	0.9
Chhattisgarh	49.4	48.7	-0.7
Jharkhand	45.3	39.1	-6.2
Assam	34.4	37.9	3.5
Uttar Pradesh	40.9	37.7	-3.2
Orissa	57.2	37.0	-20.2
Madhya Pradesh	48.6	36.7	-11.9
West Bengal	34.2	26.7	-7.5
Rajasthan	34.4	24.8	-9.6
Maharashtra	38.2	24.5	-13.7
Karnataka	33.3	23.6	-9.7
Gujarat	31.6	23.0	-8.6
Andhra Pradesh	29.6	21.1	-8.5
Haryana	24.1	20.1	-4
Uttarakhand	32.7	18.0	-14.7
Tamil Nadu	29.4	17.1	-12.3
Punjab	20.9	15.9	-5
Delhi	13.0	14.2	1.2
Kerala	19.6	12.0	-7.6
Himachal Pradesh	22.9	9.5	-13.4
Jammu & Kashmir	13.1	9.4	-3.7

Source: Planning Commission of India (2012b). Consistent Tendulkar Committee methodology based on state-wise poverty lines

the poverty ratios for some of the bigger states declined very marginally. Another striking fact is that the poverty levels increased in five of the seven north-eastern states of Assam, Meghalaya, Manipur, Mizoram and Nagaland during the corresponding period (Planning Commission of India, 2012a).

The failures of rapid economic growth to make stronger inroads into poverty reduction are linked closely to the structural composition of India's economy. Patterns of Indian economic growth have differed significantly from the norm experienced elsewhere in the developing world, particularly when compared to East and South East Asia. The key distinction has been the relatively muted contribution of manufacturing within recent growth. Contrary to development pathways of lower-income countries elsewhere across the world in the 1990s and 2000s (Memedovic and Lapadre, 2009), in India, the share of total national employment in manufacturing has stagnated, and then, from around 2007–08, actually declined (Aggarwal and Kumar, 2012: 7). India's economic take-off since the early 1990s has been predicated on a service-oriented structural transformation rather than one based around the primary role of export-oriented manufacturing, à la the East and Southeast Asian model (Aggarwal and Kumar, 2012: 24).

The relative importance of the services sector as against manufacturing has had major impacts for India's poor. A general rule revealed across East and South East Asia is that growth in export-oriented manufacturing filters widely through the domestic economy. This is because of the multiplier effects of intra-industry linkages, and the strong positive externalities associated with the upgrading of skills, infrastructure and technologies that are attached to the need to service export markets (Freeman and Bartels, 2004). Manufacturing tends to soak up large numbers of the unemployed and underemployed labour pool, incorporating them into a jobs market that generally pays higher wages than other sectors of the economy (Whitfield, 2012). Evidence suggests that these tendencies also exist in India's manufacturing sector (Aggarwal and Kumar, 2012: 23); however, because of its relatively laggard growth, the Indian economy has not been able to capitalise on these attributes.

Conversely, the most prominent engine of growth in India's recent economic history – the business services sector – exhibits relatively narrow linkages to the domestic economy. The rise of business services in India's economy is a relatively recent phenomenon. The catalytic event which is habitually used to account for its dramatic take-off was the need for companies to safeguard their operations from the potentially adverse effects of the Y2K bug during 1999. The Indian ICT sector was well placed to service these needs, having a large reservoir of trained, English-language-speaking computer and ICT engineers, especially in the southern cities of Bangalore, Hyderabad and Chennai (Kapur, 2002; Kumar and Joseph, 2005; 2007). The rapid growth of ICT activities quickly created a substantial urban middle class attached to these sectors; however, the direct benefits for poorer, geographically isolated segments of the Indian populace have been harder to glean. Econometric analysis by Bosworth et al. (2007: 3–4) concludes that the expansion of the sector "is not creating adequate job growth for the bulk of the Indian population that is not particularly well-educated". This general finding is consistent with the observation by Ferreira and Ravallion (2008) that India entered the 1990s with a large segment of its population effectively marginalised from the ability to participate in opportunities accorded by faster economic growth, because of dire livelihood conditions, low literacy and educational levels and geographical isolation. Thus, in the long period from 1972–73 to 2009–10, India's service sector increased its share in GDP by 22 percentage points, but increased its share of national employment by only 10 percentage points (Aggarwal and Kumar, 2012: 31). The growth of India's service sector, therefore, has been associated with relatively low employment intensity, a human capital bias towards highly educated individuals and a spatial clustering around a few privileged (mainly southern) urban spaces.

In terms of poverty alleviation, the problematic sectoral composition of the Indian economy is compounded by the persistence of a dual labour market between formal and informal employment. Informalisation is an important issue for poverty reduction and food insecurity in India because of its lower wages and more precarious employment conditions. The average daily wage level in the informal sector is approximately half that paid by the formal sector (Goldar and Aggarwal, 2010: 2; NSSO, 2012: iii), and of course, these workers also miss out on a raft of social security benefits that are mandatory for formal-sector employment (Dutta, 2007: 5). The situation is pithily summarised in a study of employment informalisation in Coimbatore, Tamil Nadu:

> workers in the Coimbatore informal sector face a high degree of employment and health insecurity. Workers are found to toil for long hours. Gender-based wage discrimination is widely prevalent. An interesting feature observed is the high casualisation of labour. The workers have nobody to turn to, the government is indifferent, the casual mechanism is tardy, and there is a major dilemma about the unions. Due to the unhealthy and unhygienic nature of the production process, around two-fifths of the workers are affected by occupational health hazards. No specific healthcare protection is made available to these workers either by the government or by the employers.
>
> *(Naagarajan, 2010: 359)*

Interpretation of recent trends in the incidence of informal employment in India requires brief consideration of a set of important distinctions. The conceptual definition of informal employment is somewhat complex, because informalisation can occur across various types of economic unit (Figure 5.1). Most *informal employment* occurs within the *informal sector*;[3] however, it can also exist in formally incorporated enterprises (through casualisation and temporary employment) and within households (when a member of kin is informally engaged within an economic activity wholly undertaken by household members).

Authoritative estimates of the extent of informal employment in India have been generated by the National Sample Survey Organisation (NSSO) in its 55th round

Economic units by type	Own-account workers		Employers		Contributing family workers	Employees			Members of producers' cooperatives	
	Informal	Formal	Informal	Formal	Informal	Informal	Formal		Informal	Formal
Formal-sector enterprises										
Informal-sector enterprises										
Households										

FIGURE 5.1 Conceptual definition of informal employment
Shaded cells indicate components of informal employment

Source: NSSO (2012: 32)

(1999–2000), 61st round (2004–05) and 66th round (2009–10). The release of data from the NSS 61st round occurred in close coincidence with the change of govern-ment at the national level. In 2004, the Congress-Party-led UPA coalition, under the prime ministership of Dr Manmohan Singh, formed office. A vital element in this political shift was the electorate's apparent rejection of the "India Shining" cam-paign slogan associated with the incumbent Bharatiya Janata Party (BJP). This slogan operated on the premise that India's impressive economic growth credentials were being translated into improved living standards for the bulk of the populace. Release of the NSS 61st round data exposed this deceit. It indicated that the growth of India's economy was not translating into a substantial formalisation of employment across the country, with commensurate improvements in working conditions and wages. Rather, the NSS 61st round data revealed that the proportion of workers in India defined as being in informal employment actually *increased* from 91.2 per cent in 1999–2000 to 92.4 per cent in 2004–05 (Naik, 2009: 8), in seeming contraven-tion of standard models of classical economic development theory which assumed that "the traditional or informal sector would gradually shrink with the process of industrialisation, urbanisation, and modernisation" (Maiti and Sen, 2010: 195).

This contradiction between the pattern of economic growth and employment conditions was then taken up during the UPA's first terms of office through the establishment of the National Commission for Enterprises in the Unorganised Sec-tor (NCEUS), formed under the chairmanship of the late Professor Arjun Sengupta. Crucially, the Commission connected the dots between poverty and employment informalisation. According to the Commission, in 2004–05 some 20.4 per cent of informal workers had incomes below their state-specific poverty lines, as against just 4.9 per cent of workers with regularised wages and conditions (NCEUS, 2007: 24).[4] Informal workers were found to be highly vulnerable to widespread flouting of the *Minimum Wages Act* (NCEUS, 2007: 42) and piece-rate payment regimes that were open to deception by supervisors.[5] In rural India, the majority of casual workers in key employment sectors were paid well below the minimum wage, with women faring much worse than men (Table 5.4). Crucially in terms of

TABLE 5.4 Average daily earnings of casual workers by industry and gender, rural India, 2004–05

	Rupees per day			Percentage below Minimum Wage		
	Male	Female	All persons	Male	Female	All persons
Agriculture	47.88	33.15	42.48	86.56	96.71	90.46
Manufacturing	63.85	37.63	57.59	63.86	92.89	71.37
Construction	69.49	49.81	66.94	58.25	85.99	61.91

Source: NCEUS (2007: 259)

public debate, the NCEUS told this narrative using tangible monetary comparisons. At a time when the middle class was booming and the trappings of more expensive forms of day-to-day consumption (shopping malls, modern cafes, etc.) were sprouting across India's cities, the NCEUS emphasised the fact that almost 77 per cent of workers in the informal sector in 2004–05 were earning less than Rs 20 per day. And, moreover, approximately one third of this group was attempting to survive in the "extremely poor" and "poor" range of less than Rs 11 per day (NCEUS, 2007: 6).[6] NCEUS's summary of labour market developments in India during the post-liberalisation period from the early 1990s is outlined in Box 5.1.

BOX 5.1 A SUMMARY OF LABOUR MARKET TRENDS IN INDIA FROM THE EARLY 1990s TO 2004–05

1. The record of employment–unemployment in [the period 1993–94 to 2004–05] has been unimpressive compared to the previous decade . . . and this despite higher aggregate growth. We have estimated that the annual growth rate of employment declined from 2.03% in 1983–1993/94 to 1.85% between 1993–94 and 2004–05.

2. Employment in India can be meaningfully grouped into four categories to reflect quality and its sectoral association. These are (a) formal employment in the formal or organised sector, (b) informal employment in the formal sector, (c) formal employment in the informal sector, and (d) informal employment in the informal sector. We find that the Indian economy is dominated by (d), constantly around 86% of employment as of 2004–05.

3. The net growth of employment [in the period 1999–00 to 2004–05] has been largely of an informal kind, implying that these workers are vulnerable in significant ways. This is true of both formal and informal sectors. What this means is that even the increase in employment in the formal sector is entirely that of informal employment suggesting informalisation of the formal sector as far as employment is concerned.

4. The growth rate of wages of almost all categories of workers, including casual work which concerns the bottom layer of workers, has declined during 1993–94 to 2004–05 . . . This is clearly a case of generalized slowdown in the growth of wages when the overall economy registered a higher growth in income during the second period compared to the first.
5. Informal-sector enterprises face higher constraints on growth due to lack of access to credit, technology, marketing, skills, and also incentives. . . .
6. A large proportion of the Indian workforce and the Indian population continues to be "poor and vulnerable" . . . and this segment has experienced very low rates of improvement in living standards as a whole since the early 1990s . . .
7. The growth [in living standards] that has occurred has been unequal, concentrating its benefits among the top segments of the population.

Source: NCEUS (2009: 9–10)

The recent release of data from the NSS 66th round (NSSO, 2012) seems to confirm that the tendencies identified by the NCEUS remain a prevailing feature of the Indian labour market. Unfortunately, NSSO (2012) does not present data on the incidence of employment informalisation in a way that enables direct comparison with earlier results.[7] However, examination of different components of labour market change suggests that the tendency for informalisation has continued, albeit in a roundabout way. What seems to be occurring in India is that the percentage of workers employed in the informal sector (as noted above, a subset of *informal employment*) has declined (Table 5.5) but there has been a strong surge towards the informalisation of employment (mainly via casualisation) in the formal sector. NSS data points to the fact that between 2004–05 and 2009–10, the proportion of workers with no written job contract and who were not eligible for paid leave increased from 63 per cent to 65.8 per cent (NSSO, 2012: 69), which, in the context of the data in Table 5.5, implies a substantial increase in informalisation in the formal sector. Further evidence on this point is provided in the work of Jatav (2012), who provides a detailed assessment of the rural component of the 2009–10 NSS data. Jatav's manipulation of the NSS data suggests that an unprecedented jump in casualisation occurred between 2004–05 and 2009–10, leading to an increase

TABLE 5.5 Percentage of workers employed in informal sector, 2004–05 and 2009–10

	Rural – male	*Rural – female*	*Urban – male*	*Urban – female*
2004–05 (61st round of NSS)	79.2	86.4	73.9	65.4
2009–10 (66th round of NSS)	74.2	74.4	68.5	61.6
Percentage point decline over five years	5.0	12.0	5.4	3.8

Source: NSSO (2012: 50). Note: excludes persons growing crops and tending livestock

in the proportion of casuals amongst rural non-farm workers from 26.6 per cent to 36.6 per cent. Disaggregation of these data by social category and geography points to significant associations between marginalisation, distress and the rising incidence of casual workers. Jatav argues that increases in the incidence of casualisation are strongest amongst Scheduled Tribe and Scheduled Caste populations, and in relatively disadvantaged and remoter parts of the country including central Uttar Pradesh, most of Madhya Pradesh, central parts of Bihar, mountainous regions of Jammu and Kashmir, western, southern and northern parts of Rajasthan, inland parts of Tamil Nadu, coastal and southern Orissa, the western plains of West Bengal and the Ranchi Plateau of Jharkhand. Hence, Jatav (2012) sees a convergence of economic, social and institutional factors contributing to casualisation:

> Growth of casual workers in 2009–10 seems to be a result of some distress push factors such as poverty, low levels of education, less amount [sic] of land owned etc. But during the period of 2004–05 to 2009–10, there may have been some pull factors, namely, increasing demand of labour in some particular sectors [strongly associated with temporary and casual employment practices] like construction, mining and quarrying and services.

The informalisation of formal employment by way of casualisation also raises the contentious issue of labour market rigidities in India in the form of industrial regulation. A recurring refrain in the Indian discussion of labour market casualisation is that many employers have informalised and casualised their workforces to get around prescriptions and obligations in legislation (Besley and Burgess, 2004; Sharma, 2006). However, as Kannan and Raveendran (2009) note, it is difficult to tease out the precise role of labour regulations in the hiring and firing of employees in modern India, because of the accelerated context of industry restructuring in which firms currently operate. NCEUS (2009: 174) seeks to reframe this issue in terms of a holistic perspective on the labour market, incorporating both the economic arguments about incentives to hire new workers and the need to underpin labour laws within human rights:

> A repeated comment on the labour regulations in India is that there are far too many labour laws. In fact, there are too many laws for too few in the organised sector and too few for too many in the unorganised sector. Such multiplicity of labour laws has emerged because each piece of legislation was enacted as and when the need for the regulation of some segment or an aspect of the labour market arose. An integrated view does not appear to have been taken. As each piece of legislation was drafted independently of others (often copied from similar legislation in other countries), not only did the labour legislation proliferate but it also led to various definitions, often contradictory, of the same terms.

During the past few years, the issues of employment informalisation and the mismatch between economic growth and the living standards of the poor have been brought together under the banner of "decent work". This term gathered traction in the 1990s in association with social debate over globalisation and the formation of the MDGs (ILO, 1999) and was a centrepiece of the International Labour Organisation's "Global Employment Agenda" established in 2003 (ILO, 2003). In the Indian context, the concept of decent work has numerous manifestations including gender equality, child labour, workplace safety, work and livelihoods, etc. For the purposes of this discussion, however, an important outcome from the advocacy of this concept was the way it has infiltrated national economic policy. As suggested by Papola (2008: 5), the notion of "decent work" is implicit within the shift of emphasis between the Government of India's Tenth Five-Year Plan (2002–07) and its Eleventh Five-Year Plan (2007–12). The latter plan is structured around the concept of "employment for inclusive growth". To this end, a prime policy instrument has been the Mahatma Gandhi National Rural Employment Guarantee Act (MGNREGA), which has the intention of providing every adult within rural households with 100 days of paid employment per year at the rate of Rs 120 per day (2009 prices).

From the perspective of the discussion above, the advent of MGNREGA can be read in terms of a public policy intervention that seeks to address the failures of India's labour markets to provide decent work. By providing a guarantee of employment for part of the year at a wage rate that exceeds what the private sector is often willing to pay, MGNREGA acts to counter the relative slowness of employment growth *vis-à-vis* GDP growth (i.e., low elasticity of employment to national output: Bhaduri, 2008) and the way in which the informalisation of work depresses wages growth. MGNREGA not only increases the supply of jobs in rural areas but, by providing a floor price for wages, it has the effect of bidding up the rate that private employers are required to pay for workers. Of course, the potential for MGNREGA to uplift poor incomes hinges on efficient and equitable implementation, which is an issue discussed in the next chapter. However, what is important to note presently is that the recent employment dynamics of economic growth in India, when viewed in isolation, seem not to have had minimal pro-poor orientation. As summarised by Aggarwal and Kumar, the earnings of regular workers "have increased faster than those of casual employees in both rural and urban areas and the gap has been widening" (2012: 38), which leads them to conclude that: "Poverty will decline only if the organized industry can absorb on a large scale the semi-skilled and unskilled labour released from the agriculture sector, which has not been the case in India" (2012: 52). To the extent that wage incomes for the poor may have improved in the past few years, this would seem attributable to the catalytic role of MGNREGA, rather than the wider dynamics of labour market processes.

The connection between non-agricultural livelihoods and food insecurity

To recap momentarily, so far this chapter has observed that (i) an increasing proportion of the rural population has become increasingly dependent on finding new sources of livelihood outside of the farm sector; (ii) these processes have been socially uneven, with poorer and more vulnerable households being generally exposed to a greater need to diversify their livelihoods yet being less well placed and equipped to do this; and (iii) at the same time, the attributes of national economic growth have led to a perpetuation in employment informalisation, featured by relatively poor wages, casualisation and precarious and uncertain livelihood circumstances. Of themselves, these dynamics provide a drag on the alleviation of poverty and food insecurity in India. However, the scale of these problems has been exacerbated in the past few years by food price inflation.

The capacity for food price inflation to impact with severest effect on the poor was noted right at the outset of the 2008 Global Food Crisis (von Braun *et al.*, 2008). Because poor households spend a high proportion of their income on food, the results of food price inflation are strongly regressive. According to the Asian Development Bank, poor households in Asian developing countries (defined as those earning less than US$1.25 per day at 2005 purchasing power parity) are estimated to devote 60–70 per cent of budgets to food. Economic modelling by the Bank suggests that an increase in food prices of 20 per cent would push a further 3.9 per cent of households into this category, equivalent to 129 million people (Asian Development Bank, 2011: 13). Further research by the Bank concludes that poor households in South Asia are considerably more vulnerable to food price inflation than in other parts of Asia, because of their lower absolute levels of income and greater expenditure on food within household budgets (Carrasco and Mukhopadhyay, 2012: 17). Applying the ADB models specifically to India, it is found that a 20 per cent increase in food prices would increase the number of people living under the absolute poverty (US$1.25/day in purchasing power parity) benchmark by 4.3 per cent in urban areas and 5.8 per cent in rural areas (Carrasco and Mukhopadhyay, 2012: 18). To gain deeper insight into these issues by way of particular associations between food prices and the poor, we now consider the recent history of food inflation in India.

The ongoing debate on inflation trends in India hovers around the "measure of inflation" used to gauge the volatility in general price levels. India's uses Wholesale Price Index (WPI) as its headline inflation index, which, however, does not capture the consumer price situation. On the other hand, there are four separate Consumer Price Indexes (CPI): 1) CPI for industrial workers, 2) CPI for agricultural labourers, 3) CPI for rural workers and, 4) CPI for urban non-manual employees. This makes it hard to arrive at a single representative inflation measure[8] (Subbarao, 2010: 3). For purposes of consistency, in this chapter we use the Wholesale Price Index (WPI) series published by the Ministry of Commerce and Industry (Office of the Economic Advisor, 2013). An advantage of this series is that it is a long-standing data set with month-by-month information at the level of individual commodity groups. For the general purposes of this discussion, it can be assumed that changes in wholesale prices bear close correlation to final retail prices.

Focusing on the period from January 2008 (coinciding with the Global Food Crisis) to November 2012 reveals important characteristics about the relative cost of food in India, especially for poorer segments of the population. Firstly, in overall terms food prices increased at a faster rate than underlying inflation, as measured by the WPI "All Commodities" index. For statistical purposes, the WPI includes two broad food categories: "Food Articles", which correspond to raw and unprocessed/minimally processed foods, and "Food Products" which represent foods with higher levels of processing. As indicated in Figure 5.2, during this period the "All Commodities" and "Food Products" indexes increased by approximately the same amount, but "Food Articles" rose much more steeply. This is particularly significant for the focus of the current debate because, as a general rule, the raw and minimally processed nature of many of the items which constitute the "Food Articles" category accords them greater importance within the diets of the poorer cohorts of the population. Hence, wholesale prices of (unprocessed) cereals and pulses rose by 60.1 per cent from January 2008 to November 2012, as against 44.7 per cent for "All Commodities".[9] Cereals account for 29 per cent of food expenditure for the poorest third of the Indian population, as opposed to just 12 per cent for the top third (Dev, 2009: 9).

Moreover, further investigation of these trends points to the fact that pulses experienced a much more rapid rise than cereals in this period (Figure 5.3), which would have had major impacts on the poor. Access to staple cereals is underpinned by the policy architecture of Minimum Support Prices (MSPs) for agricultural production and purchases by the government for subsidised allocation to the poor through the Public Distribution System (PDS) (see Chapter Six). However, pulses have traditionally fared much less centrally in these arrangements. In terms of the

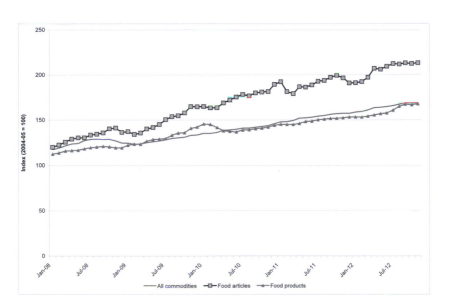

FIGURE 5.2 Wholesale food price inflation, 2008–12, all commodities versus food

Source: Office of the Economic Advisor (2013)

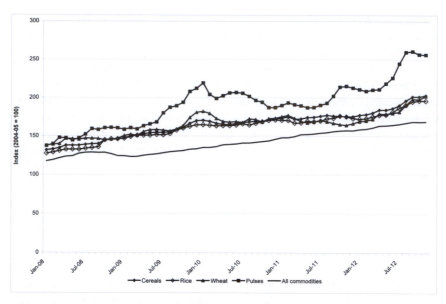

FIGURE 5.3 Wholesale food price inflation, 2008–12, cereals and pulses

Source: Office of the Economic Advisor (2013)

MSP, pricing methodologies have favoured wheat and rice cultivation. Only in the past few years have Indian policymakers specifically raised the MSP for pulses at a faster rate than for wheat and rice, in an effort to boost production (Dev, 2012). In the future, it may be expected that the effects of these policies will kick in, with one researcher forecasting "an increase in consumption of pulses as the availability increases" (Dev, 2012: 14). With respect to the PDS, in most Indian States, pulses are not included within the PDS, meaning that poor households tend to be wholly reliant on the private-sector operations of the market, if they are to obtain pulses. The increase in the price of pulses over the past few years might be expected to have induced a substantial effect on the poor population's inclusion of these items in their diets. It goes without saying that pulses play a crucially important nutritional role for poor people, as they are a major source of iron and protein within diets which, either by religious taboo or poverty, often have minimal or no meat or eggs.

Similarly, the growth in the wholesale prices of raw and unprocessed fruits and vegetables was faster than the average inflation rate for all consumption sectors, and this was more notable for vegetables than fruits. Again, as a general rule, vegetables represent a core component of diets of the poor, while fruits, although important, to a certain degree encompass a discretionary element. According to calculations by Carrasco and Mukhopadhyay (2012: 8), fruits and vegetables were the largest single contributor to food price inflation in India during the period from 2007 to 2011. These trends are captured in Figure 5.4. In this diagram, seasonal fluctuations in prices are seen to impose a strong effect, although year-to-year patterns have

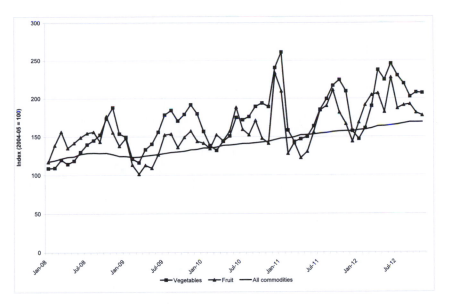

FIGURE 5.4   Wholesale food price inflation, 2008–12, fruits and vegetables

Source: Office of the Economic Advisor (2013)

not followed a precise twelve-month cycle. During the years from 2008 to 2011, prices fell during the months of March, April and May, and then began to climb from around July onwards, reaching annual heights around December–January. However, in 2012 this seasonal cycle seemed to reverse, with fruit and vegetable prices at an annual low in December 2011–January 2012, before climbing in the first half of the year and reaching a peak in June. The aberrant seasonal conditions in 2012 provoked considerable media discussion, and were linked to unusual weather patterns. India experienced low rainfall in the first half of 2012 which impacted in particular on strategic food growing areas of South India and Punjab.

With the prospective effects of future climate change, the unpredictability of seasonal weather patterns would be expected to increase with ensuing effects on price volatility. These issues pose major implications for the ability of India's poor to access fruit and vegetables. Poor people have weaker financial buffers to cope with rapid increases in prices. Yet in India, the very close associations between culinary cultures and a person's identity means, often, that the poor can be locked into dependence on particular foodstuffs notwithstanding price increases. This was observed in late 2010 and early 2011 when a nationwide shortage of onions caused prices to skyrocket (Figure 5.5). WPI data suggests that the price of onions rose by more than 500 per cent between August 2010 and January 2011. In part, this market outcome can be seen as being a product of the way the diets of many people in India are composed of a relatively narrow range of meals and foodstuffs, creating highly inelastic demand attributes for core ingredients. Thus, because onions are essential ingredients in many recipes which many people in India regard as being

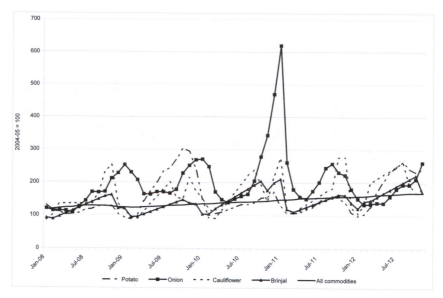

FIGURE 5.5 Wholesale food price inflation, 2008–12, individual vegetable items

Source: Office of the Economic Advisor (2013)

essential within daily life, demand for onions continued to be relatively robust through the period of national shortage, driving prices ever higher.

The rising wholesale cost of cereals, pulses and vegetables in India during recent years has important relevance for interpreting the debate on food price inflation. One pervasive argument about India's food price inflation (which gains considerable traction in the business media) is that it is being demand-driven by the emergent middle class (Farrell and Beinhocker, 2007; DBS Group Research, 2011). As a large number of researchers have observed, the 'middle-classing' of diets in India is behind much of the shifting pattern of food industry market demand over recent years (inter alia, Dastagiri 2004; Golait and Pradhan, 2006; Kharas, 2010; Gaiha *et al.*, 2010). These trends have led to the Government of India reweighting the composition of the food baskets which are used to calculate food price indexes (Golkarn, 2010), and are also evidenced in the fact that prices of the protein-rich categories of milk, eggs and meat increased at a rapid clip from 2008 to 2012; wholesale milk prices grew by 79.8 per cent and eggs, meat and fish grew by 118.5 per cent. However, the growth in prices for higher-value, protein-based foodstuffs should not lead, *ceteris paribus*, to researchers concluding that food price inflation in India is primarily caused by, and impacts on, the middle class. Although the rise of India's middle class has had a major impact on the Indian food system and is a contributor to food price inflation, the chief victims of these processes are the de-agrarianised poor, particularly individuals in urban informal-sector jobs, who are generally highly dependent on the operation of the private sector for their food security needs to be satisfied.

Conclusion

This chapter has addressed an issue that is sometimes lost in wider discussion of food security. All too often, attention focuses exclusively on questions relating to agricultural production (or "food availability", in the FAO terminology) and the fate of farmers. De-agrarianisation, however, invokes a need to reorient the food security problem to the question of how non-farm livelihood diversification connects to decent work and the ability of household members to secure their food needs from the market. In India's case, as this chapter has shown, there have been important shortcomings in the extent to which these connections have facilitated improvements to food security.

At one level, the issues at the heart of this chapter speak to the social and economic frictions which are presently accompanying de-agrarianisation in India. Farm-based households needing to diversify their sources of livelihood frequently have insufficient human capital resources. The parlous condition of education in many parts of rural India means that illiteracy remains widespread among poor population segments. Skill sets possessed by members of the rural population are often constructed within the narrow ranges expected through the community norms and conventions of caste, community and gender. As a result, too much of the impoverished, de-agrarianised population of rural India is ill-equipped to derive improved livelihoods outside of their traditional occupational domains. This issue has been summed up neatly by Justice Singvi of the Supreme Court of India in a 2011 judgement on behalf of a farmer litigant who had opposed his land being compulsorily acquired by an agency of the State of Haryana. As the justice observed: "After Independence, the administrative apparatus of the state did not make enough investment in rural areas and those who have been doing agriculture have not been educated and empowered to adopt alternative sources of livelihood" (*Raghbir Singh Serhrawat v. State of Haryana and Others*, 2011: 1120).

These arguments are important contributions to the overall argument of this book. In contemporary India, it cannot be assumed that, as agriculture exerts a lesser pull on livelihoods, people will seamlessly transition into the non-farm economy. As noted at the outset of this chapter, these processes are rarely painless, whether in the frame of Dickens's England or modern India. The inability in India's economy to soak up the excess labour demand from agriculture through decent work, coupled with the debilitating effects of food price inflation on the poor, mean that this component of food insecurity in India will continue to be a major policy headache for the foreseeable future.

Notes

1   NSS adopts the concept of "usual place of residence" (UPR), which is defined as the place where the person had stayed continuously for a period of six months or more. Accordingly, a migrant is defined as a person whose last UPR was different from the present place of enumeration (NSSO, 2010: 11).

2   The new methodology moves away from the earlier practice of estimating poverty in mere calorific terms and instead constructs implicit price indices for household

consumption expenditure on food, health and education using the 2004–05 NSSO survey data. The inclusion of non-food expenditure on education and health was in light of falling share of food in total household expenditure as a result of changing household consumption basket (Planning Commission of India, 2009). It is important to mention that even though the Tendulkar committee revised poverty line upwards, it remains far below the internationally accepted benchmark of USD 1.25 per day. Recently, the Planning Commission revised the committee's 2004–05 poverty lines, using the 2009–10 (66th round) NSSO data on household consumption expenditure. According to this revision, people spending Rs 22.4 (USD 40 cents) and Rs 28.6 (USD 50 cents) in rural and urban India, respectively are above the poverty line (Planning Commission of India, 2012a). This caused great outrage in the country, with national media and civil society groups vehemently criticising the low poverty threshold.

3   The informal sector is defined as economic units which "operate at a low level of organization, with little or no division between labour and capital as factors of production and on a small scale. Labour relations – where they exist – are based mostly on casual employment, kinship or personal and social relations rather than contractual arrangements with formal guarantees. The informal sector forms part of the household sector as household enterprises or, equivalently, unincorporated enterprises owned by households" (Naik, 2009: 2).

4   The NCEUS uses the terminology of "unorganised" and "organised" to describe these two categories.

5   Although piece-rate payment opens the door for worker exploitation, an interesting counterargument presented by Deshingkar and Farrington (2006: 125), based on their field research among rural labouring work gangs in Andhra Pradesh and Madhya Pradesh, is that "Piece-rate contracts are preferred by labourers for the increased independence, dignity, and satisfaction they confer".

6   Rs 20 was the equivalent of US$0.48 at 2007 exchange rates. Rs 11 was US$0.27 during the same period.

7   This is because, in the NSS 66th round, coverage of employment informalisation was limited to the non-agricultural economy, and to the labouring components of the agricultural sector (harvest workers, people employed in packing sheds, etc.). This excluded workers in India who defined their primary occupation as growing crops and tending livestock (i.e., the self-employed "family farmer" segment of the Indian labour market (NSSO, 2012: v).

8   The first three CPI indexes are compiled by the Ministry of Labour and Employment and the one relating to urban non-manual employees by the Central Statistics Organisation.

9   In passing, it is worth noting that this significant rise in the price of cereals occurred even though the Government of India had largely insulated the country from the effects of cereal price inflation elsewhere in the world. (Thus, for example, in 2008 the government temporarily banned wheat and rice exports.) Hence, increased prices were largely attributable to domestic factors (Dev, 2009).

6

FOOD SECURITY THROUGH SOCIAL SAFETY NET PROGRAMS

Introduction

The extensive system of food-based social safety net programs across India represents the vortex of the country's food security problems. At one level, the fact that so much of the country's population is mired in dependence to these programs is a powerful symptom of the widespread failings of India's food system. As already outlined in this book, the capacities of India's poor to meet their food and nutrition security needs through own-production entitlement systems (Chapter Four) and wage-labour entitlement systems (Chapter Five) remain beset with difficulties. As a result, for millions of people across India, day-to-day nourishment becomes hinged on food-based social safety nets. Yet, at another level, these programs can be equally understood as a problem, not a panacea, in the attainment of food and nutrition security in India. For whilst the presence of food-based social safety nets is a vital addition to the overall food security capacity of the country, gaping holes in these nets substantially mitigate their effectiveness, perpetuating food insecurity for far too many of India's poorest and most vulnerable people.

Our analysis of these issues comes at a vital juncture in India's recent history. The past few years have witnessed intensified debate about the performance and future of India's food-based social safety net systems. Whilst these debates have swirled around an array of issues, their essence can be distilled to two core questions: who should be guaranteed a right to food, and how should this right be managed?

Consideration of the first of these questions has been informed by an evident need for clearer articulation of the purposes of food-based social safety nets. The past two decades have been characterised by an ebb and flow of apparently contradictory sentiments in this policy field. On occasions there have been agendas to curtail and delimit households' access to programs, in the name of attempts to better target resources for the prime benefit of those most in need. The evolution of universal Public Distribution System (PDS) entitlements into the *Targeted* Public Distribution System (TPDS) during the 1990s represents a good example of these tendencies. On other occasions entitlement franchises have been widened irrespective of needs-based criteria. Thus, the establishment of the Mahatma Gandhi National Rural Guarantee Scheme (MGNREGS) in 2005[1] was premised on the universalist prescription that all of the rural population was entitled to 100 days paid work per year, regardless of circumstances. On myriad other occasions, moreover, the dominant logics of food-based social safety policies seem to have been driven by narrow political motivations attached to the capture of vote banks, rather than any broader programmatic rationality. It is not uncommon in India for a state government to tweak social safety net access criteria (through expanding the franchise or making one-off bonus entitlements) when an election is imminent.

These issues remain unresolved. During debates about the design of India's Food Security legislation during 2010–12, robust arguments were put both for program coverage that inclined towards universalism, and for programs structured around tighter and more efficient targeting. The details of these debates are addressed later in this chapter. However, as a framing observation we note that, unlike previous times, these considerations are girded by recognition of a legal *right to food*. This recognition transforms the question of 'who should be the beneficiaries' of food-based social safety nets from the arena of public policy discretion to the realm of a state obligation. Henceforth in India, the operation of food-based social safety programs becomes a component of the state's legal requirements to its citizenry, in line with obligations under national and international laws.

Consideration of the second core question – how should rights to food be managed? – is equally contentious. This debate is focused on the operations and future of the central program element in the Government of India's food-based social safety net system, the PDS. As briefly outlined in Chapter Three, the PDS emerged in its (relatively) modern form in the mid-1960s in the context of widespread food shortages just prior to the advent of the Green Revolution in north-west India.[2] It was tied at birth with the Green Revolution, as large surpluses of wheat and rice in Punjab and Haryana were purchased by the newly established Food Corporation of India (FCI), under Minimum Support Price (MSP) legislation, and then recycled at subsidised prices to households throughout the country via networks of state government warehouses and local Fair Price Shops. Over many years, a litany of arguments has been made regarding the overall inefficiency of these arrangements. A substantial proportion of food procured through the PDS fails to find its way to intended recipients, alternately through maladministration, corruption or theft. At the same time, the FCI's management of stocks has come under legal challenge by public interest litigants who have contended that the state should not hold large volumes of food in stock in the presence of substantial national malnourishment.

The imperative to improve the overall delivery performance of the PDS has culminated in two parallel reform agendas being initiated during the recent past. The first of these concerns the technological basis of PDS delivery, and is entwined within a broader national e-governance plan. The contours of this argument suggest that much of the present inefficiency of the PDS can be repaired through creating a digital administrative spine to replace the traditionally disparate, hard-to-verify, paper-based administration of the system. From around 2010 onwards, a range of PDS e-governance reforms was commenced with this goal in mind. The second reform agenda focuses on the transactional mode through which households receive PDS entitlements. The history of the PDS has involved beneficiaries receiving an entitlement expressed in a volume of food: for example, a particular class of household might be entitled to a certain number of kilograms of wheat per month, at a subsidised price of so many rupees per kilogram. However, during recent reform debates, loud and significant calls were made to replace this regime with one based around Cash Transfers (CTs). The push for reforms along these lines was closely implicated with an internationally mobilised set of arguments, supported by the World Bank, which advocated the superiority of cash-based over goods-based mechanisms for the delivery of social services. In this, the recent experiences of Brazil were deployed as an exemplar from which India could learn (see Chapter Seven). After considerable public debate, in late 2012 the Government of India announced its decision to trial the implementation of DCT-based delivery for a number of social welfare schemes. Given the politically sensitive nature of food subsidies they were excluded from the initial trials. However, potential expansion of DCT arrangements into the mainstream of the food-based social safety system remains an option for future policy, and this direction has strong support from some elements within government.[3]

Elaboration of these two questions – the "who" and "how" dimensions of India's food-based social safety nets – form the main body of discussion in this chapter and the next. Our division of material across these two chapters reflects an emergent sense that India's food-based social safety net system is potentially on the cusp of dramatic change. This chapter sketches the overall architecture of the food-based social safety net and addresses the "who" dimensions of the issue – the question of how widely the safety net should be cast. Then, in the next chapter, attention turns to the crucial question of how India's food-based social safety net should be designed in the future.

India's food-based social safety net system

The Government of India and its constituent states and territories operate a series of programs with the goal of seeking to ensure the food needs of its populace are met. The centrepiece of this policy area is the PDS, as noted above. Yet, although the PDS figures centrally within Indian food policy, it is supplemented by various ancillary programs, of which the most important are the Integrated Child Development Scheme (ICDS), the MGNREGS (mentioned above), and the school-based Midday Meal Scheme. Consideration of these other programs is vital for an overall perspective of India's food-based social safety net system, because of their crucial role in addressing particular shortcomings in the PDS, and the coordination challenges they present for policy coherence in this area.

(i) The Public Distribution System

The PDS is the world's largest food distribution scheme, and the largest welfare program operated by the Government of India (Svedberg, 2012). During 2011–12, the Government of India and its constituent states procured some 35 million tonnes of rice and 28.3 million tonnes of wheat from farmers which went into storage within a vast network of FCI godowns (warehouses) across the country, representing around one third of total national production (Table 6.1). Some 91.9 per cent

TABLE 6.1 Procurement and off-take of food grains from the Government of India Central Pool, million tonnes

	Rice 2011–12 (April to March)	Rice 2012–13 (six months only, April to September)	Wheat 2011–12 (April to March)	Wheat 2012–13 (six months only, April to September)
Total national production	102.0	NA	86.9	87.5
Volume of grain procured by central and state governments for allocation to the Central Pool	35.0	9.4	28.3	38.1
Off-take from Central Pool				
Public Distribution Scheme				
BPL	11.3	5.9	6.0	3.5
APL	6.4	3.4	9.8	5.1
Antyodaya	6.6	3.5	3.1	1.8
Special ad hoc and other	5.2	1.4	2.6	0.7
Subtotal	**29.5 (91.9%)**	**14.2 (91.0%)**	**21.5 (60.0%)**	**11.1 (77.6%)**
Welfare schemes				
Midday Meal Scheme	0.3	0.1	0.9	0.4
Other	1.7	1.3	0.6	0.3
Subtotal	**2.6 (8.1%)**	**1.4 (9.0%)**	**1.5 (4.2%)**	**0.7 (4.9%)**
Open/tender sale	0.0	0.0	11.8	2.2
Export	0.0	0.0	1.0	0.3
Subtotal	**(0.0%)**	**(0.0%)**	**12.8 (35.8%)**	**2.5 (17.5%)**
Off-take grand total	**32.1 (100.0%)**	**15.6 (100.0%)**	**35.8 (100.0%)**	**14.3 (100.0%)**

Source: USDA (2012) (production data); Department of Food and Public Distribution (2012: 4) (procurement data) and Department of Food and Public Distribution (2012: 7) (off-take data)

of the rice and 60 per cent of wheat was then disbursed through the PDS, finding their way to approximately half a million Fair Price Shops spread across the length and breadth of the country (Saxena, 2012). The operating cost of the PDS for 2012–13 is estimated at Rs 638 billion (US$11.7 billion) (Jha and Gaiha, 2012: 21), which represents the approximate equivalent of 0.7 per cent of Indian GDP.

Although the PDS today takes its mandate in terms of national poverty alleviation (i.e., access to basic foods at reasonable prices to vulnerable populations), its origins were wrapped in a more wide-ranging set of aspirations connected to a Nehruvian socialist vision of Indian society. According to Bapna (1990), the establishment of the PDS was inspired not only by an anti-poverty/food security agenda, but, also, as a means for the state to execute controls over food prices and to delimit the role of private traders in the domestic economy. To this end, its original formulation saw its operations largely restricted to urban areas. Among the rural populations which dominated the nation's demography, a household's access to food grains was premised on its ability to cultivate its own land holdings, or to earn sufficient income to purchase grain from private markets. In this era, PDS supplies were available only during times of scarcity, due to flood, drought, etc. In the mid-1970s, however, the scope of the PDS was expanded. A small number of states (Kerala, Gujarat, Tamil Nadu and Andhra Pradesh) extended PDS entitlements to rural populations (Janbee, 2000: 29). This lead was soon followed by other states, such that by the 1980s the scheme had come to possess a comprehensive, nationwide ambit. Clearly, this capacity for PDS expansion was underpinned by the huge increases in India's wheat and rice production through the Green Revolution. What began in the 1960s as a scheme to hold buffer stocks and to ensure the urban poor had access to food grains, by the 1980s had evolved into the basic mechanism through which the bulk of the Indian population accessed their basic food needs.

In 1997, changes were introduced to the PDS with the goal of better ensuring the program's delivery logic met the needs of the population. Thus, the PDS became transformed into what was labelled the Targeted PDS (TPDS) (although in common parlance, the simpler acronym PDS is still most regularly used). This reform was executed through the development of income criteria to demarcate "poor" and "non-poor" households. Each household was allocated to one of the following three categories and was accordingly given a PDS card which specified their entitlements for food grain subsidies. These categories were *Above Poverty Line* (APL), *Below Poverty Line* (BPL) and *Antodaya Anna Yojana* (AAY) (usually translated into English as "the poorest of the poor"). Although this was rolled out as a national scheme, state governments held responsibilities for defining the income levels at which eligibility for each of these categories kicked-in, as well as the price subsidies, volumes of food permissible for each household and range of items covered by the PDS (which also included non-food items such as kerosene). Consequently, when seen from a national perspective the advent of the TPDS soon became highly differentiated, as individual states amended program rules in line with their own political or policy objectives.[4]

The issues of eligibility and franchise in the TPDS, however, need to be interpreted within the context of parlous delivery performance of the scheme as a whole. Regardless of what state governments may legislate in terms of the PDS, all too frequently it has been the case that intended beneficiaries are either not aware of their entitlements or for various reasons the legislated disbursements do not reach Fair Price Shops or cardholders in the first place. Different studies over recent years provide a range of estimates of the percentage-wise extent of the failings of the PDS. These studies vary in their bottom-line figures dependent on their assumptions and time periods. Nevertheless, they all conclude that the problem has immense scale and has persisted for a long time. Research by Parikh (1994: 14–15) using 1986–87 NSS data concluded that for every rupee spent on the PDS, less than 22 per cent reached the poor. Examination of 1999–2000 NSS data suggested that the passage of a decade had contributed only marginally to PDS effectiveness, with just 29 per cent of allocated food grains actually reaching beneficiaries (both studies cited in Bhalla, 2011: 24). A detailed sample survey of PDS recipient households across 60 districts in 2001 by the Planning Commission of India suggested that just 42 per cent of subsidised food grains reached their intended target group (Planning Commission, 2005: ii) which, once administrative costs are taken into account, suggests a finding broadly in line with earlier studies. The situation seems not to have altered much a few years later, according to Jha and Ramaswami's (2010) assessment. Using 2004–05 NSS data, the researchers suggest that 40 per cent of rice and 73 per cent of wheat were pilfered, and that the costs of public sector transport and logistics in the PDS were 35 per cent higher than comparable private sector benchmarks (Jha and Ramaswami, 2010: 16). When this data was entered into a model, the researchers came up with the startling conclusion that the income transfer to the poor from the PDS amounted to only 10.5 per cent of the total program costs. The remaining income transfers went to the non-poor (benefiting from inclusion and exclusion errors) (18.8 per cent), persons profiteering from illegal diversions (42.8 per cent) and public servants and contractors benefiting from inflated program management costs (28.0 per cent) (Jha and Ramaswami, 2010: 21). Using the same (2004–05) NSS dataset, Svedberg (2012: 54) arrives at an even more dire set of efficiency measures, suggesting that the effects of grain diversion and exclusion errors within the cardholding population are of such magnitude that the net subsidy to all poor households through PDS equates to an increase of less than 2 per cent in their monthly consumption expenditure, and that for every Rs 9 the Government of India spends on the scheme, only Rs 1 is received by the poor.

More recent assessments, however, are less gloomy. Reetika Khera (2011b; 2011d; 2012a; 2012b) has been at the vanguard of these reappraisals. Using NSS data up to 2007–08, she provides an authoritative and comprehensive recent word on this topic (Khera, 2011b: 109). She concludes:

- The effectiveness of the PDS deteriorated starkly between 1999–2000 and 2004–05, with total leakages (due to corruption, transport losses, losses due to spoilage, etc.) increasing from 24 per cent to 54 per cent of the total PDS supply.

- From 2004–05 there has been improvement in PDS effectiveness, with leakages falling from 54 per cent to 44 per cent.
- There are significant differences in states' performance which seem to be linked to governance. Bihar and Jharkhand, two of the states at the bottom rung in Indian human development, exhibited extremely high rates of diversion and barely any progress. (From 2004–05 to 2007–08, the leakage rate in Bihar shifted from 91 per cent to 90 per cent of total stocks; in Jharkhand, from 85 per cent to 84 per cent.) Yet, at the same time, in comparable Chhattisgarh, the leakage rate fell from around 52 per cent to zero.

More recent evidence is suggestive of a more profound turnaround in PDS effectiveness. A nine-state survey undertaken in 2011 to glean levels of beneficiary satisfaction revealed a steadily improving system when compared to earlier studies (Khera, 2011d). Because this study was conducted in the context of the debate around a proposed shift to cash transfer modes of PDS delivery, we discuss its findings in detail in Chapter Seven. For the moment, our attention focuses on the historical reasons why PDS has unarguably performed so poorly.

The question of how much of this loss can be attributed to problems of logistics and poor product storage, as opposed to diversion through theft, is an important one. As anyone who has visited a large FCI godown would testify, the rat population of India maintains a healthy appetite from the operation of the PDS. However, beyond such factors, it is clearly apparent that the scale of losses in the system to a large extent reflects structural dimensions pertaining to program administration and policy logics.

One cause of these problems rests with the separation of responsibilities with regards to the enumeration and identification of beneficiaries (Ramakumar, 2010). Different institutions are responsible for estimating the number of poor at different levels of geography (State/Territory, District, Block and Gram Panchayat). Typically, officials at local levels are responsible for identifying and issuing cards to potential beneficiaries, however the number of cards that can be issued in a particular area is specified in accordance with enumerative models designed at national and state scales. Supposedly, "bottom-up" headcounts of households in need and "top-down" models distributing resources between geographical areas are coordinated through data exchange within each state government's Department of Food and Civil Supplies. However, this would seem to be the ideal rather than the reality of public administration. During 2012, we undertook a series of interviews with PDS bureaucrats at Village, Block, District and State levels to elicit details of how this policy field operated. It was plainly apparent that local allocation models (determining the flow of food grains to particular Blocks, Gram Panchayats and Fair Price Shops) often bore the distinct fingerprints of vested interests. Rent-seeking by key gatekeepers took the form of subtle (and, occasionally, not-so-subtle) over- and under-allocations to particular places, in line with arrangements to shed benefits to favoured economic constituencies.

These mismatches in the geographical targeting of entitlements are aggravated at the individual level by the political economy of card issuance. The PDS is riddled with inclusion and exclusion errors, with deserving households left out, and the better-off households having access (Swaminathan, 2000). During the household surveys in ten villages of Siwan, Bihar, conducted by Choithani (one of the present authors), a senior villager, aware of BPL enumeration process, told him:

> People who have pukka houses, 2–3 acres of land, whose members are in stable jobs (some even in government jobs), have BPL cards. On the other hand, there are families left out whose stoves do not burn the day they do not find work.

Additionally, monitoring of the social status of households perennially lags behind contemporary conditions, meaning that the names of deceased and migrated household members are often kept on cards long after they should have been deleted whilst, conversely, newborns and daughters-in-law (given that wives move into husbands' families in India) are often not included. For most households across rural India, cardholder status was enshrined in the BPL Census of 2002, and unless the household successfully applied/petitioned for changes, or administrative officers took action to revise entitlements, the original status set down in 2002 may still remain in place. Thus, in 2012, the entitlement level of many rural Indian households was based on its size and status a full ten years earlier. Although a more recent census has taken place (the Social-Economic and Caste Census, 2011), at the time of writing (February, 2013) cardholder status across India has not been updated for these results. Adding further problems to this situation is the tendency for some local officials to issue bogus cards from which they personally benefit (a phenomenon known as "ghost cards"). The Planning Commission of India (2005: vii) has noted that: "Some States have issued more cards than the number of households." There is little doubt that the scale of inclusion errors, exclusion errors and "ghosting" is massive across India.

The accuracy to which households are allocated to the appropriate card category also begs questioning. A detailed impact evaluation study conducted by the Planning Commission (2005) found that large numbers of potentially BPL households were incorrectly classified as APL households. There were many reasons for this, but two brief examples illustrate the point. Firstly, the presence of household income from a daily wage labourer was found to sometimes cause the household to be classified as APL; however, more detailed investigation by the Planning Commission revealed that household food insecurity could persist notwithstanding the contribution of wages. Contrarily, there was a tendency for some smallholder farmers to be classified as BPL on account of their low-cash incomes, without full consideration of the contribution of their own-production to their household's food security.

The PDS, therefore, has a contradictory presence within India's food system. Its shortcomings are profound and open to wide criticism. The misdirection of millions of tonnes of food grains supposedly destined for the poor represents a large part of the food security problem in India. As a number of economic studies have confirmed, its inefficiencies mean that it is a very costly way of transferring incomes to the poor (Kapur *et al.*, 2008; Panagariya, 2008; Planning Commission, 2008). Yet, notwithstanding its dire status, the PDS remains a bulwark in the Government of India's attempts improve the food security of its people. Without the PDS provisions distributed through the near-half-million Fair Price Shops in India, food insecurity would inevitably be much higher. Subsidised PDS grain accounts for approximately 40 per cent of all food grain purchases by poor households (Jha and Ramaswami, 2010: 14);[5] if these households had to pay market prices for this grain, their economic welfare and food security would be substantially reduced. These contradictions are fully on view in India's villages, where citizens demand their PDS rights yet, often in the same breath, acknowledge Fair Price Shop owners and officials as scoundrels. As Khera (2011b: 1039) observes:

> My fieldwork, conducted in Rajasthan, presented an intriguing picture of the PDS. PDS grain was not much cheaper than market grain of similar quality. Further, in Rajasthan wheat is supplied through the PDS, but in six out of eight sample villages, the staple was maize or pearl millets ("coarse cereals"). Yet, people were desperate to have access to the PDS. Those who had APL cards complained bitterly at being left out. Those with BPL cards made repeated trips to ration shops that were often quite far and queued in order to enjoy this small subsidy. In spite of this, they rarely got their full entitlement of 35 kg. Having spent some time at ration shops, I noticed that they were often cheated by their PDS dealer. Those who were aware of being cheated often complained to me, but did not protest in front of the PDS dealer.

(ii) The Mahatma Gandhi National Rural Employment Guarantee Scheme

The Mahatma Gandhi National Rural Employment Guarantee Scheme (MGNREGS) is a job guarantee scheme which emanated from the Mahatma Gandhi National Rural Employment Guarantee Act (MGNREGA), a hallmark piece of legislation from the UPA's first term of office. It was launched on 2 February 2006 for the poorest 200 districts in India, before being expanded nationwide in 2008 (Jha and Gaiha, 2012). The program sought to improve the employment opportunities for poor rural households. Its basic thrust is a guarantee of 100 days of employment a year to at least one member of any rural household who is willing to perform unskilled labour for the minimum wage. The program promises to uphold this undertaking to any rural resident within 15 days of them lodging an application to participate in the program. In the event that there is no work available for the applicant, the relevant state government is liable to pay an unemployment allowance. Administration of the program is highly decentralised, with local government institutions (Gram Panchayats/Gram Sabhas) being responsible for the identification of suitable projects and having a central role in the planning and implementation of the job programs. In 2010–11 MGNREGS provided employment for 50 million households across India, and more than half of all participants were women (Beddington *et al.*, 2012: 36).

MGNREGS is ostensibly a jobs program, rather than part of India's food-based social safety net. The unemployed are provided with work opportunities and are paid a monetary wage. Nevertheless, MGNREGS has a vital role in food security. As mentioned above, the PDS accounts for approximately 40 per cent of households' food grain needs across India, meaning that the remainder needs to be grown or procured from the market. (In volumetric terms, the PDS arrangements in most states provide between 20 kg and 35 kg of food grains per household per month [depending on cardholder status], but an average-sized household in rural India of four to five members requires approximately 60 kg/month for basic food needs.) Hence, in light of existing PDS limits and pervasive employment deficits across rural India, it can be said that "a genuinely guaranteed rural employment program is a *sine qua non* for authentic food security" (Venugopal, 2010: 580).

Furthermore, the logic behind the establishment of MGNREGA was closely connected to the politics of food insecurity in India. As discussed in the previous chapter, de-agrarianisation and the informalisation of employment generated pitfalls for the abilities of many individuals and households to construct sustainable livelihoods. This perpetuation of poverty cycles contributed directly to the incidence of under-nutrition with ensuing poorer health outcomes for the population and lesser workforce capabilities (as discussed in Chapter Two). Establishment of MGNREGS was designed as a circuit breaker for these patterns. By providing rural residents with 100 days' employment, it was assumed that (i) MGNREGS would provide a fillip to households' financial resources that would boost food consumption and potentially reduce the distress-related rural-to-urban migration, and (ii) it would induce shifts to labour force processes in the rural economy, bidding up wages and thereby addressing problems of poor working conditions and informalisation that mitigated against food security, as discussed in Chapter Five.

The extent to which MGNREGS has met these aspirations appears mixed. A number of village-level case analyses by NGOs and journalists have suggested that the scheme's commencement was associated with improved levels of consumption within poor households, reduced distress migration and some increases in lean season wages, especially for women (PACS [Poorest Areas Civil Society (Program)], 2007; Ghosh, 2008; Sainath, 2008). In an opinion piece written for the *Indian Express* newspaper, Patnaik (2011) suggests that MGNREGA has pushed up agricultural wages in some places and at some times of the year by up to 40 per cent. Analysis of the program using national-level data, however, draws a more complex set of conclusions. Using data from the Ministry of Rural Development over the period from 2006–07 to 2011–12, Jha and Gaiha (2012) assess MGNREGS using four criteria: (1) the average number of days of employment per household; (2) the percentage of households completing 100 days of employment under the MGNREGS; (3) the percentage of expenditure used in the program against total available funds; and (4) the percentage of work completed. Their analysis finds that with the exception of criteria (2), in general the performance of NREGA has been disappointing and has deteriorated over time, especially during the two most recent years under their analysis, 2010–11 and 2011–12. Their dismal assessment concludes (2012: 21):

> Reports abound of corruption at all stages with participants obtaining wages, often long delayed, unrelated to the work done. Project activity is dull or highly uneven with earmarked funds being siphoned off. Village panchayats and local officials are not silent or helpless observers of the gravy train, but key to keeping it going.[6]

Nevertheless, this is not the only view of how MGNREGS has altered the contemporary socioeconomic fabric of rural India. Dutta *et al.* (2012) paint a more optimistic picture. Contrary to Jha and Gaiha, they conclude that, despite the obstacles of program administration, the scheme is reaching the rural poor and backward classes and is attracting poor women into the workforce. They find that there is a greater demand for work in the relatively poor Indian states, which is not unexpected. There is some evidence of unmet demand for work on the scheme in all states, and more so in the poorest ones, where the scheme is needed most. They suggest that for India as a whole, 45 per cent of rural households wanted work on the scheme and, of these, 56 per cent got work – a national rationing rate of 44 per cent. However, surprisingly, they find that participation in the MGNREGS program is weakly correlated with rural poverty rates across states. In other words, if the program had worked as the Act had intended, it would have been expected that the program would be more attractive to individuals living in poorer states. However, some of the poorest states (including Bihar, Jharkhand and Orissa) have low participation rates and high levels of unmet demand. On the other hand, the situation is not wholly uniform, with other poor states such as Chhattisgarh, Rajasthan, Madhya Pradesh and West Bengal having a better record in providing employment under the scheme. Evidently, like the situation with PDS discussed above, the answer would seem to lie in the way that the institutional capacity of states interacts with the policy commitment and "good administration" of their governments. As stated by Premchander *et al.* (2008: 71), in many states and districts: "the number and quality of human resources deployed so far are completely inadequate for shouldering the complex and manifold responsibilities" of MGNREGA implementation. As the counterpoint which proves the rule, in Kerala, Khera (2012a) observes high rates of female participation and pro-poor outcomes in MGNREGA, which she attributes to the state's impressive human development credentials, including literacy and involvement in Panchayat Raj institutions.

The importance of these issues of administration and governance provides the basis for "middle-ground" assessment of MGNREGS, such as that provided by Liu and Barrett (2012). Their study suggests that although processes of self-selection for MGNREGS are strongly pro-poor (with poorer and scheduled tribe or scheduled caste households exhibiting greater rates of demand for places in the scheme) this demand is unmet in roughly half of India's states because of problematic implementation. In these states, "the administrative rationing of MGNREGS jobs is not propoor but, rather, exhibits a sort of middle-class bias" (Liu and Barrett, 2012: 16). In other words, the ability of program gatekeepers to favour the distribution of jobs within spatially and socially proximate networks of like-interests creates patterns of exclusion for households and social groups most in need. As a notable key illustration of the enacted biases in MGNREGS administration, Liu and Barrett find that male-headed households are more likely than female-headed households to seek and obtain MGNREGS jobs when income factors are normalised (Liu and Barrett, 2012: 16). This insight is consistent with the observation by Himanshu (2011: 45) that multiple sources of deprivation (in this case, gender discrimination and bias) can provide an obstacle for the realisation of pro-poor aspirations in policy.

In summary, during the short space of time in which MGNREGS has existed (it has been in place at a national level only since 2008), the scheme has exerted a powerful influence on the character of food insecurity in India. Like PDS, its effectiveness is impaired by a swathe of problems relating to maladministration and criminality. As observed by Khera (2011c), it is hobbled by the interplay of local elite capture, spatial mismatch and administrative incapability. Nevertheless, there is little doubt that it plays a crucial role as an adjunct to PDS, potentially better enabling poor households to meet their food security needs. In the context where an increasing proportion of India's rural population is becoming less attached to farming as a means to secure their food and nutritional needs, provision of rural employment must inevitably adopt a heightened role in the nation's food security equation.

(iii) The Integrated Child Development Scheme and Midday Meal Scheme

The Integrated Child Development Scheme (ICDS) and Midday Meal Scheme (MDMS) represent an important third leg of India's food-based social safety net. The nature of these interventions is that they target children under six, pregnant and lactating mothers (ICDS) and school-aged children (MDMS). Both these programs are extensive ambits. The ICDS is estimated to provide 68 million children with food (Saxena and Mander, 2009: 6). The Government of India states that the MDMS provides lunches to 120 million school children in 1.3 million schools (and like facilities) across the country (Ministry of Human Resource Development, 2013).

Although the MDMS provides food to almost twice as many children as the ICDS, the latter program has attracted a considerably larger amount of research interest and NGO investigation over the years. As such, the following discussion focuses on the ICDS. However, the broad arguments made about the ICDS apply equally to the MDMS.

The core objective of the ICDS is to improve the nutritional and health status of children in the age group 0–6 years, through supplementary feeding for undernourished children. In terms of public policy, the direction of resources to infants and young children has strong benefit–cost arguments, because of the longer-term health effects of adequate and appropriate early childhood nutrition. ICDS services are provided through a vast network of ICDS centres, better known as "Anganwadi". The term Anganwadi developed from the idea that a good early childcare and development centre could be run with low-cost local materials even when located in an "angan" or courtyard.

ICDS Anganwadi centres are located throughout the nation and, unsurprisingly for such a large and extensive program, the quality of services can vary substantially from place to place. However, as a general rule, research has tended to find that Anganwadi centres and the ICDS more generally operates more effectively and with more complete coverage in areas with relatively higher socioeconomic status (Gragnolati *et al.*, 2006; Pande and Yazbeck, 2003). According to Lokshin *et al.* (2005: 613) the program operates regressively, with:

> The states with the greatest need for the programme – the poor Northern states which account for nearly half of India's population and which suffer from high levels of child malnutrition – have the lowest programme coverage and the lowest budgetary allocations from the central government.

Thus, for the years 2000–01 and 2001–02 (the most recent years for which Lokshin *et al.* (2005: 624–25) provide data) ICDS expenditure per undernourished child was 14 times higher in Kerala (with one of the best human development records in the country) than Bihar (where over half of the children below three years of age were moderately or severely underweight). An ICDS Anganwadi centre was present in only 32 per cent of villages in Bihar, but 97 per cent of villages in Kerala.

Furthermore, access to ICDS services is socially uneven, even when an Anganwadi centre exists. Dalit and tribal communities on the fringes of hamlets and villages may not gain access to Anganwadi services, due to relative geographical isolation or informal processes of social exclusion – it is frequently the case that Centres are located in dominant caste areas of villages and have dominant caste personnel as social gatekeepers (Swain and Kumaran, 2012: 33–35). Discriminatory cultural norms relating to the preparation and eating of food among caste groups can provide a mechanism for the social exclusion of children from the ICDS in some parts of India (Mamgain and Diwakar, 2012: 28).

One important reason for the highly uneven operation of the ICDS across India resides with the political football that accompanies ICDS funding. Whilst this is a national program with core funding from New Delhi, operational management and ancillary activities is the responsibility of the states. Thus, for example, state governments are responsible for funding the construction and upkeep of Anganwadi buildings. Clearly, states with stronger economies and budgetary circumstances are better placed to support these functions. And furthermore, states with better records of program transparency are more likely to ensure that funds allocated to the construction of Anganwadi centres actually end up being used for this purpose.

A second manifestation of the political football around the ICDS pertains to the intervention of the Supreme Court of India. In response to the 2001 Writ Petition to the Court by the People's Union for Civil Liberties (PUCL), discussed in Chapter One, the Supreme Court of India over subsequent years set down a number of Interim Orders specifying minimum standards for ICDS meals and broadening of the geographical and social coverage of ICDS. This has included: banning cost recovery in the provision of Anganwadi meals, and replacing dry rations with cooked meals (Interim Order, 2 May 2003); prohibiting the exclusion of children from Anganwadi centres on the basis of their PDS status; increasing the budgetary allocations to meals from one rupee to two rupees per day (29 April 2004); prohibiting contractors from delivering supplementary nutrition through ICDS programs (7 October 2004); and, finally, nationwide universalisation of the ICDS (13 December 2006). The specificity of the Supreme Court's Interim Orders has made it a direct participant in policymaking in this area. According to two legal academics:

> By engaging in something strikingly close to lawmaking, the Supreme Court has, through its series of interim orders, gradually defined the right to food in terms of what policies are required of the state and central governments in order for them to adequately fulfil their constitutional obligation under Article 21 [which specifies the right to life and implicitly right to food]. Notable modifications to government schemes (and therefore the right to food) have evolved in subsequent orders, reflecting an interesting display of judicial activism regarding food policy.
>
> *(Birchfield and Corsi, 2010: 700)*

Yet despite the clear intent of the Supreme Court Interim Orders, implementation has remained partial. In the Ninth Report of the Supreme Court Commissioners (the body charged with oversighting the implementation of the ruling), the commissioners complained that although:

> The instructions of the Supreme Court have been categorical to ensure the coverage of all children below six years, all pregnant and lactating mothers and adolescent girls in all rural habitations and urban slums with all nutritional and health services of the ICDS in a phased manner latest by December, 2008.
>
> *(Saxena and Mander, 2009: 5)*

a study of Anganwadi coverage indicated that only 58.6 per cent of children under six were receiving the mandated supplementary nutrition. Bihar and Rajasthan were "named and shamed" as states with less than 40 per cent coverage of child supplementary nutrition. Problems of inadequate funding and spatially and socially uneven coverage in the ICDS continue to bedevil the potential of the scheme as a contributor to improved food security in India. According to the Right to Food Campaign, budget allocations to ICDS are insufficient to ensure universalisation of the scheme across India, with recent increases falling behind cost of food increases and promised pay increases for Anganwadi workers (Right to Food Campaign, 2011a). Furthermore, as with the PDS and MGNREGA discussed above, issues of theft and corruption appear as endemic features of the scheme's operations across a number of states. Hence, in a case investigated by the Office of the Supreme Court, contracts for the supply of Rs 10 billion (US$183 million) of ICDS food in Maharashtra were captured by a group of private contractors (in opposition to legislation which requires village-level institutions to hold contracts), who were alleged to have profiteered from their dominant market position by way of making illegal diversions of food and supplying poor quality foodstuffs to Anganwadi centres (*Times of India*, 2012; *Hindustan Times*, 2012).

(iv) Effective coordination and policy coherence: The ultimate goal of Indian food-based social safety net policy

To briefly conclude this section of the chapter, it needs noting that if the various schemes and programs discussed above are to comprehensively address India's problems of food insecurity, they need to cohere within a soundly developed administrative and policy logic. At one level, this can be seen to be the case: the function of the PDS is to provide households with a basic level of food grains; the MGNREGS then establishes an enabling labour market context for remaining food deficits to be more readily met, and the ICDS and MDMS ensure that the needs of infants and children are taken into account in intra–household distribution of food.

Of course, this rosy portrait of the operation of these programs belies the glaring inadequacies which impair their operations. All of these schemes are riddled by maladministration and criminality. Economists' assessments (witnessed most evidently in the case of the PDS, addressed above) suggest that because of the magnitude of these problems, these schemes tend to be quite inefficient as mechanisms to redistribute benefits to the poor. Yet at the same time, it is equally blindingly obvious that these schemes, for all their faults, remain crucial bedrocks for any attempt to improve food insecurity in India. The broad objectives to which they aspire (i.e., delivering food grains; providing jobs; caring for the nutritional needs of infants and children) will continue to have central relevance in the food politics of India.

The fulcrum of problems, it seems to us, lies in the capacities of program failure in these schemes to contribute to what Wolff and de-Shalit (2007: 133) have coined "corrosive disadvantage". In all cases discussed above, a pivotal theme is that these schemes often tend to operate less effectively within poorer districts, and for more disadvantaged social categories (Scheduled Tribes, Scheduled Castes, women, female-headed households, etc.). This relationship, whilst not absolute (it was noted that Chhattisgarh, a poor state, had a highly effective PDS), operates as a fair rule of thumb. Consequently, delivery failures of PDS, MGNREGS and

ICDS/MDMS in already disadvantaged segments of rural India can act to further entrench social and spatial cleavages across the country.

The capacity for uneven service delivery to contribute to corrosive disadvantage has been increasingly recognised within India. A pervasive theme in policy development over recent years has been a more explicit and direct tailoring of programs towards institutional and capacity building in backward districts. A prominent example of this is the "Integrated Action Plan", under which a young professional (selected through the highly prestigious "Prime Minister's Rural Development Fellowship Scheme") is placed in each of 78 backward districts across India. This strategy seeks to tap into the highly talented human resources of India's young professionals: a domestic analogy to President Kennedy's development of the Peace Corps in the early 1960s. Likewise, the National Rural Livelihoods Mission (NRLM), developed in collaboration with the World Bank and launched in 2010, has the objective of delivering services to disadvantaged districts and households through innovative, place-based strategies that bypass traditional bureaucracies. A major component of NRLM is the mobilisation of self-help groups (SHGs), the establishment of stronger linkages between SHGs and formal financial institutions, and the alignment of these interventions with sustainable livelihood strategies. A key actor in this policy field is the National Bank for Agriculture and Rural Development (NABARD), which was set up by the Government of India as an apex Development Bank with a mandate for facilitating credit flow for promotion and development of agriculture, small-scale industries, cottage and village industries, handicrafts and other rural crafts. It also has the mandate to support all other allied economic activities in rural areas.

This broadly framed agenda seeks to create a set of scenarios where incomes earned through livelihood initiatives could be saved through the SHG microcredit mechanism (with women as the custodians of the savings), with these savings, in turn, reinvested into new livelihood options. Therefore, the distinctive focus of the NRLM enables the formation of virtuous cycles in which poor households (and, especially, women in those households) can more fully participate in the rural markets as both producers and consumers.

Though arrangements within these schemes are still in infancy, they potentially represent the hallmarks of a new policy approach. As indicated in the work of Arunachalam (2013), a prevailing narrative of contemporary India is that the noble ambitions of Indian poverty programs have often met the Achilles heel of implementation shortcomings. The newer wave of initiatives takes on board these lessons explicitly. They represent a set of programs which appreciates the centrality of bottom-up capacity building as a means to ensure that nationally instituted programs do not end up generating larger divisions between advantaged and disadvantaged segments of Indian society.

Who should be included in food-based social safety nets?

Questions relating to scope and coverage have consumed a large part of recent public debate in India about the future of food-based social safety nets. This attention has been due in no small part to an increasingly legal-focused and rights-based set of perspectives on these issues.

Consideration of the evolution of legalist and rights-based discourses around food in India commences with the observation that the need to provide adequate food is referenced both in India's national Constitution, and is part of international law to which India is signatory. Rights to food and nutrition are implicit within Article 21 of the Indian Constitution – "No person shall be deprived of his life or personal liberty except according to procedure established by law" and are explicit in Article 47 – "the State shall regard raising the level of nutrition and standard of living of its people and improvement in public health among its primary duties". In 1948, the UN Declaration of Human Rights recognised the right to food as a core element of a person's human right.

As briefly noted in Chapter One the full significance of these obligations remained latent until the twenty-first century. At the international level, in 2000, the UN Commission on Human Rights appointed (for the first time) a Special Rapporteur on the Right to Food. The purpose of this office was to report on international progress on the Right to Food, thereby creating an arena in which individual countries were monitored and held to account within the strictures of UN forums. Signatory countries to the UN Declaration of Human Rights were expected to meet obligations pertaining to *respect* (not to take any measures that arbitrarily deprive people of their right to food), *protect* (enforce appropriate laws and take other relevant measures to prevent third parties, including individuals and corporations, from violating the right to food of others) and *fulfil* (proactively strengthen people's access to and utilisation of resources so as to facilitate their ability to feed themselves) (UNCESCR, 1999: 5; see also Ziegler, 2012). Recognition of these international treaty obligations helped trigger in India a shift to what can be labelled a *judicialisation* of the politics of food security (Dressel, 2012). This means that food security became to be seen as something to which individuals had legal rights, and was open to justiciable action.

These perspectives on rights to food gained tangible expression in 2001. Public debate on the moral (if not legal) obligations of the Government of India heated up during this period because of rapid growth in the volume of food grain stocks held in the Central Pool (the network of warehouses controlled by the Union and state governments). Stockholdings increased during 1999–2001 before hitting historical high levels in 2001–02. During this year, an average of 42 million tonnes of wheat and 28 million tonnes of rice were under storage, when for both commodities the recommended buffer levels (to guard against crop failure) was around 10 million tonnes for each (USDA, 2012: 8 [wheat] and 2012: 16 [rice]). The presence of such vast reserves of food grains, at a time when under-nutrition remained pervasive in the population, caused considerable popular consternation.[7]

In April 2001, an umbrella civil society organisation called the People's Union for Civil Liberties (PUCL) lodged Public Interest litigation in the Supreme Court of India to force action on the question of food security. As noted in Chapter One, the writ – *PUCL vs. Union of India and Others (Writ Petition [Civil] No. 196 of 2001)* – argued that because Article 21 of the Indian Constitution enshrined the right to life, it followed that the Government of India had a constitutional responsibility to ensure all citizens had adequate food.[8] The Supreme Court adopted a highly activist response to this Writ. It rapidly published a series of Interim Orders and established two commissioners[9] charged with wide-ranging powers in respect to:

- monitoring the implementation of interim orders issued by the Supreme Court relevant to the case;
- reviewing and analysing the performance of the central and the state governments in implementing schemes and programs related to the case;
- investigating reported complaints and local failures in the discharge of food programs, as well as starvation deaths;
- making recommendations to respective state governments and to the Supreme Court on ensuring the respect, protection and fulfilment of the right to food of the people (Supreme Court Commissioners, 2011).

Over time, the ambit of the case and the role of the commissioners expanded. A mass of court orders covered a vast array of issues (too many to recount here) ranging from specific circumstances (e.g., provision of homeless shelters in Jammu and Kashmir) to more general themes (e.g., failures of certain state governments to provide timely statistical data on hunger and PDS performance). These actions fundamentally altered the dynamic of the food security debate in India. As Mander (one of the commissioners) has noted:

> It was not enough to declare that every citizen enjoys the fundamental right to food. Each category of people has varying food needs, denials and vulnerabilities, and the Court has in effect "explicated" or unpacked the right in relation to each segment of people. For an infant, the right to food translates itself into the entitlement of supplementary nutrition of defined specifications in feeding centres. For a school-going child, the right implies hot cooked school meals at state expense. For pregnant women, it means supplementary nutrition and maternity benefits. For designated poor families, it means 35kg of state-subsidised rice or wheat every month. For the able-bodied, it means guarantee of food through wage work. For the aged, it means pensions.
>
> *(2012: 19–20)*

Hence, through the handing down of Supreme Court Orders and the funding of commissioners to monitor compliance and to undertake inquiries on their own account, food security was made a question of law.

In response to the evolution of debate along these lines, at the 2009 general election the Congress-Party-led UPA administration promised National Food Security legislation that would enshrine rights to food security. After the UPA was returned to power, policy discussions intensified on how to bring this commitment to reality. To develop the legislation, the government established a Working Group of the National Advisory Council (NAC), an apex body chaired by Sonia Gandhi with a mandate to provide inputs in India's social policy formulation. The first major official public insight into the evolution of the government's proposal occurred in July 2010, when the NAC announced that whilst "universalisation of foodgrain entitlements across the country may be desirable" the legislation would proceed by way of targeting the 150 most disadvantaged districts, roughly corresponding to 25 per cent of the total number of districts in the country (NAC, 2010). In these targeted districts, all households would be guaranteed (under threat of litigation for non-delivery) of 35 kg of food grains per month at Rs 3 per kg. Outside of these areas, there would be progressive implementation of guarantees giving priority to Scheduled Caste, Schedule Tribe, urban slum dweller and other socially disadvantaged households. Delivery commitments for these groups were also guaranteed 35 kg of food grains each month at Rs 3 per kg. For other social groups, monthly disbursements were limited to 25 kg per month at varying (unspecified) price levels. In early 2011, fuller details of the NAC's draft were made public. This included a number of steps which received generally positive endorsement from stakeholders, including:

- processes to place ration cards in the name of women;
- introduction of ration cards for migrant populations;
- establishment of an independent authority to redress complaints;
- enablement of claimants to take legal actions, with civil and criminal liabilities on officials wrongly denying rights.

However, the spatial and social targeting foreshadowed in July 2010 had been further ingrained in policy, with the immediate focus of the Bill's implementation being confirmed in terms of the 150 most disadvantaged districts and the remaining population of beneficiaries divided into 'priority' (i.e., socially disadvantaged) and "general" categories.

This narrowing of the proposed Bill away from universalism elicited considerable public debate, both from civil society and even including dissenting views from within the Committee. Jean Drèze, who was invited to join the NAC on the basis of his specialist economic knowledge of the interactions between India's food system and under-nutrition, publically distanced himself from the approach and asked that his membership of the NAC not be continued after July 2011. For much of civil society, the thrust of criticism was that the NAC proposals represented a missed opportunity for India to match the universal human right to food, with consistent legislation and program practices. In the words of the Right to Food Campaign (2011b: 2):

> By proposing to continue with the system of targeting, the NAC has failed to seize the current opportunity of a proposed food security bill which will honestly address the issue of hunger, malnutrition and food insecurity amongst the people of India.

Arguments for a universalist approach also invoked the administrative problems of targeting. As discussed above in relation to the PDS, attempts to separate out various population segments in terms of socioeconomic disadvantage in a country as large as India seem inevitably prone to substantial errors of inclusion and exclusion and opportunities for the corruption of beneficiary lists. In an article in the widely read *Outlook India* magazine, Jean Drèze and Amartya Sen put forward the case for universalism, proposing that the successful history of Tamil Nadu should provide a policy exemplar for New Delhi politicians and bureaucrats:

> Tamil Nadu was the first state to introduce free and universal midday meals in primary schools. This initiative, much derided at that time as a "populist" programme, later became a model for India's national midday meal programme, widely regarded today as one of the best "centrally sponsored schemes". The state's pioneering efforts in the field of early child care, under the ICDS, has made great strides towards the provision of functional Anganwadis accessible to all, in every habitation. Tamil Nadu, unlike most other states, also has an extensive network of lively and effective healthcare centres, where people from all social backgrounds can get reasonably good healthcare, free of cost. MGNREGA, another example of universalistic social programme, is also doing well in Tamil Nadu: employment levels are high (with about 80 per cent of the work going to women), wages are usually paid on time and leakages are relatively small. Last but not the least, Tamil Nadu has a universal PDS, in both rural and urban areas and Tamil Nadu's PDS supplies not only food grains but also oil, pulses and other food commodities, with astonishing regularity and minimal leakages.
>
> *(Drèze and Sen, 2011)*

Nevertheless, when the government's legislative proposal (the *National Food Security Bill* [NFSB]) was tabled in Parliament in December 2011, it was premised on strict socioeconomic targeting of beneficiaries. The provisions in the Bill guaranteed the distribution of food grains to 67 per cent of India's population (75 per cent of rural dwellers and 50 per cent of urban dwellers), with 46 per cent of the former and 28 per cent of the latter accorded 'priority' status, which entitled them to 7 kg of food grains per person per month at Rs 3 per kg (rice), Rs 2 per kg (wheat) and Rs 1 per kg (coarse grains). Eligible households in the "general" category were to be entitled to 3 kg of food grains per person per month at a price which was to be calculated at "half the minimum support price offered to farmers by government during procurement" (*Times of India*, 2011).

In early 2012 the NFSB was referred to a Parliamentary Committee, which took a full year to consider the legislation. The eventual set of recommendations to emerge from the Committee altered the original Bill in two key ways (Standing Committee on Food, Consumer Affairs and Public Distribution, 2013). Firstly, it recommended abandonment of the "general" and "priority" categories in favour of a single entitlement. Evidently, the Committee's support for this view was swayed by the incorrigible problem of accurately targeting beneficiaries. A single entitlement would make for a far simpler system. Secondly, it recommended reducing the quantity of food grain entitlement from 7 kg to 5 kg per person per month. This recommendation was founded on budgetary concerns. However, the fact that the Committee stood firm in endorsing the 67 per cent population coverage proposed in the Bill attracted immediate fire from civil society groups. The Right to Food Campaign (2013) saw this as a fundamental retreat from a commitment to the right to food, arguing that its "reasoned position" was to prefer no law at all than a flawed one. The organisation also pointed to what it believed was a series of other limitations in the Committee's response to the Bill, including legal guarantees on the inclusion of pulses and coarse grains in the PDS, the need for local community control of PDS distribution and the absence of an independent authority to enforce the legislation.

These gaps identified by the Right to Food Campaign represent missing pieces in the Government of India's attempt to enshrine a legislative right to food. Nevertheless, if politics is the art of the possible then the legislation proposed by the Standing Committee reflects a series of compromises within the scope of budgetary and administrative limits. Indeed, the problem of crafting a legislative response that walked a fine line between the competing goals of government was foreshadowed at the commencement of the legislative debate by the government's Chief Economic Advisor, Dr Kaushik Basu (2010: 31–32), who identified the difficulty of designing a law that would enshrine this right but in a financially feasible and clearly enforceable manner:

> we have to be careful in granting rights too easily, since if we grant rights that are impossible to satisfy, then this simply devalues the meaning of a right and also perpetuates the culture of having laws that are meant to be violated. This can devalue the efficacy of all the laws in a nation. But the right to food is an achievable right, with some qualifications carefully spelled out and so, to that extent, is a move in the right direction [sic] that India is about to take.

Without seeking to diminish the legitimacy of arguments by the Right to Food Campaign, if legislation broadly along the proposed lines is eventually passed, there is little doubt it will make an historic contribution to India's food security policy. Without undue hyperbole, Haddad *et al.* (2012: 1) suggest that "India stands on the threshold of potentially the largest step toward food justice the world has ever seen". This is the result both of the resources devoted to this task and the qualitative character of change. In terms of the former, in one fell swoop it would deliver a quantum of additional resources – both in terms of the volume of subsidised food grains and the financial resources – to the task of redressing food insecurity. As of January 2013, unofficial estimates suggest that 62 million tonnes of food grains will be required to meet the annual obligations of the proposed legislation. This compares with 51 million tonnes lifted from the Central Pool in 2011–12 for provisioning the PDS (see Table 6.1). The additional annual budgetary cost associated with this policy is anticipated to be in the order of Rs 275 billion (or US$5 billion) annually (*Hindustan Times*, 2013). In terms of the character of food security policy, the justiciable rights that are at the heart of the legislation are conceived as imposing direct and binding commitments which delivery agencies risk missing at their legal peril. During the past decade, the actions of the Supreme Court commissioners have emboldened and empowered the large and active civil society component of contemporary India to act on behalf of beneficiaries whose rights to food are not being met. The anticipation behind making the provision of food grains a justiciable obligation of government is that civil society will quickly mobilise to expose and take legal action.

Conclusion

It is difficult to conceive any discussion of food security in India without detailed consideration of the country's food-based social safety nets. They continue to have a vital, indeed, expanding, role to play, notwithstanding the rapid growth of the national economy during the past decade. It is not coincidental or anomalous that legislative proposals to enlarge and strengthen this system have provided one of the most wide-ranging and important national debates over recent years. As discussed in the previous two chapters, the shifting social basis of agriculture and the inability of non-agrarian segments of the rural population to find decent work in the non-farm sector has meant that a large proportion of India's population has little choice but continue to rely on social safety net arrangements.

Yet although these arrangements are a crucial foundation of India's food system, their operational inadequacies also make them a liability for the attainment of improved food security. The flagship programs of the Government of India – PDS, MGNREGS, ICDS and MDMS – are all riddled with problems of maladministration and criminality. Their policy design and program attributes often leave much to be desired. For these reasons they exude a contradictory presence in the Indian food economy. They are crucial aspects of the institutional architecture but equally in need of substantial reform. Our consideration of their operations comes at a critical juncture, as mentioned earlier in this chapter. The past decade has been witness to discussion about these issues increasingly through the lens of legal obligations and human rights. As noted by the Supreme Court Commissioner Harsh Mander:

> The unique experience in India since 2001 demonstrates the practical ways in which a right as fundamental as the right to food can become legally enforceable, and have extraordinary impacts on the massive redeployment of state expenditures in favour of the dispossessed.
>
> *(Mander, 2012: 16)*

These discourses have flowed through the channels of international organisations, to the Supreme Court of India, and finally into the national Parliament. In its attempt to redraft national food policy in terms of the public's legal right to food, the Government of India has had to confront thorny issues such as the question of what proportion of the Indian population should have their food security needs underwritten by the state.

These issues continue to be a live debate within India. However, in the next chapter we turn to an equally contentious set of issues that is central to the future of food security policy: the question of how legal rights to food should be administered.

Notes

1 MGNREGS legislation was enacted in August 2005 and implemented in February 2006.
2 The PDS has a somewhat longer history, being conceived and implemented during the Second World War as a wartime rationing measure in a few major cities. In 1950, it evolved into a welfare measure for urban residents, with limited extension to rural areas that had food deficits (Swaminathan, 2000b). However, for all intents and purposes, it gained the semblance of its modern form only in the 1960s.
3 The rollout was in 20 districts and included 26 schemes. Initially it was planned in 51 districts, but absence of adequate infrastructure led to its scaling down by way of geography and program scope (*Times of India*, 2013).
4 Whilst it is certainly the case that individual states administer the PDS in quite different ways, consideration of this point should not be blind to the overarching impact of the PDS in terms of nutritional standardisation across India. As discussed in Chapter Three, the advent of the PDS has enshrined wheat and rice as the staple cereals of Indian diets. Coarse grains, including traditional millets such as jowar (pearl millet), ragi (finger millet), etc. have largely remained outside the ambit of the PDS, have not received subsidies and have witnessed reductions in levels of per capita consumption during the "PDS era" of the Indian food economy. Likewise, the subsidisation of wheat and rice has arguably crowded out pulses in Indian diets. The Right to Food campaign in India argues that nutritional security requires the inclusion of millets in the PDS (Right to Food Campaign, 2010: 10).
5 The level of subsidy provided by the PDS (when operating without significant leakage) has been calculated in Tamil Nadu (probably the best-performing state in terms of PDS performance) to equate to Rs 112.8 per person, or approximately Rs 500 per household (Khera 2012b). Comparably, the total food grains supplied through the PDS (35 kg/month of wheat and rice) equates to 233 g of rice/wheat per person per day. Data from the 2005 Indian Human Development Survey (IHDS) examined by Srinivas (2011) suggests that, at a national average, BPL and Antyodaya households consumed a total of 434 g of wheat and rice per person per day.
6 It might also be noted that there have been numerous cases of physical violence associated with the administration of MGNREGA, due to the need for officials to juggle vested interests. As described by Datta and Sharma (2008: 31) in an NGO report: "The 'suicide' of a Block Development Officer in West Bengal, who was honestly trying to implement NREGA, and the murder of activist Lalit Mehta in Jharkhand, within a month of each other, shows the extent of vested interest in the misuse of this program."
7 It might be noted that, in response to outcries, this stock level was drawn down over the following years, but recently has crept up again, such that as of 1 November 2012 when the Central Pool held 28.9 million tonnes of rice and 40.6 million tonnes of wheat (Department of Food and Public Distribution, 2012: 7), levels that are well beyond buffer stock needs.
8 The concept of Public Interest litigation is a distinctive feature of the Indian court system. According to Gauri (2009: 2): "PIL or 'social action litigation', as some call it,

originated in the late 1970s when the judiciary, aiming to recapture popular support after its complicity in Indira Gandhi's declaration of emergency rule, encouraged litigation concerning the interests of the poor and marginalized, and to do so loosened rules and traditions related to standing, case filing, the adversarial process, and judicial remedies."

9 The two originally appointed commissioners were Dr N.C. Saxena, former Planning Secretary, Government of India, and Mr S.R. Shankaran, former Secretary, Rural Development, Government of India. After the first few years, Mr Shankaran was replaced by Mr Harsh Mander, a social activist and former Indian Administrative Service officer with extensive background working in tribal areas.

7

INDIA'S BRAVE NEW WORLD OF FOOD SECURITY POLICY: E-GOVERNANCE AND CASH TRANSFERS

Introduction

The lived reality of India's food-based social safety nets is a world of ration cards, distribution queues and unadorned depots which serve as village-level Fair Price Shops. To receive their monthly entitlement, beneficiaries take their ration card booklets to their local Fair Price Shop. The local ration distributor weighs the volume of food specified in the entitlement, stamps the beneficiary's book and records the distribution in a matching ledger. The beneficiary pays the sum of money that is due[1] and then walks away with their food entitlement.

Current reform proposals in various stages of development and trial, however, would turn these arrangements upside down. One aspect of reforms involves replacement of the paper-based regime of booklets and ledgers with e-governance arrangements. The ensuing digitisation of all records would have the intended effect of improving system-wide efficiency and transparency with the effect of cracking down on corruption, theft and mismanagement. The second key aspect in current reform debates relates to implementation of cash transfer (CT) programs. The application of these programs in the field of food security policy would imply that the state would no longer provide beneficiaries with a physical supply of food grains, but, instead, would provide cash which could be used to purchase food items.

These two areas of policy reform are highly contentious. Whilst both serve the important purpose of seeking to repair the gaping holes in the food-based safety net system as discussed in Chapter Six, a range of questions exist about whether their means justify their ends, and indeed, whether their enactment would merely shift around the metaphorical deckchairs of policy implementation, causing problems of maladministration and criminality to reappear in other guises.

This chapter traverses these issues. When viewed side by side, it is apparent that e-governance acts as a precursor to CTs. It provides the information capabilities that enable a potential shift to CTs. Thus, the chapter firstly addresses the issue of e-governance, and then, in longer fashion, assesses the background and current status of the CT reform agenda. This extended treatment of CTs brings in two defining aspects of the contemporary character of this area of policy reforms: the role of neo-liberal moral formulations about social safety nets, and the demonstration effect of Latin America (and especially Brazil) within the Indian policy imagination. Bringing these themes together in the last major section of this chapter, we caution against inchoate applications of these agendas. The widely heralded successes of Brazil in bringing down levels of food insecurity hold important relevance for India; however, equally, policymakers need to be on guard against proposals which cherry-pick aspects of Brazilian policy and implement these out of context in India.

E-governance: digitising the right to food

It is perhaps no surprise that e-governance looms large in the public policy imagination of contemporary India. The nation's hugely energetic and financially successful software industry provides an extensive repository of ideas and human capital which can potentially be tapped and put into service for public administration. During the past decade there has been a vast number of experiments and trials which have applied e-governance to different aspects of the public service delivery challenge (Tandon, 2005; Paul, 2007; Monga, 2008; Bhatia *et al.*, 2009; Gorla, 2009; Madon, 2009; Bhatnagar and Singh, 2010; Gupta, 2010; Saeed *et al.*, 2012).[2] These initiatives gave rise to the development of more holistic and strategic approaches (Second Administrative Reforms Commission, 2008) and the first National e-governance Plan, released in 2006.

In recent years, food security policy has emerged as a key site for e-governance. A wide body of initiatives has been developed ranging across logistics, public accounting and cardholder management. This has involved, for instance, GPS monitoring of delivery trucks, the creation of web portals detailing delivery schedules, initiatives to text-message beneficiaries when supplies arrive in their village, and point-of-sale weighing machines connected to thumb print identification for beneficiaries.

In key respects, the evolution of e-governance in India's food security programs has mirrored the broader set of issues facing these reforms. Projects and trials are prone to the problem of being set up as 'islands' of initiatives without adequate recourse to the issue of how they interact with wider administrative systems (Gupta, 2010). Individuals championing particular initiatives frequently originate from technocratic worlds and can be unfamiliar with the village-level social contexts into which proposals are placed. As Banerjee and Duflo (2011: 235) note: "Even the most well-intended and well-thought-out policies may not have an impact if they are not implemented properly. *Unfortunately, the gap between intention and implementation can be quite wide*" (italics added). Madon (2009: 159) typecasts this as a major pitfall of e-governance, which can often result in projects "losing all sense of actual reality". Examples of these tendencies are legion across rural India.

It is not uncommon when visiting a panchayat office to see a dusty, disconnected computer in the corner of a room, surrounded by reams of paperwork. In one example we witnessed, a senior bureaucrat in the capital of one of India's poorest states championed the fact that, under his watch, all the PDS warehouses had been linked electronically enabling him to personally monitor stock levels and transport flows. A day or two later we visited a warehouse and observed a disconnected computer. When we enquired about this, we were told that the machine had a virus and was not working, no one knew how to repair it and there were no funds allocated for computer repair, in any case. Such anecdotes emphasise the disjuncture that often exists between head office imaginaries and the capabilities of personnel at the district and block levels.

The simple issue of electricity supply warrants forthright consideration in this regard. Most of rural India suffers from intermittent electricity. It is not uncommon for villages to receive just a few hours of power each day, and for the supply to unexpectedly cease without notice. Moreover, the supply of electricity has considerable social and spatial unevenness, with villages and hamlets inhabited by Scheduled Caste and Scheduled Tribe communities often missing out while adjacent communities have access to power (Planning Commission Expert Group, 2008: 10). These uneven and inadequate service levels persist despite specific programs providing funds for the erection of poles and wire infrastructure to disadvantaged communities. As argued by the Planning Commission Expert Group (2008: 73):

> Rural electrification has to mean households actually receive electricity, not merely an electric pole with a line going to BPL households . . . [If] money is used for building poles and laying lines to BPL households, without the actual supply of electricity, experience shows that both the poles and wires are stolen; at the very least, it is wasted investment, since there is no electricity flow for years after the investment in transmission lines.

The centrality of these problems within e-governance agendas is highlighted in Ripley's (2012) assessment of the PDS reform agenda in Karnataka. Not surprisingly for a state whose capital is Bangalore, the Government of Karnataka has an ambitious program of e-governance with particular reference to food-based social safety net programs. This includes the establishment of an Internet portal to carry real-time, publically accessible information about PDS deliveries to every district and block; reissuance of all PDS cards in digitally readable formats; and the distribution of electronic point-of-sale weighing machines in all Fair Price Shops, so that every PDS transaction is digitally captured and uploaded daily. The success of this agenda is however contingent on the degree of fit between the hi-tech attributes of policy and the physical and social environments in which they will be implemented. Ripley's research documented the case of a village community just 80 km from Bangalore with intermittent power supply and no Internet connectivity to speak of, which nevertheless was the site of a trial of the new e-governance PDS infrastructure.

Hurdles presented by the limitations of physical infrastructure notwithstanding, it might reasonably be expected that successful implementation of e-governance reforms would engender greater levels of transparency and reduced opportunities for corruption. Such conclusions are consistent with some field-based case research evidence, such as that from Shanker (2008), who found that a range of e-governance applications in the village of Bellandur, Karnataka, were successful in transferring some power away from corrupt and exploitative middlemen. However, consideration of these issues within wider terms suggests a different set of conclusions. Analysis by Bussell (2012: 256–57) on the relationship between digital-based administrative reforms in India and corruption concludes:

> reforms of public services are likely to threaten petty corruption entrenched in the delivery of services, but should have little effect on corruption in contracting or misuse of public funds. Instead, reforms that incorporate a one-stop service centre model actually provide a new opportunity for politicians to extract rents from potential partners. In addition, these reforms allow politicians to target the services they provide selectively, so as to maximise electoral benefits while minimising the threat to rents.

Further complicating these issues, the trajectory taken by e-governance in India is now throwing up important questions about civil rights. A crucial component of India's move towards e-governance in food-based social safety net programs is the capture of biometric information from all beneficiaries and recording this on cards which can be read digitally. This initiative is intended to address two key problems in current programs: the wide number of fraudulent "ghost cards" in circulation and the inability of migrants (e.g., people who move from rural to urban areas) to access PDS entitlements (both discussed in Chapter Six). These aspirations are currently incorporated within a much wider agenda by the Government of India to provide a Unique Identification Number (UID) for every citizen. This program, called *Aadhaar*, ultimately envisages that all aspects of an individual's dealings with the government are recorded against a single card containing a range of relevant biometric information. Legislation enabling these plans was introduced to the national Parliament in 2010 and implementation commenced soon afterwards (even before the legislation was voted on) via pilots across the nation. Collection of biometric data in this format clearly poses crucial implications in terms of the potential for identity theft and abuse by corrupt and/or despotic state agencies. The future of these agendas would seem to rest with the outcome of the raft of legal challenges highlighted by civil rights organisations which will inevitably follow the passage of legislation. Some key thinkers within India's food security policy debate support these plans (e.g., Saxena, 2012); however, many remain opposed. In January 2013, a total of 208 leading food security researchers and activists, including such figures as the "father of the Green Revolution" M.S. Swaminathan, Jean Drèze, Bina Agarwal and Utsa Patnaik, attached their names to a petition which called for UID to be voluntary, not compulsory, and to be excluded from the PDS and MGNREGS (Swaminathan *et al.*, 2013). At the time of writing, its precise future with regards to food-based social safety net policies remains unclear.[3]

Cash transfers

In current reform discourse, proposals to reform India's food-based social safety system through e-governance are closely entwined with proposals to introduce a system of cash transfers (CTs). Although implementation of the former does not necessarily imply a move towards the latter,[4] the information capabilities generated by e-governance provide the preconditions for a shift to CTs. It is difficult to envisage a shift to CTs without comprehensive digitisation of entitlements (through smart cards or a similar technology) linked to beneficiaries' UIDs. Thus, e-governance reforms have opened up a new arena of reform possibilities based around the replacement of physical deliveries with financial equivalents.

The evolution of CT proposals in India is integrally interconnected with a wider, global agenda. Depending on one's perspective, policy shifts along these lines represent either a revolutionary opportunity to address poverty and food insecurity (Hanlon *et al.*, 2010) or "the latest fad of the international development industry" (Ghosh, 2011: 67). As will be discussed below, the introduction of this arena of policy reform came to India specifically via Latin America. As early as 2006, a World Bank publication assessing under-nutrition in India noted the Latin American experience and argued: "The possibility of introducing [cash transfer] programs in India should be explored" (Gragnolati *et al.*, 2006: 82). The Government of India publically endorsed this thinking in its *Economic Survey for 2009–10* (Government of India, 2010), suggesting that the PDS could and perhaps should be replaced with direct cash transfers. Also in 2010, the Chief Minister of Delhi, Sheila Dikshit, launched a discussion paper arguing specifically for a shift to cash transfers for social safety net benefits in the national capital (cited in Basu, 2010: 35). These arguments then gained substantive momentum with the release of the Government of India's Budget for 2010–11. The then Finance Minister Pranab Mukherjee announced in the Budget a Task Force to recommend reforms to LPG, kerosene and fertiliser subsidies. The ensuing report recommended transition to direct transfer of through cash payments that would be connected to beneficiaries' UID cards (Task Force on Direct Transfer of Subsidies, 2011). The unspoken assumption in the reform agenda for these subsidies was that it could provide the launch pad for a much wider implementation of CTs, encompassing the PDS and related food-based social safety net schemes. This evolution of policy thinking progressed hand-in-hand with the views of the Expert Committee charged with assessing the National Advisory Council's proposals on Food Security Bill. In its report, the Committee stated:

> As an alternative to the existing PDS we may switch over to the use of smart cards which simply means that the food subsidy may be directly transferred to the beneficiaries instead of to the owners of the PDS stores. This in turn

gives the people an opportunity to go to any store of their choice and use their smart cards or food coupons to buy food.

(Economic Advisory Council, 2011: 15)

The impending shift of the government in this direction prompted a flurry of public commentary and studies during 2011–12. Key contributions from these efforts are unpacked below. However, in terms of the evolution of policy, a key milestone in this period was the announcement, in late 2012, that the government would replace the existing in-kind social welfare benefits with cash transfers. The prime minister of India constituted the "National Committee on Direct Cash Transfer", which, in its first meeting on November 26, 2012, agreed on the phased implementation of CT reforms. This included implementation of 34 schemes (chiefly including scholarships and pensions) in 51 districts across the country in the initial phase, with the entire country to be covered by the end of 2013. The slogan adopted by the government to popularise the CT schemes was, "*Apka Paisa, Apke Haath*" (*Your money in your hands*). On 1 January 2013 the government reacted to problems with infrastructure and capacity and scaled down the scope of the initial implementation to 26 schemes in 20 districts. As mentioned in Chapter Six, the in-kind subsidies on food and fertilisers were excluded from the initial phase of CT reforms; however, their potential inclusion in a future phase of CT reforms was kept open.

In order to critically evaluate the implications of CT policies, it is necessary to firstly set out how they would work.[5] The basic principle behind CT reforms is to replace beneficiaries' physical (in-kind) entitlements to food with financial equivalents. The right to food, thus, is exchanged for a right to buy food. However, amending policy along these lines can occur through various degrees and dimensions; CTs are not a single approach, but an umbrella term for a policy shift that can be executed via various means.

This can occur through two general means. The first of these involves the use of vouchers. Under this option, beneficiary households would receive a monthly voucher entitling them to spend the subsidy amount on approved food items. Assuming that vouchers could be used at any approved outlet, this would presumably inspire competition between suppliers, which may include the existing Fair Price Shops or, if regulators wished to go down this path, any new entrant that met approval. Also, assuming vouchers were decoupled from individual food items (that is, they allowed the beneficiary to spend the total amount on approved food commodities but in whatever combination best suited them), beneficiaries would gain the freedom to spend their food subsidy in ways dictated by their own desires, rather than from the set combination of foods established by bureaucratic edict. Nevertheless, the use of vouchers implies an ongoing *conditionality*: the subsidy has been transformed into a financial payment, but on the condition that beneficiaries use these monies for food. In India, some states (notably Bihar) have trialled barcoded vouchers to bring in greater transparency, but in these policy reforms the supplier has remained the same. The next stage of proposed reform along these lines would involve providing beneficiaries with the freedoms to use vouchers in the open market, but the potential for shifts in this direction have been overtaken by the altogether more liberalised direct cash transfer (DCT) option. Under this scenario, subsidy benefits are wholly fungible. Recipients would receive a cash amount every month, which would represent the Government of India's commitment to providing households with the means to ensure their food security. Whether households spent this amount on food would, of course, be up to them.

The option of progressing CT reforms either through vouchers or DCTs emphasises one of the benchmark ideological decisions in this policy area. The voucher option is indicative of a program logic and design which sees CTs primarily as a means of countering maladministration and criminality. The aim of a voucher-based regime is to continue to guarantee a physical flow of food to households, delivered, however, through different (more efficient) administrative means. The DCT option also pursues these aspirations, however within a robustly libertarian view of the role of the state. In this option, the state delivers on its commitment to provide households with the monetary resources to potentially meet their food security needs, but otherwise interferes minimally in their lives. From this perspective, the question of how households go about deploying these monetary resources, including the vital issue of whether they use them to purchase food or for other purposes, is essentially a matter for individual households and not the state. This philosophy is encapsulated neatly in the title of Hanlon et al.'s (2010) position-defining book *Just Give Money to the Poor,* and has emerged as the Government of India's apparent default policy option for progressing reforms in this area. This being the case, we now assess the chief lines of argument used by proponents of the shift to CTs, and then counter this with those advocating a more cautionary approach.

(i) Arguments in support of cash transfers

As a general rule, the strongest advocacy of the more hands-off, libertarian view of CTs tends to emanate from mainstream economists whose world views are informed by principles of individual utility optimisation (inter alia, Basu, 2010; Jha and Ramaswami, 2010; Kotwal et al., 2011; Ramaswami et al., 2012). These researchers tend to outline their advocacy of CTs on two broad grounds. Firstly, they contend that current in-kind provisioning is a suboptimal set of arrangements reflecting policy capture by the vested interests of political lobbies associated with Fair Price Shop owners and PDS distributors. Implementation of CTs would smash the influence of these interests and therefore enable rents to be redistributed to beneficiaries. In their articulation of this set of arguments, CT advocates combine a broadly libertarian perspective with a set of hard-nosed arguments about the practical advantages of direct cash payments over and above some kind of mediated voucher regime or the status quo. Thus, Basu (2010: 33) argues that attempts to reform and improve the current Fair Price Shop/in-kind allocation regime are simply not worth the effort:

It is easy to respond to [arguments about the need to clamp down on malad-ministration and criminality] by asking for better policing. Here again we have to be realistic. Trying to police such a large system by creating another layer of police and bureaucracy will come with its own problems of corruption and bureaucracy. This is where the question of systems design arises. An economic system is like an engineering system. We may and should lecture people on the importance of honesty and integrity but till that message sinks in, it would be foolish to work on the assumption that people are robotic units that do the job they are supposed to do flawlessly. We have to take the laws of the market and the incentives people respond to and then design an optimal system for doing the job we want to get done.

Secondly, proponents contest claims that CTs would give rise to socially inferior patterns of food consumption; in the words of Ramaswami *et al.* (2012: 18), "paternalistic arguments in favour of in-kind distribution are weak". A range of factors is used in defence of this point. Influentially, an economic experiment conducted during 2010–11 in 12 blocks of Raghubir Nagar (West Delhi) involved researchers randomly selecting 450 households and for a portion of this sample (the "Treatment" group) their monthly PDS benefits were replaced with CTs (Gangopadhyay *et al.*, 2012). Consumption patterns for this sample of households were monitored over a two-year period in three stages: mid-2010 (baseline), mid-2011 (midline) and January 2012 (final). For the present discussion, the key conclusion from this experiment is as follows:

> We find that with CT, food security is not compromised. In particular we find that households with CT are no worse off than households with PDS. We even find that unconditional cash transfers provide opportunities for households to shift to other nutritious options in the non-cereal segment. We also test the hypothesis that cash transfers lead to wasteful expenses, but do not find any statistical evidence for this. Hence, our experiment provides evidence that unconditional cash transfers do not compromise on food security, nor do they induce households to increase wasteful expenses.
>
> *(Gangopadhyay et al., 2012: 31)*

Yet, even if beneficiary households were to replace food with non-food expenditure following the implementation of CTs, advocates suggest that this would not necessarily be problematic. Basu (2010: 35) makes this point candidly, by metaphorically shrugging his shoulders and suggesting that even if beneficiaries decided to use their cash for non-food items, the fact that so much of the PDS is diverted under the present system might suggest that households are not worse off, in any case. He argues:

> If they choose not to take the benefit in the form of food and buy something else, then it is not as big a tragedy as the benefit going to the owners of PDS stores as often happens in the current system.

And finally on this point, as Ramaswami *et al.* (2012) argue, policy analysts should not assume that under the present arrangements beneficiary households necessarily consume the food they receive from their Fair Price Shops. As the authors suggest, once a beneficiary picks up their allocation, it is not inviolate from being resold. Indeed, in our own fieldwork in a remote part of Orissa, we observed wide-scale reselling of PDS rations of rice. Beneficiaries held the quality of rice delivered to the local Fair Price Shop in disdain, and only worthy of being used in toddy (rice-based alcoholic drink). In cahoots with the Fair Price Shop owner, they would receive an amount of cash in lieu of their allocation, and the Fair Price Shop owner would use the uncollected rice for toddy manufacturing, which would then often be sold back to the original beneficiaries. Thus, what was intended to be a food staple for impoverished households was consumed in the form of alcohol. These issues suggest that the question of *who* receives benefits is potentially more important than the shape these benefits take (i.e., cash or in-kind). Previous studies in India have documented the fact that when benefits are paid in the name of women, there is a greater probability that their use will be more in line with policy intentions (Mencher, 1988; Agarwal, 1990; Kanbur and Haddad, 1994; Basu, 2006; Pankaj and Tankha, 2010). The importance of this issue is heightened in the case of CTs, because of their direct fungibility. Thus, implementation plans for CTs need to be alert to the household politics of gender, if these reforms have any chance of meeting their promise.

(ii) Arguments for a cautionary approach

The prospect of replacing in-kind PDS entitlements with CTs has triggered important reappraisal of this scheme. In Chapter Six, we presented and discussed the series of studies that documented high levels of diversion and maladministration in the PDS. To briefly recap, an investigation by the Planning Commission (2005) found that in 2001, only 42 per cent of PDS grain actually found its way to beneficiaries, and that excessive program administration expenses undermined the entire cost-efficiency of the scheme. In the early years of the twenty-first century the situation appeared to deteriorate further, with data from the 2004–05 NSS round being interpreted by researchers to suggest that almost 90 per cent of the program effort from the PDS failed to reach the poor (Jha and Ramaswami, 2010; Svedberg, 2012).

Nevertheless, there seems to be an accumulating body of evidence that the performance of the PDS has improved over recent years. In Chapter Six we introduced Khera's (2011a) analysis of the PDS using 2007–08 NSS data. Her research revealed improvement in nationwide PDS effectiveness, with leakages falling from 54 per cent to 44 per cent between 2004–05 and 2007–08 and (importantly for the current discussion) dramatic improvements in some states linked to governance reforms. More recent analysis (Khera, 2012b) demonstrates a continuation of these trends. Her examination of data for nine states for 2009–10 indicates that PDS performance improved substantially in all the states under consideration with the sole exception of Bihar (Table 7.1).

TABLE 7.1 Incidence of PDS grain diversion, 2004–05 and 2009–10

	2004–05	*2009–10*	
Andhra Pradesh	23.2	8.2	
Bihar	90.9	74.5	
Chhattisgarh	51.8	10.4	
Himachal Pradesh	27.0	22.2	
Jharkhand	85.2	46.3	
Orissa	76.3	30.2	
Rajasthan	93.9	66.0	
Tamil Nadu	7.3	4.1	
Uttar Pradesh	58.0	57.5	

Source: Khera (2012b) using NSS data

The question of system-wide improvement is at the heart of the wider debate on the merits of CTs. Evidence of dramatic improvement to the existing PDS would take the wind out of the sails of arguments for wholesale reform. This being the case, one of the most vital pieces of evidence for the present debate is provided by Khera's (2011d) nine-state survey undertaken in 2011. In each state, two districts were selected and two blocks within each district chosen. Within each block, three villages were randomly selected and 12 households in each village randomly identified to be interviewed. This gave a total survey size of 1,227 households.

The survey indicated a much more efficient system than suggested by previous research. The benchmark measurement of PDS efficiency used by Khera is the Purchase-Entitlement Ratio (PER) (the proportion of full entitlement that is actually obtained by eligible households). Across the nine states, the PER was found to be between 84 and 88 for BPL households, and 87 for Antyodaya households (Table 7.2). For more than 75 per cent of beneficiaries surveyed, the PER was 100; these

TABLE 7.2 Purchase-Entitlement Ratios for PDS food grain deliveries, 2011

	BPL	*Antyodaya*	
Andhra Pradesh	100	97	
Bihar	45	47	
Chhattisgarh	95	97	
Himachal Pradesh	92–100[a]	94–100[a]	
Jharkhand	71	68	
Orissa	97–100[a]	100	
Rajasthan	86–100[a]	100	
Tamil Nadu	92	88	
Uttar Pradesh	77–88[a]	85	
All the above states	84–88[a]	87	

Source: Khera (2011d: 37). Note: (a) Entitlements are reported as a range by Khera to account for an additional 5 kg of food grains that was ordered by the Supreme Court in the Right to Food case. The range represents the upper and lower limits of the PER, depending on whether this additional entitlement is included.

households knew their ration entitlements and fully received them. Moreover, the survey revealed a substantially lower extent of inclusion and exclusion errors than had been found in previous research (Khera, 2011d: 38) and "hardly any instances of overcharging" by Fair Price Shop owners (Khera, 2011d: 41). With the notable exception of Bihar and, to a lesser extent, Jharkhand, a picture was painted of the PDS that was starkly different from pre-existing assumptions. As Khera (2011d: 36) argued, the study confounded assertions of the PDS as "an irreparably dysfunctional scheme".

The strongly positive interpretation of the PDS efficiency which emanates from Khera's survey prompts the question of how and why this scheme has apparently been turned around so effectively. Khera (2011: 36) identifies the change to a revival of political interest by state governments in PDS performance, which is manifested in initiatives to (i) expand and simplify coverage, (ii) reduce prices (or set them at zero, as has occurred in Tamil Nadu since June 2011) and use various e-governance reforms to ensure better inventory management and reduce the potential for corruption. To this end, the survey reveals the performance problem of the PDS as a technical and bureaucratic challenge, rather than a systemic issue related to the allegedly inherent failings of in-kind modes of benefit delivery (cf. the quote by Basu (2010: 33) above). Following from this perspective, the debate on PDS reform should focus on the administrative issue of how different state governments have managed this program. To this end, a brief comparison of Chhattisgarh and Bihar provides important insights.

Chhattisgarh is an important case to consider because of its dramatically improved PDS. The popular view of these reforms is their close association with the 2003 election of the BJP Government led by Chief Minister Raman Singh (Puri, 2012). Soon after taking office, the new administration enacted the *Chhattisgarh Public Distribution System (Control) Order 2004*, which mandated that Gram Panchayats, self-help groups and local cooperatives operate Fair Price Shops, and replaced the private transport of PDS grains with government trucks, each painted yellow to facilitate community transparency. Then, in 2007 the government radically extended the scope of the PDS by adding in all households that were excluded from the 2002 BPL survey. This led to a further 1.9 million Chhattisgarh households being included as PDS beneficiaries, more than doubling the coverage of PDS in the State so that it encompassed approximately 80 per cent of the rural population (Puri, 2012: 22). Finally, to reduce bogus cardholding, the government painted signs outside each house specifying the name and ration status of the occupants: a strategy to "name and shame" those households falsely claiming Antyodaya status. The energy given to improving the operation of the PDS in Chhattisgarh has spilled over into a wider commitment to food security, with the state passing its own *Food Security Act* in 2012, in advance of national legislation.[6] This legislation judicialises the right to food in the State in alignment with PDS entitlement levels.

On the other hand, in Bihar, the wide-ranging governance reforms that accompanied the election of new state government in 2005 have hardly changed the grounded realities of social welfare delivery to the poor. Findings from household surveys conducted by one of us (Choithani) in ten villages of the Siwan District revealed that rent-seekers continue to find new ways to undermine efforts to revamp the dysfunctional state of social provisioning. In order to make PDS more transparent, in 2007 the Chief Minister of Bihar, Nitish Kumar, introduced the system of PDS coupons (which, from 2011 onwards, were barcoded and contained useful information about the PDS beneficiaries and Fair Price Shops). Under the coupon regime, each beneficiary household is provided with a total of 12 coupons each year for wheat, rice and kerosene that specify their PDS entitlements[7] as well as the price they have to pay. These coupons are distributed, usually, through the village camps, organised jointly by the local Block Development Office and Gram Panchayat. The way the system was envisaged to work was that each month the beneficiary redeems one coupon against each of the specified PDS commodities at the local Fair Price Shop. The Fair Price Shop licensee then has to submit these coupons every month to the block/district administration in order to get the next month's supply. The coupon system was a well-intentioned attempt by the government to stop the PDS supplies from being sold in the open market. During his field research, however, Choithani found that most of the Antyodaya and BPL households were being forced to give Fair Price Shop licensees coupons for two months (or more) just in order to receive the food rations for one month, thus still allowing the diversion of grains in the open market. Moreover, the quantity of food grains provided to the beneficiary households was less than their entitlement.[8] With the exception of one village, recipients seemed to accept these frauds without resistance. To quote one of the villagers:

> It is not us who get less than what they are entitled to, but all families in the village. And no one speaks up against this practice. We don't think an individual voice of ours could make any difference but if we unite, collective action could change things for good.

While culprits, the local ration distributors are not solely responsible for these anomalies. For example, in one of his study villages, villagers told Choithani that when they protested against the local ration dealer and demanded that they get their full quota on regular basis, the dealer got his license transferred to another village because the bribes demanded by the authorities in the PDS supply chain system meant that the full quota regime was not sustainable from his business viewpoint. Furthermore, the local ration dealers themselves were provided with less grain from the block/district warehouses. Most PDS dealers Choithani interviewed told him that each 50 kg bag of wheat and/or rice given to them typically weighs between 44 kg and 46 kg. This lower off-take by PDS dealers then gets passed on the beneficiaries. Added to this were the transportation costs incurred by the local dealers to procure the grains from the government warehouses, which were also indirectly borne by the beneficiaries. The sister of a PDS dealer in a study village, who was also the headmistress of a high school in a nearby village, remarked, "Everyone is wise enough to understand that nobody will pay this transportation cost from their pocket. The government must fix it, if they have to set the system straight."

Clearly, these findings highlight that the problems of PDS governance in Bihar run deep through various layers of administration, ultimately preventing the deserving poor from realising their welfare entitlements. It is no surprise that, dejected by dysfunctional PDS, the surveyed households in Siwan showed a marked preference for cash over food, a finding consistent with Khera's PDS survey results in Nalanda and Katihar districts.

The differences between Chhattisgarh and Bihar underline the considerable variation between states in Khera's survey. A key aspect of this variation is in regards to the question of attitudes towards the PDS. Each respondent household was asked their opinion about a shift from in-kind to cash benefits.[9] Across-the-board there was a strong preference for in-kind over cash – 67.2 per cent of respondents preferring food entitlements against 17.9 per cent preferring cash (Table 7.3). However, there are major differences between states. In states with functioning PDS the status quo was preferred, while in those with poorer levels of performance (Bihar, Uttar Pradesh, Jharkhand and Rajasthan) support for cash transfers was stronger. Khera (2011d: 44) explains these findings as follows:

> People's preferences depended on a combination of pragmatism, shrewdness and deep understanding of the local circumstances. For example, a widow in a remote Maoist-affected block of Nuapada district (Orissa) with no local transport but with a functional PDS was as likely to opt for food as a widow from a Bharatpur village (Rajasthan) with easy access to banks and markets where she suspected the PDS dealer was cheating her was to opt for cash.

These concerns are clubbed with the important issue of financial sector functionality in rural India. Many parts of the country suffer from an extremely rudimentary banking infrastructure that is riddled with high levels of mistrust from would-be users. A graphic illustration of this was provided in January 2013 by a journalist accompanying bank officials in Rajasthan charged with implementing the government's CT pilots:

TABLE 7.3 Preference for in-kind or cash PDS delivery

	Prefer food (%)	*Prefer cash (%)*
Andhra Pradesh	91.3	5.6
Bihar	20.8	54.2
Chhattisgarh	90.3	2.1
Himachal Pradesh	81.4	9.3
Jharkhand	66.0	22.2
Orissa	88.3	5.8
Rajasthan	59.6	14.7
Tamil Nadu	70.6	10.5
Uttar Pradesh	41.5	34.1
All the above states	67.2	17.9

Source: Khera (2011d: 44)

one family, petrified to see the bank officers, shut the door in their faces and wouldn't deal with the officers until the village head man intervened . . . [According to a State Bank of India representative] "They feel insecure to see officers at their place, they fear we might rob them of their money . . . it takes a lot to convince them."

(Pandey, 2013)

These issues of local institutions and infrastructure flow into concerns about how a shift towards CTs would expose beneficiaries to new forms of market vulnerability. In an article which otherwise is highly supportive of CTs, Kotwal *et al.* (2011: 74) admit that this is "the most serious objection" to the introduction of these measures. As Shah (2008: 78, cited in Svedberg, 20102: 60) asks: "it is not clear how transfers of cash to the poor would allow them to buy grains from the open market in times of steep inflation." During Choithani's surveys in Siwan, Bihar, where he found an otherwise marked preference for cash over food as a result of dysfunctional PDS, a middle-aged woman told him, "No matter how much money the government provides, the grain prices in the open market can never be as low as those offered by the PDS shop". Theoretically this concern could be addressed by policies guaranteeing that cash entitlements are indexed to price increases; however, from a beneficiary's perspective, commitments by the Government of India to maintain the real price of food subsidies may be seen as less than ironclad. A cash-strapped government could potentially delay or cancel inflation adjustments to the PDS under the rationale of needing to impose emergency financial measures. Market vulnerabilities could also be generated through the collusion of local retailers. Although CT advocates emphasise the potential for cash to induce competition and lower prices for beneficiaries, it is perhaps not unrealistic to suggest that this represents an idealised vision of market processes in small, remote Indian villages. As suggested by Khera (2012b) "context matters!" – competition for the "food subsidy market" would evolve in varying ways across rural India depending on the quality and depth of local commercial infrastructure, the number of market participants and the relationships between them and the extent of oversight by government regulation. If local shops or distributors collude on price, the food equivalent of CTs is devalued and poor households may have little scope for redress.

The final area for caution relating to the implementation of CTs relates to dietary diversity. As argued in Chapters Three and Five, the dominance of wheat and rice within the PDS has had the overall effect of distorting the Indian food economy towards these commodities, a situation which has encouraged the country's achievements in "cereal security" to run ahead of its capacity to provision its citizens with nutritionally diverse and appropriate diets. On the one hand, CT proponents suggest that liberalising the food choice aspect of the food-based social safety net may assist dietary diversification and micronutrient intakes, notably with respect to coarse grain and pulse consumption. They contend that, under current arrangements, beneficiaries' diets are locked into a heavy dependence on wheat or rice. Whether or not CTs may alter food consumption patterns is a highly speculative question. There is scant evidence of how the decoupling of food-based safety nets from specific items may impact on nutrition. In one of the very few investigations of this issue, a study from Indonesia of the links between CTs, dietary diversity and nutrition failed conclusively to identify clear relationships (Skoufias *et al.*, 2011). Moreover, consistent with the discussion above, such concerns in any case may be able to be addressed through administrative reforms to in-kind PDS delivery regimes. Some states have added coarse grains and pulses to the list of subsidised PDS entitlements, and the National Food Security Bill also proposes a shift in this direction. Whatever trajectory is taken, however, there is an undeniable need to improve the dietary diversity of poor Indian households. Khera's (2011d: 43) survey of PDS recipients found that 7 per cent of respondents ate only rice or roti in the previous day's evening meal. A total of 8 per cent of respondent households did not eat dal at any time during the previous week; 68 per cent did not eat fruit; and 58 per cent did not eat eggs or meat. Half of all households did not consume vegetables daily. These findings have dire implications for micronutrient, vitamin, iron and protein intakes, with longer-term implications for health and human capabilities.

International evidence on food policy cash transfers: what can Indian policymakers learn from Brazil?

> Cash transfers are increasingly seen as a potential cornerstone of social policy in India, often based on a distorted reading of the Latin American experience.
>
> *(Drèze and Sen, 2011)*

The discussion in the previous section set out the key arguments that have been deployed in the contemporary Indian debate on the potential use of CTs to meet the nation's food security obligations. Importantly, however, this debate has not been occurring in a national vacuum. As noted earlier in this chapter, the CT policy model was introduced to India as part of a development policy discourse advocated by the World Bank and strongly informed by the Latin American experience, especially Brazil. A comprehensive understanding of the Indian policy options is incomplete without close examination of these international influences. In this section we outline the Latin American roots of the CT model and highlight the lessons this holds for any potential translation into Indian contexts.

According to Banerjee and Duflo (2011: 78–81) the policy take-off of CTs can be traced to education and health reforms undertaken in Mexico between 1994 and 2000. Mexico's deputy minister of finance, Santiago Levy, launched a series of pilot programs which made the payment of welfare monies conditional on recipients meeting school attendance requirements and participating in preventative health-care programs. In these permutations, the chief purpose of CT reforms was to encourage behavioural changes in recipients that would, in holistic terms, reduce the cost to government; better health would reduce the state's hospital and medical expenses, and better education would help impoverished households to break out of poverty cycles. The apparent success of this shift to conditionality in government payments (soon generalised under the label "conditional cash transfers" (CCTs)) then led to its emulation in an array of programs and initiatives across Latin America during subsequent years. The underlying premise of the CCTs is that, whereas the state provides benefits for the upliftment of the weak and vulnerable, the recipients of such benefits must commit to their own development by the same token. According to Fiszbein *et al.* (2009: 10), "The state is seen as a partner in the process, not a nanny".

Even though Mexico was the first country to have a nationwide CCT program called *Progresa* (renamed *Oportunidades* in 2001) as early as 1997, this was in turn inspired by the local-level initiatives in Brazil.[10] For the purpose of this discussion, we focus on the way this model helped shape food security policy in Brazil. Our choice of focusing on Brazil is primarily guided by its influence in shaping the international policy discourse on the nature and scope of social safety nets, including India where the proposed transition to CTs frequently cites the experience of Brazil. Besides, several other important considerations guide us to discuss the Brazilian case from the Indian perspective. Firstly, notwithstanding the differences in the magnitude of hunger between India and Brazil, the social, cultural and geographical correlates of hunger in both countries appear somewhat similar. For example, levels of poverty and inequality vary as markedly by skin colour in Brazil as by caste status in India. Secondly, hunger exists in India and Brazil despite both countries being net exporters of food, which suggests that the issue of hunger is situated in a broader set of livelihood circumstances of people. Finally, while the remarkable growth of the Indian economy has failed to translate into the nutritional well-being of its population, Brazil's success in reducing hunger, by contrast, has occurred despite its far-from-ideal rate of economic growth. Hence, insights from Brazil might play a crucial role in deciphering the "Indian Enigma" of a rather weak negative correlation between economic growth and hunger, introduced in Chapter One.

The introduction of CCT programs in Brazil occurred in a highly adverse national social context. Until recently, the narrative about Brazil in the international development discourse characterised it as being one of the most unequal societies in the world. During 1977–99, the Gini coefficient for Brazil mostly stayed within the range of 0.58–0.62, which led some analysts to describe this phenomenon as "the unacceptable stability" of Brazil's inequality (World Bank, 2004: 13). The persistence of high inequality in Brazil over this period can be traced to an inequitable social development model. From the 1930s, the contributory model of social protection, chiefly pensions, formed a dominant feature of Brazil's social safety nets (Soares, 2011), but these arrangements only safeguarded the interests of formal sector workers. The disregard of the dual nature of labour markets, comprising a parallel and significantly sized informal sector, led to the exclusion of the bulk of poor and marginalised populations from state protection and opportunities for upwards social mobility (Sánchez-Ancochea and Mattei, 2011: 301). Over time, these inequalities in life opportunities became increasingly entrenched.[11]

While Brazil continues to be affected by high levels of inequalities, progressive social reforms initiated since the mid-1990s have drastically altered the country's image, making it a role model for social development. Following the end of 21 years of military rule (1964–85), in 1988, constitutional reforms widened social and citizenship rights. Although the prevailing economic stagnation around the same time prevented any immediate boost in social-sector spending for the poor, acknowledgement of the complementary role of inclusive social development appeared widespread among policy circles. The economic reforms of the 1990s, therefore, while conforming largely to the structural adjustment policies of the "Washington Consensus", were accompanied by major reforms to social protection systems which targeted the poor better (Ravallion, 2011: 84).

The first key plank of these reforms was the proposal of a guaranteed "citizen income". In 1991, Senator Eduardo Suplicy from the Worker's Party presented a "Basic Income" proposal in the Senate. The bill sought to provide supplementary income to all citizens aged 25 years and above whose monthly earnings fell 2.5 times below the country's minimum wage, though its implementation was planned in a phased manner over a period of eight years, targeting extremely vulnerable groups at the outset (Brito and Soares, 2011: 2). Alongside the basic income proposal, the policy deliberations of the time also stressed the need to devise strategies that address the structural causes of intergenerational poverty – the second key plank of social protection reforms. In particular, the role of education in breaking the vicious cycle of poverty and enhancing the living standards of the poor was considered crucial, given that it accounted for significant income disparities. These parallel discussions, therefore, directed policy thinking towards the idea of linking the cash benefits with a long-term vision of human capital accumulation, in what later came to be known as CCTs.

The initial experiments with CCTs in Brazil were small in scale and implemented at the sub-national level. The first set of CCT programs largely focused on improving educational outcomes among the poor. Later initiatives then incorporated health and food and nutrition security. In 1995, the then governor of the Federal District of Brasilia, Cristovam Buarque, started the first CCT program linked with child education. Named as the *Programa Bolsa Famíliar para a Educação* (Family Allowance Program for Education), it targeted poor families with children aged between 7 and 14 years. Cash incentives were provided (up to the equivalent of one minimum wage) for beneficiaries whose children fulfilled a school attendance rate of 90 per cent. Later programs also included conditionalities on health. Following the lead from these municipal initiatives, the federal government initiated two CCT programs with coverage limited to select municipalities: *Programa para a Erradicação do Trabalho Infantil* (Program for the Eradication of Child Labour) in 1996 and *Programa de Renda Mínima* (Minimum Income Program) in 1997 (Soares, 2011: 56). The encouraging results from these local-level initiatives soon inspired wider experimentation with CCTs, and encouraged a near-unanimous political consensus in Brazil in favour of CCTs as the most effective way of redistributing income and alleviating poverty (Brito and Soares, 2011: 3). As a result, three major nationwide CT programs were launched in 2001 by the federal government under the administration of the then president Fernando Henrique Cardoso (1995–2002):

- Bolsa Escola: A program of cash payments to poor families conditional on children maintaining a school attendance rate of at least 85 per cent.
- Bolsa Alimentação: A program of cash payments to poor families (defined on the same basis as *Bolsa Escola*) conditional on health behaviours of women (prenatal and antenatal care) and children (regular vaccinations).
- Auxílio Gás: Unlike the other two programs, this was an unconditional income transfer to compensate for the in-kind cooking gas subsidies, which were later phased out. The benefits included a bi-monthly payment for each eligible household which fell below the minimum income threshold.

In all these programs, women were made the ultimate beneficiaries. This served to influence the wider political acceptability of cash transfers within Brazil and among the international development policy planners and donors. The positive results emerging from the concurrent evaluations of these CCTs gave further credence to this mode of social assistance. The social policy reforms in Brazil, therefore, resulted in the fully fledged embracement of CCTs and they soon became an integral feature of Brazil's social protection system.

In 2003, the political landscape in Brazil witnessed a dramatic change. For the first time in history, the Worker's Party (*Partido dos Trabalhadores*) assumed power at the federal level. This change altered political priorities. The new president, Luiz Inácio Lula da Silva (2003–2010), put hunger-elimination at the top of his political agenda. Carrying on his party's image as socially forward-looking, Lula, in his now widely famous inaugural speech, pledged:

> We are going to create appropriate conditions for all people in our country to have three decent meals a day, every day, without having to depend on donations from anybody. Brazil can no longer put up with so much inequality. We need to eradicate hunger, extreme poverty, and social exclusion. Our war is not meant to kill anyone – it is meant to save lives.
>
> *(cited in da Silva et al., 2011: 9)*

Within a month of assuming power, Lula created a special ministry in his office named "Extraordinary Ministry of Food Security and Fight Against Hunger" (Portuguese acronym MESA) and launched the "Zero Hunger" (ZH) program. At the time Lula assumed office, 44 million people in Brazil were existing on a per capita income below US$1 per day and thus possessed extreme vulnerability to hunger (da Silva *et al.*, 2011: 19). The tragic irony of this statistic is that Brazil's is one of the world's largest food exporters and, by one estimate, annual per capita food availability in the country is approximately 35 per cent more than the requirements needed to provide every Brazilian citizen with adequately nutritious diets (do Amaral and Peduto, 2010). Given the widespread political support for the CCT model of social assistance, Lula retained the cash transfer programs initiated under the Cardoso administration and added new ones. In alignment with the primary objective of his ZH strategy, the most immediate addition was *Cartão Alimentação*, a food card program under the purview of the newly created MESA. This provided uncondi-tional financial assistance to individuals/households on the brink of hunger, with a particular focus on the disadvantaged north-eastern region which accounted for half of the nation's rural poverty. In the 2003 budget, *Cartão Alimentação* accounted for 70 per cent of the new funds earmarked for food security (Takagi, 2011: 56). Then, later in 2003, the Lula administration restructured and merged the various CCT programs initiated under the Cardoso regime with the food card program to create the umbrella CCT program, *Bolsa Familia* (Family Grant). The hunger-combat ministry MESA was merged with the Ministry of Social Development and renamed as the "Ministry of Social Development and Fight Against Hunger", (MDS) which was responsible for the overall coordination of *Bolsa Familia*.

In its initial phase, *Bolsa Familia* targeted the households which received the benefits under the previous four separately managed CCTs, with new households qualifying if they registered with their respective municipalities and met program eligibility criteria. The unified *Bolsa Familia* grouped the households in two broad categories based on predetermined income criteria, "extremely poor households" and "poor households", and benefits to households varied according to the cat-egory to which they belonged. The creation of these arrangements established a more efficient targeting mechanism, underpinned by *Cadastro Único* de Programas Sociais *(Cad Único)*, a single registry system which has enabled the collection of data on the social, demographic and economic conditions of poor households.

Since its implementation, the scope and reach of *Bolsa Familia* has continually expanded by the means of raising both the minimum income threshold to cover more households as well as the benefits offered. In 2004, 6.3 million households benefited from the support provided through the program (Soares *et al.*, 2010: 176). By 2008, this had risen to 11 million (World Bank, 2009: 32). More than 50 per cent of beneficiaries are concentrated in drought-prone north-eastern Bra-zil. Although some studies point to the high unmet need (exclusion of potential beneficiaries) in *Bolsa Familia* (Sánchez–Ancochea and Mattei, 2011: 305), its wide coverage and successful targeting of the poor have ensured the program has made an impressive dent on the Brazilian incidence of poverty and hunger. Soares *et al.* (2010: 179) find that *Bolsa Familia* accounted for at least 10 per cent of the total income of poorest 5 per cent of the population. According to the Brazilian Insti-tute of Applied Economic Research (2008), between 2002 and 2007 the per capita income of the poor households grew at an annual average rate of 9 per cent, more than double the rate of their richer counterparts (cited in Sánchez–Ancochea and Mattei, 2011: 306). Estimates by the World Bank suggest that *Bolsa Familia* has lifted 20 million individuals out of poverty and resulted in a marked reduction in inequality, which now stands at a 30-year low (World Bank, 2010). Similarly, there is strong evidence that *Bolsa Familia* has had positive outcomes in terms of school enrolment, grade progression, child vaccination and food consumption patterns (IFPRI, 2009; Lingani *et al.*, 2010).

It is important to note that although CCTs became the defining public face of Brazil's food-based social safety net agenda, the scope of initiatives under

President Lula expanded well beyond the original ambit of *Bolsa Familia*. Recognising the multifaceted nature of poverty and hunger, more than 50 closely interlinked policy initiatives have been added as part of Brazil's ZH strategy. These include the *Programa Nacional de Fortalecimento da Agricultura Familiar* (National Program for Strengthening Family Farming), which provides financial and technical assistance to smallholder farmers and aims to promote family farming; *Alimentação Escolar*, a school meal program providing cooked meals to 47 million children every day, and subsidised kitchens for low-income workers. These initiatives greatly complemented the direct cash assistance programs and therefore represented a "whole approach" to enhancing food and livelihood security among the vulnerable in Brazil. As a result, Brazil has exhibited an impressive performance on the hunger reduction front. Between 1999–01 and 2010–12, the percentage of hungry in Brazil declined almost by half, from 12.1 per cent to 6.9 per cent of the population. In absolute numbers, this translates into a reduction of 8 million food-insecure people (FAO, 2012: 49). The prevalence of child malnutrition and child deaths also reduced by 73 per cent and 45 per cent respectively during the period 2002 to 2008 (Special Rapporteur on the Right to Food, 2009: 13).

This brief narrative of the history of CTs and food security policy in Brazil illuminates key lessons for consideration in the comparable Indian debate on these issues. Brazil's success in combating hunger has been drawn upon by advocates of CTs in India and, as already mentioned, the World Bank has advocated this template as a mode of reform. However, the assumption that cash transfers provide a magic bullet must be treated cautiously, for their effectiveness and efficiency is highly context-dependent. In a report published by the World Bank, Fiszbein *et al.*, (2009: 48) note: "In the face of arguments both for and against, it cannot be stated categorically that every country in the world should have a cash transfer program in place to help reduce poverty." A close reading of the Brazilian case renders the need for equal consideration of the broader political and administrative contexts in which Brazil's CT programs have been situated. Most importantly, CTs were introduced by the Cardoso administration with the purpose of encouraging positive behavioural changes among beneficiaries, and then, with the Lula Government, these programs were strongly augmented by unconditional cash transfers that had the purpose of bolstering the financial resources of poor households. Both these aspects of the Brazilian experience seem to have gone missing in the Indian debate. In India, the debate is anchored around the issue of *replacing* in-kind benefits with unconditional CTs. This approach writes out the two elements that have been most central to the Brazilian experience. Brazil's successes are emblems of an interventionist state flexing its muscles, both in terms of using its benefit payments to encourage behavioural changes in recipients and in the substantial budget increases which have accompanied an expanded social safety net. Yet in India, advocacy of CT reforms is immersed in policy agendas attached to a shrinking of the state. Indeed, for some analysts, part of the explicit attraction of introducing CTs is that it would trigger wide-ranging change across the Indian food system that would substantially reduce the logic of government involvement in agricultural policy, food storage and distribution. As argued by Basu (2010: 37): "In such a scenario [i.e., CTs] the state's involvement in the market will be much smaller and will pertain mainly to holding stocks for emergencies and unexpected food shortages."

Secondly, over the course of the Lula administration in Brazil, CCTs were used strategically as one aspect of a multi-pronged food security policy. In India these policies are being advocated in quite different policy circumstances. As observed by Drèze and Sen (2011):

> In Latin America, conditional cash transfers usually act as a complement, not a substitute, for public provision of health, education and other basic services . . . In India, however, these basic services are still largely missing, and conditional cash transfers cannot fill the gap.

Thirdly, the implementation of CCT programs in Brazil was preceded by the wide-ranging public debates on its implications for the millions of poor Brazilians. Additionally, numerous pilot projects were conducted to assess how the recipient households reacted to such programs, and what impact they made on household welfare outcomes, before they were widely embraced, whereas in the case of India, barring the notable exception of a PDS survey (Khera, 2011), there is a dearth of empirical evidence on the beneficiary households' perceptions of cash transfers. Without an appreciation of the varying contextual realities under which these programs do or do not work, it is likely that they may fall well short of meeting their desired objectives of strengthening the food security of India's populace. As Banerjee and Duflo (2011: 35) note: "The poor often resist the wonderful plans we think up for them because they do not share our faith that these plans work or work as well as we claim."

Finally, in Brazil, the broader food security vision for the nation has been defined in ways that place emphasis on the decentralisation of program administration and recognition that local-scale initiatives provide a key ingredient in the attainment of national goals. Thus, the *Programa Nacional de Fortalecimento da Agricultura Familiar* (National Program for Strengthening Family Farming) is premised on the recognition of the role of own-production as a key means for poor households to meet their food and nutritional needs. Urban agriculture has been supported, and land redistribution has also been in the policy frame during this period, with the robust civil society efforts of the *Movimento dos Trabalhadores Rurais Sem Terra* (Landless Workers' Movement) playing a key role in advocating and protesting on behalf of vulnerable Brazilians. Again, these complementary policy agendas have been notably absent from the policy debates on these issues in New Delhi.

In summary, nuanced consideration of the Brazilian experience tells a story that is highly relevant to contemporary India, though in a way that departs from a simple endorsement of CTs/CCTs. The Brazilian case suggests there is a potential place for CTs in food security policy, but as part of wider "whole of system" strategies. In Brazil the key innovation in this policy field involved the addition of a *conditionality* component to welfare schemes that were already cash-based. This had the intention of encouraging behavioural changes among recipients as part of a strategy to combat the structural roots of intergenerational poverty. However, these initiatives on their own remained insufficient to comprehensively address Brazil's problems of food insecurity: an expanded, unconditional set of welfare payments for the poor was also required. To date, the Indian debate on CTs has not embraced these lessons.

Conclusion

This chapter has continued the analysis in Chapter Six of India's food-based social safety nets. In terms of the broader structure of this book, this discussion has corresponded to the need to understand what Sen (1981) labels the "exchange system entitlement" component of food security. As indicated in Chapter Six, discussion of these issues reveals their contradictory position in the Indian food system; the dependence on these arrangements by such a large proportion of the Indian population is both a symptom of the country's food security failings, and evidence of their importance in abating (what otherwise would be) nationally debilitating levels of under-nutrition.

This chapter has focused on the theme of program reform. The two central aspects of current reforms involve the implementation of e-governance initiatives, and proposals to restructure the way that entitlements are managed, through the replacement of in-kind arrangements with direct cash transfers. The direction these two reform paths take will shape significant aspects of India's social safety system into the future. In both cases, this chapter has assessed their transformative potentials and their potential pitfalls. In the case of CTs, it has argued that key lessons from the Brazilian experience can and should influence the policy imagination.

In the next chapter, which concludes the book, we bring together the issues addressed in this and previous chapters, generating an overarching assessment of the food security challenges facing India into the future.

Notes

1 Entitlements in some states are provided at zero price to some beneficiaries; however, for most beneficiaries in most states, they are priced at a heavily subsidised rate. Thus, a typical PDS entitlement of rice or wheat would be in the range of Rs 2 to Rs 5 per kilogram, whereas a private market price would more likely be between Rs 12 and Rs 20 per kilogram, depending on quality.

2 Some ideas in this discussion draw from research originally undertaken by Ripley (2012).

3 The implementing agency for this scheme, Unique Identification Development Authority of India (UIDAI), was established by an executive order and the legislation – UIDAI Bill, 2010 – seeking its statutory status has not yet been passed by the parliament. After the bill was tabled in the Upper House (Rajya Sabha), it was referred to the "Parliamentary Standing Committee on Finance", which, in its recommendations, asked the government to consider it afresh (Standing Committee on Finance, 2011).

4 The logic of e-governance reforms is consistent with the status quo being maintained (i.e., continuance of entitlement deliveries in physical form).

5 Quite deliberately, this book uses the phrase "cash transfer" and the acronym CT. This is in order to distinguish this policy field as a broad area including both conditional cash transfers (CCTs) and direct cash transfers (DCTs), and in the Indian context, inclusive both of voucher and direct cash payment proposals.

6 It should be noted that party politics also played a role in this, with Chhattisgarh's BJP administration seeking to demonstrate its superiority in this policy area over and above the Congress-led coalition government at the centre.

7 While Antyodaya and BPL households in Bihar are entitled to 35 kg (21 kg rice and 14 kg wheat) and 25 kg (15 kg rice and 10 kg wheat) of grains and 2.75 litres of kerosene each month, APL households receive only 2.75 litres of kerosene.

8 It must be noted that irrespective of the card type, i.e., Antyodaya/BPL/APL, most households reported getting kerosene entitlements on a month-to-month basis, albeit a little less than their entitlements – 2.5 litres as against the entitled quota of 2.75 litres.

9 Specifically, they were asked "how they would feel if the FPS was closed and, instead of PDS grain, the government opened an account for them and deposited cash each month in that account. The amount deposited would be equal to the market value of the commodities they currently purchase from the FPS (i.e., whatever it would cost them to buy these commodities on the market). It was clarified that this amount would be adjusted with price increases, so that it always enabled people to buy from the market whatever they are getting today from the PDS" (Khera, 2011d: 43).

10 In 1996, a Mexican government delegation visited Brazil to learn about the municipal-level CCT initiatives on boosting child education, which subsequently inspired the adoption of Progresa in 1997 (Lindart et al., 2007: 12).

11 For example, differentials in levels of education and the corresponding differentials in wage returns to education account for about half of the income inequality in Brazil compared to the United States and Mexico (World Bank, 2004: 25). Further, based on household income distribution data from the 1999 round of the Pesquisa Nacional por Amostra de Domicílios (PNAD) survey, Bourguignon, Ferreira and Leite (2008) find that retirement pensions in Brazil are "inequality-increasing", contributing between 4 and 6 percentage points to Gini index.

8

CONCLUSION

The previous seven chapters have portrayed the challenge of "feeding India" as a multidimensional problem. Using an analytical method based around the concepts of livelihoods, entitlements and capabilities, they have focused on the lives of the poor and asked questions about how different social segments gain access to food. In this final chapter we bring together the main insights from the book. We first revisit and review the key insights in the narratives told in previous chapters and, in the final section of the book, we seek to look into the future of India's food challenge.

Revisiting the Indian food security enigma

This book opened with the vignette of a food-insecure individual ("Raju") we interviewed in an Indian village. Raju survives on a meagre diet that falls well short of his long-term needs. Its calorie content barely meets his Minimum Daily Energy Requirements, its composition does not fulfil requirements for nutritional diversity, and its continuation is highly vulnerable to adverse changes in Raju's (already tenuous) livelihood circumstances. Raju is in his mid-50s, and heading towards the end of his working life. For the entire period of his infancy, childhood and adulthood, he has faced food and nutrition insecurity. He was born into disadvantage, experienced the trauma of losing his mother and then his father, and was cut adrift from his family's traditional land. Along with his wife, he now lives a hand-to-mouth existence picking up casual rural labouring duties and relying on whatever support his sons can provide.

Raju represents a human face of India's food security enigma. During the past two decades India's economy has boomed, but barely any of this wealth or opportunity seems to have trickled down to Raju or, indeed, Raju's village. This is the case notwithstanding the fact that Raju lives in Haryana, one of India's wealthier states, and is only 200 km or so from New Delhi. Indeed, Raju's circumstances are a microcosm which lends support to Krishna and Bajpai's (2011) assessment that economic growth since the early 1990s has shed benefits in an identifiable spatial pattern in which city-dwellers have achieved the largest gains, followed by inhabitants of small towns and villages close to towns and, finally, people living in villages located more than 5 km from the nearest town (whose circumstances, if anything, have deteriorated).

Our compressed telling of Raju's life story is intended to act as a palliative to discourses about food security that focus exclusively on agricultural production and economic growth. Whilst these issues are crucially important, they are only part of the food security jigsaw. As we have emphasised in several places throughout this book, agricultural production is a fundamental plank of the food security challenge, but its ability to generate improved nutritional outcomes within a population hinges on social and economic arrangements. In India's case, the vehicles for converting food production self-sufficiency into food security for the population as a whole have remained incomplete. Raju has remained food insecure in spite of the fact that during his lifetime, Indian food grains production has more than doubled in per capita terms, and in absolute terms has increased sevenfold.

Moreover, Raju has remained food insecure in the midst of data which suggests rapid income growth at a national level. In the six years from 2004–05 to 2010–11, per capita private consumption expenditure increased by 47 per cent in inflation-adjusted terms; that is, on average, households across the country in 2010–11 were spending roughly one and a half times the amount they spent in 2004–05 (Ministry of Statistics and Program Implementation, 2012). A different story, of course, has unfolded in India's villages. Thus, the statistical relationship between GDP growth and reductions in under-nutrition which has been seen in other developing countries has not seemed to hold for India (Gillespie and Kadiyala, 2011).

Therefore, to understand the reasons for the food insecurity of Raju (and hundreds of millions like him across India), we must see through the headlines of agricultural production and economic growth, and dig deeper into the contextual environment which has framed his life. As outlined in this book, this task is facilitated by an approach that is structured around the concepts of livelihoods, entitlements and capabilities. The concept of livelihoods, as developed through the Sustainable Livelihoods Approach, asks questions about the reasons for how and why individuals and households assemble a combination of activities in the attempt to sustain or improve their well-being. The concept of entitlements refers to the bundle of attributes which a person or household can draw upon to meet their food needs. The concept of capabilities refers to the means by which entitlements can be translated into substantive freedoms by people or households to "promote or achieve objectives they value" (Alkire, 2002: 4). Seen in these terms, Raju's food security circumstances are an outcome of the unfolding of his livelihood strategies and circumstances, the bundle of food entitlements (legal, economic and cultural) he is in possession of and his capabilities to redress these conditions. To then extrapolate from the individual to the societal, the problem of food insecurity in

India can be understood to require a holistic frame of reference that understands nutritional outcomes as the product of a complex interplay of economic, social, political, environmental and cultural processes. Depending on their grounded contexts, these interactions serve either to restrict or empower the capabilities of different segments of India's population to be nourished by safe, nutritionally adequate and culturally appropriate food. Thus, the question of "how to feed India" is fundamentally about the security of livelihoods and provision of an expanded notion of justice for its most vulnerable people.

This framework has informed and guided the previous chapters. In Chapters Two and Three the scene was set by establishing the dimensions of food insecurity in India. Chapter Two focuses on the question of under-nutrition, and Chapter Three on the recent history of agricultural production trends. The following chapters then were organised in accordance with Sen's (1981) articulation of the different forms of food entitlement: own-production (Chapter Four); wage-labour (Chapter Five); and exchange-system entitlement (Chapters Six and Seven). In turn, these chapters were also structured to respond to the different components of Chambers and Conway's (1992) framing of sustainable livelihood strategies. The overarching logic of how different chapters relate to one another was set out in Figure 1.1.

In Chapter Four we asked how the post-Green-Revolution context of Indian agriculture has shaped opportunities for agricultural intensification or extensification for different components of the rural Indian population, and what this has meant for food security. In ways that are broadly sympathetic and consistent with the TANDI analysis developed by IFPRI, our interpretation of these issues emphasised the increasingly restrictive character of agriculture as a pathway for many households in rural India to improve their livelihood and food security status. This is quite unlike the situation which existed in the 1960s and 1970s during the Green Revolution in its north-west India heartland, as described in Chapter Three. In that earlier period, a comparatively "poor-friendly" churning of land ownership and employment arrangements enabled a relatively wide array of rural households (including poorer rural households) to engage successfully in agriculture-based livelihood strategies. Many relatively smaller-sized landowners were able to participate in productivity gains from the Green Revolution, and some previously landless households were able to acquire land holdings for the first time. However, the particularities of rural India in recent years have been more problematic for a repeat of such socially benign, pro-poor, agricultural advancement.

Chapter Five then reviewed the challenges facing poor segments of the Indian population to attain their food security requirements through non-farm livelihood strategies. An increasing proportion of the rural population has become increasingly dependent on finding new sources of livelihood outside of the farm sector, both locally and non-locally (through permanent and circular migration), but these processes have been socially uneven, with poorer and more vulnerable households being generally exposed to a greater need to diversify their livelihoods yet being less well placed and equipped to do this. At the same time, while the national economy has grown rapidly, this growth has been associated with a relatively weak enlargement of employment opportunities for vulnerable groups, especially in relation to formal-sector, "decent work". Thus, the growing numbers of poor and marginal people in search of livelihood opportunities outside of agriculture have predominantly ended up in the informal sector, in casualised, temporary or precarious livelihood situations. The result has been to perpetuate a high incidence of poverty within an expanding class of the population that is increasingly detached from the capacity to meet their food requirements through own-production (on their own agricultural land holdings). The food security of this expanding class is highly dependent on obtaining food through the market. Yet, during the recent period in which this process has unfolded, food prices have increased at a relatively rapid rate, with the overall effect of creating a major new obstacle to progress against food insecurity in India.

Finally, in Chapters Six and Seven, attention was turned to the vexed question of food-based social safety nets. These chapters posed the question: *what determines the extent to which food security in India is met through social safety net programs?* The focus in Chapter Six was the current operation of these arrangements. It was pointed out that the key components of the Government of India's social safety net system hold a contradictory place in current policy debates. On the one hand, their shortcomings ensure they are held up by critics as representing the wrongheadedness of food security arrangements in India. Critics attached to pro-free-market liberalist views excoriate these programs because of their inefficiencies. Critics from social justice movements equally lambast them because of their failures to deliver food entitlements to the poor. Yet, on the other hand, despite their failings, food-based social safety nets are seen as an essential part of India's food security challenge. Thus, they are both part of the problem and part of the solution for better food security in India.

The future of these arrangements is currently in a state of flux on account of three entwined reform agendas. The first of these concerns the Right to Food. Following the Indian Supreme Court's interventions, since 2009 the Government of India has reacted to a judicialisation of people's food rights, in broad concurrence with international human rights obligations. In any case, actions by the Supreme Court in the Right to Food case (*People's Union for Civil Liberties vs. Union of India and Others 2001*) had already moved India along this path. Making these rights a reality involves legislative action, which, at the time of writing this book, remains unfinished. In 2011 the UPA Government tabled a *National Food Security Bill* in the National Parliament, and in January 2013 a Parliamentary Review Committee completed its review of the legislation. In some form or another, it seems likely that food security legislation will eventuate. However, to the chagrin of civil society activists such as the Right to Food Campaign, it seems likely that the government will not embrace a commitment to provide everyone in India with a legal guarantee to a full, nutritionally appropriate diet. Instead, at the time of writing, the government is proposing a partial rendering of the food security commitment. It will guarantee 67 per cent of the population with a monthly food grain ration that will satisfy approximately half their needs. Beneficiary households will need to rely on self-provisioning or the market for the remainder of their food grain needs, and for other components of their diet (vegetables, pulses, meat, eggs, etc.). Of course, moreover, the merit of this (or any other) commitment depends on whether it actually delivers: whether it ensures a *substantive right* to food. The other two reform agendas currently facing India's food-based social safety nets are described in Chapter Seven as the "brave new world" of food policy. E-governance potentially invokes radical alteration to the ways in which beneficiaries' food entitlements are manifested. These agendas are being pursued via technologies based around smart cards linked to a UID, and greater transparency of food administration via the use of public Internet portals, GPS-based monitoring of deliveries, etc. There is little doubt that these innovations have the potential to dramatically improve program administration and delivery; however, they raise important issues of citizenship rights and privacy. Moreover, the problems of navigating hi-tech policies into the lifeworlds of village India should not be understated. It is in these contexts that proposals for cash transfers have been advanced. E-governance provides a potential medium for the allocation of food entitlements by way of cash disbursements rather than in-kind. Yet, as the discussion of this topic in Chapter Seven unveiled, there are highly fraught aspects of this agenda. The success of cash transfer programs in Brazil has been used to advocate their introduction to India; however, the substantial differences between the policy contexts in these two countries makes this a questionable exemplar.

Consistent with the overall perspective of this book, we contend that consideration of all these issues should be framed from a people-centric perspective. The food security question for India is: *how can the substantive freedoms of the poor and undernourished be improved so that these segments of the population can better meet their food security needs?* There is no single answer to this question, but the mere fact of framing the problem in this way opens up the need for holistic analysis that is fundamentally about the security of livelihoods and provision of an expanded notion of justice for the most vulnerable of its population. With this in mind, attention now turns to the future challenge of feeding India in a way that prioritises the food and nutrition security of the poor.

. . . into the future

Previous chapters have set out a rich description of the social and economic forces that have lain behind India's food security enigma. Out of those discussions, we identify six key issues which are centrally important in determining India's food security outcomes in the immediate future. In each case, these issues are interpreted through the lens of livelihoods, entitlements and capabilities.

The first key issue relates to the sustainability of India's current agricultural system. In Chapter Three we noted the recent difficulties in maintaining yields in the wheat-rice rotation agricultural heartlands of north-west India. Since the mid-1990s, the Green Revolution boosts to production have tapered off. Additional yields have tended to come only with great effort and expense, through a process that has been dubbed as the agrichemical treadmill. Yet these responses have been viable only through extensive subsidisation of agrichemicals, via a system in which farmers have paid fixed (heavily subsidised) prices that have been delinked from market trends. With prices of fossil fuel agrichemicals rapidly inflating in the post-2007 period, the budgetary cost of these subsidies skyrocketed, forcing the Government of India to revisit the existing arrangements in order to contain the subsidy burden. These proposed policies (Kelkar *et al.*, 2012) will likely place increasing burdens on farmers' financial abilities to maintain yields through the increased agrichemical applications. Added to these problems has been an alarming rate of groundwater depletion, exacerbated by perverse agricultural policies of state governments (free or subsidised electricity, for example) that have benefited larger farmers at the expense of smallholders. Over time, it is also likely that these subsidies will be steadily removed by state governments. Representatives of relevant voter communities (in urban areas and smallholders and non-farming populations in rural areas) will agitate for the removal of these expensive budgetary outlays to which their constituencies receive no substantial benefit. As agrichemical and electricity subsidies are pared back, farmers in north-west India will be increasingly exposed to the economic and environmental contradictions at the heart of their post-Green-Revolution condition.

Unsustainable wheat and rice cultivation in north-west India has dramatic repercussions through the Indian food system because of this region's central role in provisioning the nation with food grains. To this end, considerable recent policy attention has been focused on the potential for "Green Revolution"-type investments and reforms to boost wheat and rice production in other parts of India and, notably, in the eastern states of Bihar, Chhattisgarh, Orissa and West Bengal. Bihar occupies a strategically important position within these debates as it has traditionally been the poorest major state, despite its possession of sizeable natural resources. A highly influential recent report to the Government of India has argued that "Bihar can possibly be the next granary of India and the seat of the second green revolution" (Gulati *et al.*, 2011: 45). From a livelihoods perspective, however, this advocacy needs to be treated with caution. As argued in Chapter Three, the original Green Revolution in Punjab and Haryana had relatively benign impacts on socioeconomic inequality because of the way it disrupted pre-existing sharecropping arrangements, encouraged large landowners to move into the non-agricultural economy (providing opportunities for previously landless households to take up agricultural holdings) and provided employment for migrant rural workers. However, the evolved character of agriculture in India now means that any new "Green Revolution" may have quite dissimilar effects. Because of its increased scarcity, agricultural land has now gained considerably greater value as an asset. Therefore, it may be likely that agricultural productivity gains in a state like Bihar in the twenty-first century could be associated with land-grabbing by elites, rather than land churning, as occurred in the 1960s and 1970s in Punjab. Traditional forms of policy redress to these tendencies (notably land redistribution and land ceiling laws) appear unlikely, given that they espouse philosophical intents contrary to the dominant ideology of liberalisation, seen elsewhere in India's contemporary Indian political economy. Managing the unsustainable character of agriculture in the original Green Revolution states, and facilitating a transition towards small-holder-inclusive cereal production systems elsewhere across the nation, would thus appear a key challenge for India's future food security.

Following on from these points, a second key issue concerns the need to find ways of better incorporating smallholders within the new growth segments of India's agricultural economy. As discussed in Chapter Four, the shift towards high-value horticulture in India has been the key shift in the overall composition of the sector during the past decade (Chengappa, 2012). Although there are many examples of smallholder involvement in high-value horticultural chains in contemporary India, the inherent tendency of buyers is to deal with fewer and larger agricultural suppliers. Thus, unless smallholders are provided with appropriate institutional supports, it is often the case they can be excluded or marginalised within this lucrative growth sector.

This is a live debate in India (and, indeed, across the developing world). Much of the policy discourse around this issue invokes the concept of partnership, expressed either in the sense of large companies partnering with smallholders, or public–private partnership arrangements designed to facilitate these developments. This was a pivotal theme in *Agriculture for Development*, the World Bank's influential 2008 World Development Report (World Bank, 2008a), and was the centrepiece of an assessment of global agriculture by the World Economic Forum (2013). Of course, this usage is highly loaded – when global agribusiness engages with smallholders it is partnership of a "David-meets-Goliath-type" (Nally and Vira, 2013). Moreover, from a smallholder's perspective, involvement in high-value horticulture does not come without risks. Whilst a buyer might encourage a smallholder to devote all of her/his land and efforts to the production of a single crop, smallholders might deduce their livelihood options as being better served through a strategy of carrying on with subsistence production in parallel to servicing the market with high-value horticulture. All too often, policy discourse about smallholder inclusion in high-value chains is premised on the question of "what can be done to encourage involvement?" rather than the more appropriate question of "what would attract smallholders to participating in chains?" Answering this second question reframes the debate on this issue along the lines of a livelihoods perspective. It requires an appreciation of how high-value production might fit within smallholders' broader bundle of livelihood strategies.

The third major issue facing India's food security future relates to gender. As argued throughout this book, food insecurity in India is highly gendered. These outcomes derive from the persistence of cultural practices in intersections with the travails of modernity. Preference towards men and boys in the intra-household allocation of food remains a reality across much of India. In Chapter Two, we noted the debate about how these practices appear to permeate into gender-based differences in under-nutrition between girls and boys. Modernity has complex effects on these outcomes. The Western idealisation of gender equality has considerable power to execute intra-household behavioural changes within urban middle classes. However, these ideals don't necessarily trickle down to poorer and rural segments of India's population. Ideals of gender equity are immersed in the more broadly based arena of change associated with modernity. One important example relates to the gender effects of the rise of the cash economy over the subsistence economy. As discussed already in Chapter Three, researchers such as Bina Agarwal (1984; 1990; 2003) have identified that the introduction of cash cropping in northern India tended to empower men at the relative expense of women, because it gave new forms of economic resources (cash) in men's hands and devalued the range of subsistence activities that was traditionally the domain of women. Another example (discussed in Chapter Five) concerns the heightened role of migration within household livelihood strategies. Migration is undertaken more commonly by men than women, leading to the phenomenon of "left-behind" wives and mothers in rural villages. The impact of these processes on the gendered basis of food security is presently unknown; however, it would seem to be an important area for future research.[1]

The fourth key issue for Indian food security in the immediate future pertains to demographic change and its effects on the labour market. Relatively high rates of fertility during previous decades have produced what has been labelled as "demographic dividend" for the economy; a bulge in the nation's working population. From a food security perspective, however, this trend is potentially problematic. The increase in labour supply implicit within the demographic dividend will put downwards pressure on wages, all things being equal. And as discussed in Chapter Five, this will occur in a national labour market context already dominated by informalisation. For new labour market entrants to secure the livelihoods sufficient to ensure their food and nutrition security, Indian economic growth will need to continue at a fast clip, and its composition will need to change in ways that provide proportionate increases in formal-sector, decent employment.

Fifthly, during the next few years the Government of India will need to confront and resolve an important set of social safety net policy reforms. As the core dimensions of this challenge have been outlined in Chapters Six and Seven, there is little benefit in revisiting these issues again here. It should nevertheless be re-emphasised that the outcomes from these debates will crucially shape the manifestations of food security across the country in future years. In this regard, of pivotal significance is the extent to which reforms will be designed to embrace national uniformity, or designed to empower state-level variation and experimentation in program delivery. As discussed in Chapters Six and Seven, there is considerable differentiation among the states in terms of the ways that social safety net programs are implemented. The various state governments bring their own philosophies and agendas to this task, producing quite dissimilar outcomes. The examples of Chhattisgarh and Bihar were used in Chapter Seven to demonstrate the capacity of state governments to be either change-agents or dead hands (respectively) in the reform of policy. The experience of Brazil suggests that decentralisation is a key ingredient for policy architecture and it seems to us that the Government of India would be well advised to heed this insight.

Finally, but certainly not least importantly, is climate change. Although climate change is already being felt in India,[2] its key implications for the nation's food security lie in the future. Understood in terms of social science, it represents an exogenous change-agent which has the potential to dramatically destabilise the existing set of social, economic and environmental relations in the Indian food system. At a global level, climate change is forecast to induce net reductions in total agricultural productive capacity, due mainly to its effects in altering temperature, rainfall and the incidence of extreme weather events in the tropics (Cline, 2007). India is highly exposed to these threats. A recent assessment of the Indo-Gangetic Plain by Ericksen *et al.* (2011) concludes that populations in the area possess high sensitivity to climate change but low coping capacity. The rural population has high dependence on the cropping of wheat and rice as agricultural staples, but with household food insecurity, low incomes and resource pressures greatly inhibit their coping capacities. Climate change forecasts indicate that the region will have a greater number of extreme heat days and a reduced length of growing season, which may induce a "tipping point" that undermines the basis of this agricultural economy (Ericksen *et al.*, 2011: 42–43). As noted above, if the wheat and rice economy of the Indo-Gangetic Basin falters, the implications across the entire country are far and wide.

Bihar is at the epicentre of these vulnerabilities. Its dense rural population, highly skewed landholding pattern and extreme levels of poverty suggest that the adversities of climate change in the state will reap a significant human toll. Changes to rainfall patterns (and, in particular, the forecast tendency for sharper, more extreme rainfall events: Ericksen *et al.*, 2011: Figure 4.1) are expected to make Bihar (already the most flood-prone state in India) even more vulnerable. The past decade has witnessed an accelerating trend of major flooding in Bihar, including the calamitous 2008 Kosi River flood which inundated 340,000 hectares of cropland (United Nations, 2008). Flooding is a major climate change threat not only because of its direct impacts in terms of disrupting agricultural production and causing damage to physical infrastructure, but because it has the effect of magnifying disadvantage across lines of income, gender and age (Thielemans, 2012). As suggested by Douglas (2009: 127): "the most vulnerable groups in terms of food security during floods in South Asia under climate change will be the poor, women and children."

From a livelihoods perspective, the relevance of climate change correlates to its implications for vulnerability, adaptive capacities and resilience among the poor. A case in point is provided in research on environmental and climate-related vulnerability within fisheries communities in Chilika lagoon, Orissa (Iwasaki *et al.*, 2009). This research highlights the connectivity between economic security and climate change. This is the largest coastal lagoon in India, and provides marine stocks that support many thousands of fisherfolk. Exogenous environmental change, however, has severely imperilled the sustainability of these relations. Firstly, deforestation in upstream regions of the Eastern Ghats and related siltation of the lagoon mouth have altered the water composition and caused depletion of the fishery.

Additionally, now, increases in average sea temperatures linked to climate change will change the ecological balance of fish species and the higher risk of cyclones will likely dramatically reshape the coastline and estuary. Taking these factors into account, the authors explore how climate change may execute far-ranging livelihood responses for these communities. In a similar way, research on drought adaptation in Rajasthan emphasises the importance of understanding climate change from a livelihoods perspective (Chatterjee and Chatterjee, 2005). The study revealed that the coping mechanisms that enabled villagers to sustain their livelihoods during dry years in the past were increasingly insufficient to sustain them in present contexts of higher populations, more fragmented land holdings, sparser vegetation and depleted groundwater reserves. In these situations, an evolved set of adaptive capacities are required, linked crucially to the ability to network into state and non-state actors. Thus, capabilities within a population to galvanise networks of support also become essential tools of climate change adaptation. In brief, as the relationship between climate change and food security unfolds in India, research and policy focus needs to be placed on the question of how vulnerable populations are navigating these new threats and how their adaptive strategies reshape the bundle of entitlements they possess which enables them access to food.

Final words

The World Food Summit in 1996 was attended by representatives from 185 countries, and its Declaration was endorsed by 112 governments and 70 international organisations (FAO, 1996). It was the highest-level meeting on food and hunger since the World Food Conference in 1974, convened also by the FAO and attended by 133 nations and 161 NGOs (United Nations, 1975). At the time of the Summit, it was estimated that there were still more than 780 million undernourished people worldwide (FAO, 2010: 9). However, this number was falling both as a proportion of the world's population and in absolute terms and, in the afterglow of the Green Revolution, there were optimistic prospects about its future trajectory. At the Summit, the FAO looked to a future where there were fewer than 680 million hungry people in the world by 2010, and exhorted countries to "do more" so that this number could be reduced further (FAO, 1996).

As it turned out, these expectations were hopelessly incorrect. In 2010–12 there were an estimated 868 million undernourished people across the world – an *increase* of 86 million hungry people on the planet since 1996. Far from hunger being combated, the problem was deteriorating. With hindsight, when the Food Summit delegates gathered, world hunger actually represented the low point of a trend. The global number of undernourished people fell steadily from 1969 (when FAO estimates were first published) to 1996. Thenceforward, it began to rise. The FAO estimated that the number of undernourished people had jumped to 850 million by 2006, and then, with a spike in food prices the following year, exceeded 1 billion in 2009. Even when measured in relative terms, the size of the world's food problem appeared to get bigger. In 1969, undernourished people accounted for 33 per cent of the population of developing countries. Progress associated with the Green Revolution saw this fall to around 17 per cent by 1996. However, in the following decade and a half it budged hardly at all. Except for the temporary spike in 2009 (when it was estimated that 20 per cent of developing countries' populations was undernourished) the incidence of undernourishment in the developing world has remained stubbornly within a range of 15–17 per cent of the population (all data, FAO, 2010: 9). It was as if the triumphal aspirations of the 1996 World Food Summit marked an ironic harbinger of a more blighted future.

India has provided a national-scale laboratory for observing these outcomes. Its dramatic successes in boosting food grains production (from the 1960s to the 1980s) and then the economic reforms that have created unparalleled national wealth (1990s–2000s) might have been expected to have provided the foundations for rapid progress in combating food insecurity. Yet whilst some progress has been made, it has been at a slower rate than what might have been anticipated had international trends prevailed. The reasons for this, put simply, lie in the dilemmas of livelihoods, entitlements and capabilities. The Indian economy has not provided sustainable livelihood prospects for sufficient numbers of the vulnerable segments of its population, the entitlements to food held by these people have not been manifested in substantive rights and, all too often, food-insecure segments of the population have not possessed the capabilities (expressed in financial resources, human capital, social and political influence, etc.) to counter these obstacles.

Notes

1   This is the topic for the PhD thesis currently being researched by one of the present authors (Choithani).
2   For example, by 2010, average maximum and minimum temperatures in Punjab were approximately 1°C higher than the 1971–2000 baseline (Government of Punjab, 2012: 29).

REFERENCES

Agarwal, B. (1984) Rural women and high yielding variety rice technology, *Economic and Political Weekly*, 19, A39–A52.

Agarwal, B. (1990) *Structures of Patriarchy: State, Community and Household in Modernizing Asia*, Zed Books, London.

Agarwal, B. (2003) Gender and land rights revisited: Exploring new prospects via the State, family and market, *Journal of Agrarian Change*, 3 (1 &2): 184–224.

Agarwal, B. (2011) *Twelfth Plan Working Group on Disadvantaged Farmers Including Women*, Final report submitted to the Planning Commission of India, online, http://indiagovernance.gov.in/files/working_group-report-farmers.pdf (accessed 29 January 2013).

Aggarwal, A. and Kumar, N. (2012) Structural change, industrialization and poverty reduction: The case of India, *UNESCAP South-West Asia Discussion Papers*, 1206 (New Delhi).

Aksoy, M.A. and Isik-Dikmelik, A. (2008) Are low food prices pro-poor? Net food buyers and sellers in low-income countries, *World Bank Policy Research Working Paper*, 4642.

Ali, M., and Byerlee, D. (2002) Productivity growth and resource degradation in Pakistan's Punjab: A decomposition analysis, *Economic Development and Cultural Change*, 50 (4): 839–63.

Alkire, S. (2002) *Valuing Freedoms: Sen's Capability Approach and Poverty Reduction*, Oxford University Press, Oxford.

Arnold, F., Parasuraman, S., Arokiasamy, P. and Kothari, M. (2009) *Nutrition in India. National Family Health Survey (NFHS-3), India, 2005–06*, International Institute for Population Sciences, Mumbai and ICF Macro, Calverton, Maryland, USA.

Arora, S. (2012): Farmers' participation in knowledge circulation and the promotion of agroecological methods in South India, *Journal of Sustainable Agriculture*, 36 (2): 207–35.

Arunachalam, R. (2011) The National Rural Livelihood Mission (NRLM) should take charge of dry-land farming now, *Money Life*, October 15, online, www.moneylife.in/article/the-national-rural-livelihood-mission-nrlm-should-take-charge-of-dry-land-farming-now/20608.html (accessed 17 January 2013).

Asian Development Bank (2011) *Global Food Price Inflation and Developing Asia*, ADB, Manila.

Athreya, B.V., Bhavani, R.V., Anuradha, G., Gopinath, R. and Sakthi Velan, A. (2008) *Report on the State of Food Insecurity in Rural India*, M.S. Swaminathan Research Foundation and World Food Programme, Chennai.

Baker, K. and Jewitt, S. (2007) Evaluating 35 years of Green Revolution technology in villages of Bulandshahr district, western UP, North India, *Journal of Development Studies*, 43 (2): 312–39.

Baker, K. (1975) Changes in patterns and practices of wheat farming since the introduction of the high yielding varieties; a study in six villages of the Bulandshahr District Uttar Pradesh Northern India 1965–66 to 1971–71, unpublished PhD Dissertation, School of Oriental and African Studies, London.

Banerjee, A.V. and Duflo, E. (2011) *Poor Economics: A Radical Rethinking of the Way to Fight Global Poverty*, Public Affairs Books, New York.

Banik, D. (2007) *Starvation and India's Democracy*, Routledge, London.

Bapna, S.L. (1990) *PDS and Food Security in India*, Centre for Management of Agriculture, IIM, Ahmedabad.

Barah, B.C. (2005) Dynamic of rice economy in India: Emerging scenario and policy options, *National Bank for Agriculture and Rural Development (NABARD) Occasional Paper*, 47, Mumbai, online, http://www.nabard.org/fileupload/DataBank/OccasionalPapers/OC%2047.pdf (accessed 2 April, 2012).

Bardhan, P.K. (1988) Sex disparity in child survival in Rural India, in Srinivasan, T.N. and Bardhan, P.K. (eds) *Rural poverty in South Asia*, Columbia University Press, New York: 473–80.

Barnerjee, A.V. (1999) Prospects and strategies for land reforms, in Pleskovic, B. and Stiglitz, J. (eds) *Annual World Bank Conference on Development Economics*, World Bank, Washington DC: 253–84.

Barrett, C.B, Reardon, T. and Webb, P. (2001) Nonfarm income diversification and household livelihood strategies in rural Africa: concepts, dynamics, and policy implications, *Food Policy*, 26 (4): 315–31.

Basu, A.M. (1989) Is discrimination in food really necessary for explaining sex differentials in childhood mortality?, *Population Studies*, 43, 193–210.

Basu, A.M. (1993) How pervasive are sex differentials in childhood nutritional levels in South Asia?, *Social Biology*, 40 (1–2): 25–37.

Basu, D. and Basole, A. (2012) The calorie consumption puzzle in India: An empirical investigation, *Political Economy Research Institute (PERI) Working Paper*, 285, University of Massachusetts, Cambridge, online, http://www.peri.umass.edu/fileadmin/pdf/working_papers/working_papers_251–300/WP285.pdf (accessed 14 August 2012).

Basu, K. (2006) Gender and say: A model of household decision-making with endogenous power, *Economic Journal*, 116, 558–80.

Basu, K. (2010) The economics of foodgrain management in India, *Ministry of Finance Working Paper*, 2/1010, online, http://www.finmin.nic.in/WorkingPaper/index.asp (accessed 25 January 2013).

Basu, P. and Scholten, B.A. (2012a) Technological and social dimensions of the Green Revolution: connecting pasts and futures, *International Journal of Agricultural Sustainability*, 10 (2): 109–16.

Basu, P. and Scholten, B.A. (2012b) Crop–livestock systems in rural development: linking India's Green and White Revolutions, *International Journal of Agricultural Sustainability*, 10 (2): 175–91.

Beddington, J., Asaduzzaman, M., Clark, M., Fernandez, A., Guillou, M., Jahn, M., Erda, L., Mamo, T., Van Bo, N., Nobre, C.A., Scholes, R., Sharma, R. and Wakhungu, J. (2012) *Achieving Food Security in the Face of Climate Change: Final Report from the*

Commission on Sustainable Agriculture and Climate Change, CGIAR Research Program on Climate Change, Agriculture and Food Security (CCAFS), Copenhagen, Denmark. Available online at: www.ccafs.cgiar.org/commission.

Behrman, J.R. (1988) Intrahousehold allocation of nutrients in rural India: are boys favored? Do parents exhibit inequality aversion?, *Oxford Economic Papers*, 40: 32–54.

Besley, T. and Burgess, R. (2004) Can labour regulation hinder economic performance? Evidence from India, *The Quarterly Journal of Economics*, 119 (1): 91–134.

Bhaduri, A. (2008) Growth and employment in the era of globalisation: Some lessons from the Indian experience, *ILO Working Paper Series* (not numbered), International Labour Organisation Subregional Office for South Asia, New Delhi.

Bhalla, G.S. and Singh, G. (2009) Economic liberalisation and Indian agriculture: A statewise analysis, *Economic and Political Weekly*, 44 (52): 34–44.

Bhalla, S. (2011) Inclusion and growth in India: Some facts, some conclusions, *LSE Asia Research Centre Working Paper*, 39, London School of Economics, London.

Bhalla, S. (2012) Notes on land, long run food security and the agrarian crisis in India, *IHD Working Paper Series*, 02/2012, Institute for Human Development, New Delhi.

Bhatia, D., Bhatnagar, S.C. and Tominaga, J. (2009) How do manual and e-Governance services compare? Experiences from India, *Information and Communications for Development*, 2009: 67–82.

Bhatnagar, S.C. and Singh, N. (2010) Assessing the impact of e-Government: A study of projects in India, *Information Technologies and International Development*, 6 (2): 109–27.

Bhutta, Z.A., Gupta, I., d'Silva, H., Manandhar, D., Awasthi, S., Hossain, S.M.M. and Salam, M.A. (2004) Maternal and child health: is South Asia ready for change?, *British Medical Journal*, 328: 816–19

Birchfield, L. and Corsi, J. (2010) Between starvation and globalisation: Realising the Right to Food in India, *Michigan Journal of International Law*, 31: 691–764.

Birner, R. and Resnick, D. (2010) The political economy of policies for smallholder agriculture, *World Development*, 38 (10): 1442–52.

Birner, R., Gupta, S. and Sharma, N. (2011) *The Political Economy of Agricultural Policy Reform in India: Fertilizers and Electricity Supply for Groundwater Irrigation*, IFPRI (Research Monograph), Washington DC.

Birner, R., Sekher, M. and Raabe, K. (2012) Reforming the public administration for food security and agricultural development: Insights from an empirical study in Karnataka, *IFPRI Discussion Paper*, 00175, IFPRI, Washington DC.

Birthal P.S., Joshi P.K. and Gulati, A. (2005) Vertical Coordination in High Value Food Commodities: Implications for Smallholders, *Discussion Paper*, 85, Markets Trade and Institutions Division (MTID), IFPRI, Washington DC.

Birthal, P.S., Joshi, P.K. and Narayanan, A.V. (2011) Agricultural diversification in India: Trends, contribution to growth and small farmer participation, unpublished paper, cited in Dev, S.M. (2012) Agriculture–nutrition linkages and policies in India, *Indira Gandhi Institute of Development Research Working Paper*, 2012–006, online, www.igidr.ac.in/pdf/publication/WP-2012–006.pdf (accessed 21 January 2013).

Bolt, R. (2004) Accelerating agriculture and rural development for inclusive growth: Policy developments for Developing Asia, *Asian Development Bank Economics and Research Department Policy Brief*, 29, online, http://216.109.65.20/Documents/EDRC/Policy_Briefs/PB029.pdf (accessed 11 January 2012).

Bosworth, B., Collins, S.M.. and Virmani, A. (2007) Sources of growth in the Indian economy, *National Bureau of Economic Research (NBER) Working Paper Series*, 12901, Cambridge MA, online, http://www.nber.org/papers/w12901.pdf?new_window=1 (accessed 5 December 2011).

Bourguignon, F., Ferreira, F.H.G. and Leite, P.G. (2008) Beyond Oaxaca–Blinder: Accounting for Differences in Household Income Distributions, *Journal of Economic Inequality*, 6: 117–48.

Breman, J. (2010) *Outcast Labour in Asia: Circulation and Informalization of the Workforce at the Bottom of the Economy*, Oxford University Press, Oxford.

Brito, T. and Soares, F.V. (2011) Bolsa Familia and the citizen's basic income: A misstep, *International Policy Centre for Inclusive Growth Working Paper*, 77, United Nations Development Program.

Brulé, R.E. (2012) Gender equity and inheritance reform: Evidence from rural India, unpublished manuscript, online, http://rachelbrule.files.wordpress.com/2012/09/brule_paper1_final.pdf (accessed 25 November, 2012).

Bryceson, D.F. (1999) African rural labour, income diversification and livelihood approaches: A long-term development perspective, *African Studies Centre Working Paper*, 35, Leiden, The Netherlands.

Bussell, J. (2012) *Corruption and Reform in India: Public Services in a Digital Age*, Cambridge University Press, Cambridge.

Carrasco, B. and Mukhopadhyay, H. (2012) Food price escalation in South Asia: A serious and growing concern, *ADB South Asia Working Paper Series*, 10, ADB, Manila.

Central Statistical Organisation, Ministry of Statistics and Programme Implementation, Government of India (2005) *Millennium Development Goals Country Report – India*, Government of India, New Delhi.

Central Statistical Organisation, Ministry of Statistics and Programme Implementation, Government of India (2007) *Millennium Development Goals Country Report – India*, Government of India, New Delhi.

Central Statistical Organisation, Ministry of Statistics and Programme Implementation, Government of India (2009) *Millennium Development Goals Country Report – India*, Government of India, New Delhi.

Central Statistical Organisation, Ministry of Statistics and Programme Implementation, Government of India (2011) *Millennium Development Goals Country Report – India*, Government of India, New Delhi.

Chambers, R. and Conway, G.R. (1992) *Sustainable Rural Livelihoods: Practical Concepts for the 21st Century*, IDS Discussion Paper, 296, Brighton: Institute of Development Studies at the University of Sussex.

Chambers, R. (1984) Beyond the Green Revolution: A selective essay, in Bayliss-Smith, T.B. and Wanmali, S. (eds) *Understanding Green Revolutions: Agrarian Change and Development Planning in South Asia*, Cambridge University Press, Cambridge.

Chambers, R., Pacey, A. and Thrupp, L.A. (eds) (1989) *Farmer First – Farmer Innovation and Agricultural Research*, Intermediate Technology Publications, London.

Chandrasekhar (2012) India's triumph in rice, *The Hindu*, 23 December, online, http://www.thehindu.com/opinion/columns/Chandrasekhar/indias-triumph-in-rice/article4231844.ece (accessed 30 January 2013).

Chandrasekhar, S. (2011) Workers commuting between the rural and urban: Estimates from NSSO data, *Economic and Political Weekly*, 46 (46): 22–25.

Chatterjee, K. and Chatterjee, A. (2005) Case Study 2: India, Community Adaptation to drought in Rajasthan, *IDS Bulletin*, 36 (4): 33–52.

Chatterjee, P (2007) Child malnutrition rises in India despite economic boom, *The Lancet*, 369 (9571), 1417–18.

Chaudhri, D.P. and Dasgupta, A.K. (1985) *Agriculture and the Development Process*, Croom Helm, Washington DC.

Chengappa, P.G. (2012) Secondary agriculture: A driver of growth of primary agriculture in India, *Presidential Address to the 72ⁿᵈ Annual Conference of the Indian Society of Agricultural Economics*, Banaras Hindu University, Varanasi, 17–19 November.

Clark, D.A. (2009) Adaptation, poverty and well-being: Some issues and observations with special reference to the capability approach and Development Studies, *Journal of Human Development and Capabilities*, 10 (1): 21–42.

Cline, W. (2007) *Global Warming and Agriculture*, Center for Global Development and Peterson Institute for International Economics, Washington DC.

Cochrane, W.W. (1958) *Farm Prices: Myth and Reality*, University of Minnesota Press, Minneapolis.

Cohen, M.J., Tirado, C., Aberman, N-L, and Thompson, B. (2008) Impact of Climate Change and Bioenergy on Nutrition, Joint FAO/IFPRI paper prepared for the High Level Conference on Food Security and Climate Change, online, http://www.fao.org/ag/agn/agns/files/HLC2_Food_Safety_Bioenergy_Climate_Change.pdf (accessed 4 May 2012).

Corbridge, S. (2002) Development as freedom: the spaces of Amartya Sen, *Progress in Development Studies*, 2 (3): 183–217.

Cunningham, K. (2009) *Rural and Urban Linkages: Operation Flood's Role in India's Dairy Development, IFPRI Discussion Paper*, IFPRI, Washington DC.

da Silva, J.G., del Grossi, M.E., de França, C.G. (2011) *The Fome Zero (Zero Hunger) Programme: The Brazilian Experience*, Ministry of Agrarian Development, Brasília, Brazil.

Dantwala, M. Visaria, P., Mujumdar, N. and Sundaram, T. (1996) *Dilemmas of Growth: The Indian Experience*, Sage, New Delhi.

Dastagiri, M.B. (2004) Demand and supply projections for livestock products in India, *National Centre for Agricultural Economics and Policy Research Policy Papers*, 21, NCAEPR, New Delhi.

Datta, S. and Sahai, P. (2008b) Possibilities: Livelihood opportunities and potential, in Datta, S. and Sharma, V. (eds) *State of India's Livelihoods: The 4P Report*, Access Development Services, New Delhi: 88–100.

Datta, S. and Sharma, V. (eds) *State of India's Livelihoods: The 4P Report*, Access Development Services, New Delhi.

DBS Group Research (2011): India: Food inflation demand-driven, *DBS Group Research Note*, 24 January, DBS Group, Singapore.

de Haan, A. (1997) Migration as family strategy: rural–urban labour migration in India during the twentieth century, *The History of the Family*, 2 (4): 481–505.

de Haan, A. (2002) Migration and livelihoods in historical perspective: a case study of Bihar, India, *Journal of Development Studies*, 38 (5): 115–42.

de Janvry, A. and Sadoulet, E. (2002) World Poverty and the Role of Agricultural Technology: Direct and Indirect Effects, *Journal of Development Studies*, 38 (4): 1–26.

de Janvry, A. and Sadoulet, E. (2012) Subsistence farming as a safety net for food-price shocks, in Cohen, M.J. and Smale, M. (eds) *Global Food-Price Shocks and Poor People: Themes and Case Studies*, Routledge, London: 18–26.

de Walt, K.M. (1993) Nutrition and the commercialization of agriculture: Ten years later, *Social Science and Medicine*, 36 (2), 1407–16.

Deaton, A. and Drèze, J. (2009) Food and nutrition in India: Facts and interpretation, *Economic and Political Weekly*, 44 (7): 42–65.

Deaton, A. and Drèze, J. (2010a) Nutrition, poverty and calorie fundamentalism: Response to Utsa Patnaik, *Economic and Political Weekly*, 45 (14): 78–81.

Deaton, A. and Drèze, J. (2010b) From calorie fundamentalism to cereal accounting, *Economic and Political Weekly*, 45 (47): 87–92.

Deininger, K., Goyal, A. and Nagarajan, H. (2010) Inheritance law reform and women's access to capital: Evidence from India's Hindu Succession Act, *World Bank Policy Research Working Paper* 5338, World Bank, Washington DC.

Deneulin, S. (2002) Perfectionism, liberalism and paternalism in Sen and Nussbaum's Capability Approach, *Review of Political Economy*, 14 (4): 497–518

Deneulin, S. (2006) *The Capability Approach and the Praxis of Development*, Palgrave Macmillan, Basingstoke, UK.

Department of Food and Public Distribution (2012) *Foodgrains Bulletin*, September, online, http://dfpd.nic.in/fcamin/bulletion/annual-sep2012.pdf (accessed 14 December 2012).

Deshingkar, P. and Farrington, J. (2006) Agricultural livelihoods in an era of economic reform and globalisation, in Deshingkar, P. Farrington, J., Johnson, C. and Start, S. (eds) *Policy Windows and Livelihood Futures: Prospects for Poverty Reduction in Rural India*, Oxford University Press, New Delhi: 74–151.

Deshingkar, P. and Farrington, J. (eds) (2009) *Circular Migration and Multilocal Livelihood Strategies*, Oxford University Press, New Delhi.

Deshingkar, P., and Akter, S. (2009) Migration and human development in India. *Human Development Research Paper 2009/13*, United Nations Development Fund.

Deshingkar, P., and Grimm, S. (2005) Internal migration and development: a global perspective. *IOM migration research paper 19*, Geneva: International Organization for Migration.

Deshingkar, P., and Start, D. (2003) Seasonal migration for livelihoods in India: coping, accumulation and exclusion. *ODI Working paper 220*, London: Overseas Development Institute.

Dev, S.M. and Rao, N.C. (2006) Food processing and contract farming in Andhra Pradesh: A small farmer perspective, in Rajmanohar, T.P. and Kumaravel K.S. (eds) *Contract Farming in India: An Introduction*, Icfai University Press, Hyderabad: 166–93.

Dev, S.M. (2009) *Rising Food Prices and Financial Crisis in India: Impact on Women and Children and Ways for Tackling the Problem*, Paper prepared for UNICEF Social Policy Programme, online, www.unglobalpulse.org/sites/default/files/reports/Rising%20Food%20Prices%20in%20India%20UNICEF%20Final.pdf (accessed 7 July 2011).

Dev, S.M. (2012) Agriculture–nutrition linkages and policies in India, *Indira Gandhi Institute of Development Research Working Paper*, 2012–006, online, www.igidr.ac.in/pdf/publication/WP-2012–006.pdf (accessed 21 January 2013).

do Amaral, W.A.N. and Peduto, A. (2010) Food security: The Brazilian case, *Series on Trade and Food Security Policy Report*, International Institute for Sustainable Development, Winnipeg, Canada.

Douglas, I. (2009) Climate change, flooding and food security in South Asia, *Food Security*, 1: 127–36.

Dressel, B. (ed.) (2012) *The Judicialization of Politics in Asia*, Routledge, London.

Drèze, J. and Khera, R. (2012) Regional patterns of human and child deprivation in India, *Economic and Political Weekly*, 48 (39): 42–49.

Drèze, J. and Sen, A. (2011) Putting growth in its place, *Outlook India*, 14 November, online, http://www.outlookindia.com/article.aspx?278843 (accessed 22 December 2011).

Dutta, P.V. (2007) Accounting for wage inequality in India, *Poverty Research Unit at Sussex (PRUS) Working Paper*, 29, University of Sussex, online, http://www.sussex.ac.uk/Units/PRU/wps/wp29.pdf (accessed 1 March, 2012).

Dutta, P.V., Murgai, R., Ravallion, M. and van de Walle, D. (2012) Does India's employment guarantee scheme guarantee employment?, *Economic and Political Weekly*, 47 (16): 55–64.

Economic Advisory Council (2011) Report of the Expert Committee on National Food Security Bill, online, http://eac.gov.in/reports/rep_NFSB.pdf (accessed 24 October 2011).

Ellis, F. and Briggs, S. (2001) Evolving themes in rural development 1950s–2000s, *Development Policy Review*, 19 (4): 437–48.

Ellis, F. (2000) The determinants of rural livelihood diversification in developing countries, *Journal of Agricultural Economics*, 51 (2): 289–302.

Ericksen P., Thornton, P., Notenbaert, A., Cramer, L., Jones, P. and Herrero, M. (2011) Mapping hotspots of climate change and food insecurity in the global tropics, *CCAFS Report*, 5, CGIAR Research Program on Climate Change, Agriculture and Food Security (CCAFS), Copenhagen, Denmark.

FAO (1996) *World Food Summit Declaration on World Food Security*, FAO, Rome, online, http://www.fao.org/wfs/index_en.htm (accessed 11 November 2011).

FAO (2005) *Voluntary Guidelines to Support the Progressive Realization of the Right to Adequate Food in the Context of National Food Security*, Adopted by the 127th Session of the FAO Council, FAO, Rome, online, http://www.fao.org/docrep/meeting/009/y9825e/y9825e00.HTM (accessed 11 November 2011).

FAO (2006) *Food Security: Policy Brief*, online, ftp://ftp.fao.org/es/ESA/policybriefs/pb_02.pdf (accessed 11 November 2011).

FAO (2007) Understanding the dynamics of food insecurity and vulnerability in Himachal Pradesh, *ESA Working Paper*, 07–22, Agricultural and Development Economics Division, Rome.

FAO (2012) International Scientific Symposium on Food and Nutrition Security Information: From valid measurement to effective decision-making, 18 January, Rome, online, http://www.foodsec.org/fileadmin/user_upload/eufao-fsi4dm/docs/iss-abstract-book.pdf (accessed 6 December 2012).

FAO Statistics Division (2008) *FAO Methodology for the Measurement of Food Deprivation. Updating the MDER*, online, www.fao.org/faostat/foodsecurity/Files/undernourishment_methodology.pdf (accessed 6 December 2012).

FAO-SoFI (various years) *The State of Food Insecurity*, FAO, Rome.

Farlex (2012) Undernourishment, *The Free Medical Dictionary*, online, http://medical-dictionary.thefreedictionary.com/undernourishment (accessed 2 July 2012).

Farrell, D. and Beinhocker, E. (2007) Next big spenders: India's middle class, *Business Week*, 19 May http://www.mckinsey.com/insights/mgi/in_the_news/next_big_spenders_indian_middle_class (accessed 6 January 2013).

Ferreira, F.H.G. and Ravallion, M. (2008) Global poverty and inequality: A review of the evidence, *World Bank Policy Research Working Paper*, 4623.

Fiszbein, A., Schady, N., Ferreira, F.H.G., Grosh, M., Kelleher, N., Olinto, P. and Skoufias, E. (2009) *Conditional Cash Transfers: Reducing Present and Future Poverty*, World Bank, Washington DC.

Freebairn, D. (1995) Did the Green Revolution concentrate incomes? A quantitative study of research reports, *World Development*, 23 (2): 265–79.

Freeman, N.J. and Bartels, F.L. (eds) (2004) *The Future of Foreign Investment in Southeast Asia*, Routledge Curzon, London.

Fuchs, D. and Glaab, K. (2011) Material power and normative conflict in global and local agrifood governance: The lessons of 'Golden Rice' in India, *Food Policy*, 36 (6): 729–35.

Fujita, K. (2010) The Green Revolution and its significance for economic development: The Indian experience and its implications for sub-Saharan Africa, *JICA Research Institute Working Paper* 17, JICA, Tokyo, online, http://jica-ri.jica.go.jp/publication/assets/JICA-RI_WP_No.17_2010.pdf (accessed 6 August 2012).

Gaiha, R., Jha, R. and Kulkarni, V.S. (2010) Demand for nutrients in India, 1993–2004, *Australia South Asia Research Centre Working Paper*, 2010/16, Australian National University, Canberra.

Gangopadhyay, S., Lensink, R. and Yadav, B. (2012) Cash or food security through the Public Distribution System? Evidence from a randomized controlled trial in Delhi, India, unpublished paper, online, http://ssrn.com/abstract=2186408 (accessed 25 January 2013).

Gauri, V. (2009) Public interest litigation in India: Overreaching or underachieving, *World Bank Policy Research Working Paper*, 5109, World Bank, Washington DC.

Geelhoed, D., Agadzi, F., Visser, L., Ablordeppey, E., Asare, K., O'Rourke, P., Van Leeuwen, J.S. and van Roosmalen, J. (2006) Maternal and fetal outcome after severe anemia in pregnancy in rural Ghana, *Acta Obstet Gynecol Scand*, 85 (1): 49–55.

Ghatak, M. and Roy, S. (2007) Land reform and agricultural productivity in India: A review of the evidence, *Oxford Review of Economic Policy*, 23 (2): 251–69.

Ghosh, J. (2008) Two years of NREGA – far from failure, *Transparency Review/ Journal of Transparency Studies*, I (4): 5–7.

Ghosh, J. (2011) Cash transfers as the silver bullet for poverty reduction: A sceptical note, *Economic and Political Weekly*, 46 (21): 67–71.

Gillespie, S. and Kadiyala, S. (2011) *Leveraging Agriculture for Improving Nutrition and Health, 2020*, Conference Brief 20, IFPRI, Washington DC, online, http://2020conference.ifpri.info/publications/briefs/ (accessed 4 March 2011).

Gillespie, S., Harris, J. and Kadiyala, S. (2012) The agriculture–nutrition disconnect in India: What do we know?, *IFPRI Discussion Paper*, 001187, IFPRI, Washington DC, online, http://www.ifpri.org/sites/default/files/publications/ifpridp01187.pdf (accessed 2 September 2012).

Giovannucci, D., Scherr, S., Nierenberg, D., Hebebrand, C., Shapiro, J., Milder, J. and Wheeler, K. (2012) *Food and Agriculture: the Future of Sustainability*. A Strategic Input to the Sustainable Development in the 21st Century (SD21) Project, United Nations Department of Economic and Social Affairs, Division for Sustainable Development, New York, online, http://www.un.org/esa/dsd/dsd_sd21st/21_pdf/agriculture_and_food_the_future_of_sustainability_web.pdf (accessed 19 November 2012).

Glover, D. (2011) Science, Practice and the System of Rice Intensification in Indian agriculture, *Food Policy*, 36 (6): 749–55.

Gokarn, S. (2010) The price of protein, *Reserve Bank of India Monthly Bulletin*, November: 2313–22.

Golait, R. and Pradhan, N.C. (2006) Changing food consumption pattern in rural India: Implication on food and nutrition security, *Indian Journal of Agricultural Economics*, 61 (3): 374–88.

Goldar, B. and Aggarwal, S.C. (2010) Informalization of industrial labour in India: Are labour market rigidities and growing import competition to blame?, Unpublished paper presented at the 6th Annual Conference on Economic Growth and Development, December 16–18, Indian Statistical Institute, New Delhi.

Government of India (2010) *Economic Survey 2009–10*, Ministry of Finance/Oxford University Press, New Delhi.

Government of India (2012) *Agriculture*, online, http://india.gov.in/sectors/agriculture/index.php (accessed 14 November 2012).

Government of India – Ministry of Agriculture (2012) *Agricultural Statistics at a Glance*, online, http://eands.dacnet.nic.in/latest_2006.htm (accessed 25 September 2012).

Government of Punjab (2012) *Punjab State Action Plan for Climate Change*, Department of Science, Technology and Environment and Non-Conventional Energy, Chandigarh.

Gragnolati, M., Shekar, M., Das Gupta, M., Bredenkamp, C. and Lee, Y.-K. (2006) India's undernourished children: a call for reform and action, *Health, Nutrition and Population (HNP) Discussion Paper*, World Bank, Washington DC.

Griffiths, P.L. and Bentley, M.E. (2001) The nutrition transition is underway in India, *Journal of Nutrition*, 131 (10): 2692–700.

Gruère, G. and Sengupta, D. (2011) Bt cotton and farmer suicides in India: An evidence-based assessment, *Journal of Development Studies*, 47 (2):316–37.

Gulati, A., Ganguly, K. and Shreedhar, G. (2011) *Food and Nutritional Security in India: A Stocktaking Exercise*, IFPRI and ICAR, New Delhi.

Gupta, A. (1998) *Postcolonial Developments: Agriculture and the Making of Modern India*, Duke University Press, Durham NC.

Gupta, A. (2011) An evolving science–society contract in India: The search for legitimacy in anticipatory risk governance, *Food Policy*, 36 (6): 736–41.

Gupta, D. (2008) India's Lagging Sector: Indian Agriculture in a Globalising Economy, Australian National University, Australia South Asia Research Centre Working Papers, 2008–05, online, http://www.crawford.anu.edu.au/acde/asarc/pdf/papers/2008/WP2008_05.pdf (accessed 14 March 2012).

Gupta, I., and Mitra, A. (2002) Rural migrants and labour segmentation: micro-level evidence from Delhi slums, *Economic and Political Weekly*, 37 (2): 163–68.

Gupta, M.P. (2010) Tracking the evolution of e-Governance in India, *International Journal of Electronic Government Research*, 6 (1): 46–58.

Haddad, L., Alderman, H., Appleton, S., Song, L. and Yohannes, Y. (2003) Reducing child malnutrition: how far does income growth take us?, *World Bank Economic Review*, 17 (1): 107–31.

Haddad, L., Chandrasekher, C.P. and Swain, B. (2012) Overview. Standing on the threshold: Food justice in India, *IDS Bulletin*, 43 (S1): 1–7.

Hall, A., Bockett, G., Taylor, S., Sivamohan, M., Clark, N. (2001) Why research partnerships really matter: Innovation theory, institutional arrangements and implications for developing new technology for the poor, *World Development*, 29 (5): 783–97.

Hanlon, J., Barrientos, A. and Hulme, D. (2010) *Just Give Money to the Poor: The Development Revolution from the Global South*, Kumarian Press, Sterling, Virginia.

Harriss, B. (1999) The intra-family distribution of hunger in South Asia, in Drèze, J., Sen, A. and Hussain, A. (eds) *The Political Economy of Hunger: Selected Essays*, Clarendon Press, Oxford: 224–97.

Harriss-White, B. (2008) Introduction: India's rainfed agricultural dystopia, *European Journal of Development Research*, 20 (4): 549–61.

Harvey, M., Pilgrim, S. (2010) Competition for land: food and energy, paper prepared for UK Government Foresight Project on Global Food and Farming Futures, UK Government, London.

Hazell, P.B.R. and Haggblade, S. (1990) Rural–urban growth linkages in India, *PR Working Paper*, 430, World Bank, Washington DC.

Hazell, P.B.R. (2009) The Asian Green Revolution, *IFPRI Discussion Paper*, 00911, IFPRI, Washington DC.

Headey, D., Chui, A. and Kadiyala, S. (2011) Agriculture's role in the Indian enigma: Help or hindrance to the undernutrition crisis, *IFPRI Discussion Paper*, 01085, IFPRI, Washington DC, online, http://www.ifpri.org/sites/default/files/publications/ifpridp01085.pdf (accessed 1 October 2012).

Himanshu, A.S. and Sen, A. (2011) Why not a universal food security legislation?, *Economic and Political Weekly*, 46 (12): 38–47.

Hindustan Times (2012) ICDS scam: second report says quality of food supplied low, 1 December, online, http://www.hindustantimes.com/India-news/Mumbai/ICDS-scam-second-report-says-quality-of-food-supplied-low/Article1-966746.aspx (accessed 14 December 2012).

Hossain, M. (1988) *Nature and Impacts of the Green Revolution in Bangladesh*, IFPRI Research Report 65.

IFPRI (2010) Study Finds Bolsa Familia Children Healthier, Doing Better in School, *International Food Policy Research Institute Press Release*, August 10, IFPRI, Washington DC, online, http://www.ifpri.org/pressrelease/study-finds-bolsa-familia-children-healthier-doing-better-school (accessed 15 December 2012).

Imai, K.S., Annim, S.K., Gaiha, R. and Kulkarni, V.S. (2012) Nutrition, activity intensity and wage linkages: Evidence from India, *Discussion Paper Series, Research Institute for Economics and Business Administration, Kobe University, Japan*, DP2012–10, online, http://www.rieb.kobe-u.ac.jp/academic/ra/dp/English/DP2012–10.pdf (accessed 8 October 2012).

Indian Express (2011) Skyrocketing tomato prices compete with onion, *Indian Express*, 17 January, online, http://www.indianexpress.com/news/skyrocketing-tomato-prices-compete-with-onion/738602/ (accessed 10 January 2013).

Indian Express (2012) UP to provide direct subsidy to farmers, *Indian Express*, 10 October, online, http://www.indianexpress.com/news/up-to-provide-direct-subsidy-to-farmers/1014620 (accessed 10 January 2013).

International Foundation for Agricultural Development (IFAD) (2001) *Rural Poverty Report*, Oxford University Press, Rome and Oxford.

International Institute for Population Sciences (IIPS) (1998–1999) National Family Health Survey, Mumbai: Macro International.

International Institute for Population Sciences (IIPS) ORC Macro (2007). National Family Health Survey (NFHS-3), 2005–06: India, Vol. I. Mumbai: IIPS.

International Labour Organisation (1999) *Decent Work: Report of the Director General*, International Labour Organisation, Geneva.

International Labour Organisation (2003) *Global Employment Agenda*, International Labour Organisation, Geneva.

Iwasaki, S., Razafindrabe B.H.N. and Shaw, R. (2009) Fishery livelihoods and adaptation to climate change: a case study of Chilika lagoon, India, *Mitigation Adaptation Strategies Global Change*, 14: 339–55.

Jaishankar, Y. and Drèze, J. (2005) *Supreme Court Orders on the Right to Food: A Primer for Action*, Right to Food Campaign, New Delhi.

Janaiah, A., Achoth, L. and Bantilan, C. (2005) Has the Green Revolution bypassed coarse cereals? The Indian experience, *electronic Journal of Agricultural and Development Economics*, 2 (1): 20–31, ftp://ftp.fao.org/docrep/fao/008/ae691e/ae691e00.pdf

Janbee, S.K. (2000) Debates on food security and Public Distribution System in India, unpublished Master of Political Science dissertation, Department of Political Science, University of Hyderabad, online, http://shodhganga.inflibnet.ac.in/handle/10603/1638 (accessed 6 January 2013).

Jatav, M. (2012) Extent of casualisation in rural non-farm workforce of India: what does recent national sample survey data reveal?, *Journal of Social and Economic Development* (Institute of Social and Economic Change, Bangalore), 14 (1), online, http://www.freepatentsonline.com/article/Journal-Social-Economic-Development/307789019.html (accessed 5 December 2012).

Jewitt, S. and Baker, K. (2007) The Green Revolution re-assessed: Insider perspectives on agrarian change in Bulandshahr District, Western Uttar Pradesh, India, *Geoforum*, 38: 73–89.

Jha, R. and Gaiha, R. (2012) NREGS: Interpreting the official statistics, *Economic and Political Weekly*, 42 (40): 18–22.

Jha, S. and Ramaswami, B. (2010) How can food subsidies work better? Answers from India and the Philippines, *Asian Development Bank Working Paper*, 221, (ADB, Manila).

Jodhka, S. S. (2012) Agrarian changes in the times of (neo-liberal) 'crises': Revisiting attached labour in Haryana, *Economic and Political Weekly (Supplement)*, 48 (26 and 27): 5–13.

Johl, S.S. (2012) Farming in Punjab: Change does not come by wishing alone, *The Tribune* (Chandigarh), October 18, www.tribuneindia.com/2012/20121018/edit.htm#4 (accessed 20 January 2013).

Johnson, S. (1972) *The Green Revolution*, Hamish Hamilton, London.

Jose, S. (2011) Adult undernutrition in India: Is there a huge gender gap?, *Economic and Political Weekly*, 46 (29): 95–102.

Joshi, P.K., Birthal, P.S. and Minot, N. (2006) Sources of agricultural income growth in India: Role of diversification towards high-value crops, *MTID (Markets, Trade and Institutions Division) Discussion Paper*, 98, IFPRI, Washington DC.

Kanbur, R. and Haddad, L. (1994) Are better off households more equal or less equal?, *Oxford Economic Papers*, 46 (3): 445–58.

Kannan, K.P. and Raveendran, G. (2009) Growth sans employment: A quarter century of jobless growth in India's organised manufacturing, *Economic and Political Weekly*, 44 (10): 80–91.

Kapur, D. (2002) The causes and consequences of India's IT Boom, *India Review*, 1 (2): 91–110.

Kapur, D. Mukhopadhyay, P. and Subramanian, A. (2008) The case for direct cash transfers to the poor, *Economic and Political Weekly*, 43 (15): 37–43.

Kelkar, G. (1981) *The Impact of the Green Revolution on Women's Work Participation and Sex Roles*, International Labour Office, Mahabaleshwar, India.

Kelkar, V.L., Rajaraman, I. and Misra, S. (2012) Report of the Committee on Roadmap for Fiscal Consolidation, Government of India, New Delhi, online, http://finmin.nic.in/reports/Kelkar_Committee_Report.pdf (accessed 3 February 2013).

Keshri, K., and Bhagat, R. B. (2012) Temporary and seasonal migration: Regional pattern, characteristics and associated factors, *Economic and Political Weekly*, 47 (4): 81–88.

Kharas, H (2010) The emerging middle class in developing countries, *OECD Development Centre Working Paper*, 285 (OECD, Paris).

Khera, R. (2011a) Trends in diversion of PDS grain, *Economic and Political Weekly*, 46 (21): 106–14.

Khera, R. (2011b) India's Public Distribution System: Utilisation and impact, *Journal of Development Studies*, 47 (7): 1038–60.

Khera, R. (2011d) Revival of the Public Distribution System: Evidence and explanations, *Economic and Political Weekly*, 46 (44 and 45): 36–50.

Khera, R. (2012a) Putting Kerala to work, *The Hindu*, 1 August, online, www.thehindu.com/opinion/lead/article3708704.ece (accessed 10 August 2012).

Khera, R. (2012b) Revival of the PDS and the cash alternative, unpublished presentation to Growth Week Conference, London School of Economics, London, 24–26 September, online, www.theigc.org/sites/default/files/sessions/Reetika%20Khera_IndiaCentral_GW2012.pdf (accessed 28 January 2013).

Khera, R. (ed.) (2011c) *The Battle for Employment Guarantee*, Oxford University Press, Oxford.

Kotwal, A., Murugkar, M. and Ramaswami, B. (2011) PDS forever?, *Economic and Political Weekly*, 46 (21): 71–76.

Krishna, A. (2010) *One Illness Away: Why People Become Poor and How They Escape Poverty*, Oxford University Press, Oxford.

Krishna, A. and Bajpai, D. (2011) Lineal spread and radial dissipation: Experiencing growth in rural India, 1993–2005, *Economic and Political Weekly*, 46 (38): 44–51.

Kumar, N. and Joseph, K.J. (2005) Export of software and business process outsourcing from developing countries: Lessons from the Indian experience, *Asia-Pacific Trade and Investment Review*, 1 (1): 91–110.

Kumar, N. and Joseph, K.J. (2007) *International Competitiveness and Knowledge Based Industries in India*, Oxford University Press, New Delhi.

Kumar, P. and Mittal, S. (2006) Agricultural productivity trends in India: Sustainability issues, *Agricultural Economics Research Review*, 19: 71–88.

Kumar, P., Kumar, A. and Mittal, S. (2004) Total Factor Productivity of crop sector in the Indo-Gangetic Plain of India: Sustainability issues revisited, *Indian Economic Review*, 39 (1): 169–201.

Kumar, S. (1977) Role of the household economy in determining child nutrition at low income levels: A case study in Kerala, *Department of Agricultural Economics, Cornell University Occasional Paper*, 95, Ithaca, US.

Kundu, A. and Chakrabarti, S. (2010) Non-agricultural informal sector in India: Impacts of agrarian conditions, *The Indian Journal of Labour Economics*, 53 (2): 199–224.

Kuznets, S. (1971) *Economic Growth of Nations*, Harvard University Press, Cambridge MA.

Landy, F. (2009) *Feeding India: The Spatial Parameters of Food Grain Policy*, Manohar/ Centre de Sciences Humaines, New Delhi.

Lanjouw, P., and Shariff, A. (2004) Rural nonfarm employment in India, *Economic and Political Weekly*, 39 (4): 4429–46.

Lignani, J de B., Sichieri, R., Burlandy, L. and SallesCosta, R. (2011) Changes in food consumption among the Programa Bolsa Família participant families in Brazil, *Public Health Nutrition*, 14 (5): 785–92.

Lindert, K., Linder, A., Hobbs, J., and de la Brière, B. (2007) The nuts and bolts of Brazil's Bolsa Família program: Implementing Conditional Cash Transfers in a decentralized Context, *Social Protection Discussion Paper*, 709, World Bank, Washington DC.

Lipton, M. and Longhurst, R. (1989) *New Seeds and Poor People*, John Hopkins University Press, Baltimore.

Lipton, M. (1978) Inter-farm, inter-regional and farm–non-farm income distribution: the impact of the new cereal varieties, *World Development* 6 (3): 319–37.

Lipton, M. (2001) Reviving global poverty reduction: What role for genetically modified plants?, *Journal of International Development*, 13: 823–46.

Lipton, M. (2007) Plant breeding and poverty: Can transgenic seeds replicate the 'Green Revolution' as a source of gains for the poor?, *Journal of Development Studies*, 43 (1): 31–62.

Liu, Y. and Barrett, C.B. (2012) Heterogeneous pro-poor targeting in India's Mahatma Gandhi National Rural Employment Guarantee Scheme, *IFPRI Discussion Paper*, 01218, IFPRI, Washington DC.

Lokshin, M., Das Gupta, M., Gragnolati, M. and Ivaschenko, O. (2005) Improving child nutrition? The Integrated Child Development Services in India, *Development and Change*, 36 (4): 613–640.

Madon, S. (2009) *E-Governance for Development: A Focus on Rural India*, Palgrave Macmillan, New York.

Maiti, D. and Sen, K. (2010) The informal sector in South Asia: Introduction, *The Indian Journal of Labour Economics*, 53 (2): 195–98.

Maitra, P. and Rammohan, A. (2011) The link between infant mortality and child nutrition in India: Is there any evidence of a gender bias?, *Journal of the Asia Pacific Economy*, 16(1): 81–110.

Mamgain, R.P. and Diwakar, G.D. (2012) Elimination of identity-based discrimination in food and nutrition programmes in India, *IDS Bulletin*, 43 (S1): 25–31.

Mander, H. (2012) Food from the courts: The Indian experience, *IDS Bulletin*, 43 (S1): 15–24.

McMichael, P. (1997) Rethinking globalization: The agrarian question revisited, *Review of International Political Economy*, 4 (4): 630–62.

MedIndia (2012) Calories in Indian Foods, online, http://www.medindia.net/calories-in-indian-food/Common_Foods/Cereal_grains_and_products.asp (accessed 24 September 2012).

Memedovic, O. and Lapadre, L. (2009) Structural change in the world economy: Main features and trends, *Research and Statistics Branch Working Paper*, 24/2009, United Nations Industrial Development Organization, Vienna.

Mencher, J. (1988) Women's work and poverty: Women's contribution to household maintenance in South India, in Dwyer, D. and Bruce, J. (eds) *A Home Divided: Women and Income in the Third World*, Stanford University Press, Palo Alto: 99–142.

Menon, P., Deolalika, A. and Bhaskar, A. (2009) *India State Hunger Index: Comparison of Hunger Across States*, IFPRI, Welthungerhilfe and UC Riverside, Washington, Bonn and Riverside, online, http://www.ifpri.org/sites/default/files/publications/ishi08.pdf (accessed 7 October 2012).

Ministry of Agriculture, Government of India (2012) Agricultural census data, online, http://www.indiastat.com/agriculture/2/agriculturalarealanduse/152/stats.aspx (accessed 1 July 2012).

Ministry of Finance, Government of India (2010) Economic Survey, Ministry of Finance, New Delhi.

Ministry of Human Resource Development (2013) Midday Meal Scheme, online, http://mdm.nic.in/ (accessed 10 December 2012).

Ministry of Statistics and Programme Implementation (2012) Quick estimates of national income, consumption expenditure, saving and capital formation, 2010–11, *Ministry Release*, 79973, online, http://pib.nic.in/archieve/others/2012/jan/d2012013101.pdf (accessed 31 January 2013).

Minot, N. and Goletti, F. (1998) Rice export liberalization and welfare in Vietnam, *American Journal of Agricultural Economics*, 80 (4): 738–49.

Mishra, S. (2006) Suicide of Farmers in Mahrashtra, Report submitted to the Government of Maharashtra, Indira Gandhi Institute of Development Research, Mumbai.

Mishra, S. and Gopikrishna, S.R. (2010) Nutrient based subsidy (NBS) and support systems for ecological fertilization in Indian agriculture, *Policy Brief : Greenpeace India*, Bangalore.

Mishra, S. (2008) Risks, farmers' suicides and agrarian crisis in India: Is there a way out?, *Indian Journal of Agricultural Economics*, 63 (1): 38–54.

Mollinger, P.P. (2010) The material conditions of a polarised discourse: Clamours and silences in critical analysis of agricultural water use in India, *Journal of Agrarian Change*, 10 (3): 414–36.

Monga, A. (2008) e-Governance in India: Opportunities and challenges, *Journal of Administration and Governance*, 3 (2): 52–61.

Mujumdar, N.A. (2006) Introduction, in Mujumdar, N.A. and Kapila, U. (eds) (2006) *Indian Agriculture in the New Millennium: Changing Perceptions and Development Policy*, Academic Foundation, New Delhi: 21–35.

Mujumdar, N.A. and Kapila, U. (eds) (2006) *Indian Agriculture in the New Millennium: Changing Perceptions and Development Policy*, Academic Foundation, New Delhi.

Murgai, R., Ali, M. and Byerlee, D. (2001) Productivity growth and sustainability in postgreen revolution agriculture: The case of the Indian and Pakistan Punjabs, *World Bank Research Observer*, 16 (2): 199–218.

Murray, C. J. L. and Lopez, A. D. (1997) Mortality by cause for eight regions of the world: Global burden of disease study, *The Lancet*, 349 (9061): 1269–76.

Naagarajan, R. (2010) Social security of informal sector workers in Coimbatore District, Tamil Nadu, *Indian Journal of Labour Economics*, 53 (2): 359–80.

Naandi Foundation (2011) *HUNGaMA: Fighting Hunger and Malnutrition*, Naandi Foundation, Hyderabad, online, http://www.naandi.org/CP/HungamaBKDec11LR.pdf (accessed 29 January 2013).

Naik, A.K. (2009) Informal sector and informal workers in India, unpublished presentation to the IARIW-SAIM Conference on Measuring the Informal Economy in Developing Countries, Kathmandu, online, http://www.iariw.org/papers/2009/5a%20naik.pdf (accessed 5 May 2012).

Nair C.V. (2010) Study of chronic energy deficiency among women labourers in Rajasthan (India), *The Internet Journal of Epidemiology*, 8 (1) (not paginated).

Nair, K.N., Paul, A. and Menon, V. (2007) Livelihood risks and coping strategies: A case study in the agrarian village of Cherumad, Kerala, *Centre for Development Studies Working Paper*, 394.

Nally, D. and Vira, B. (2013) Davos 2013: new vision for agriculture is old news for farmers, *The Guardian*, 25 January, online, www.guardian.co.uk/global-development/poverty-matters/2013/jan/25/davos-2013-vision-agriculture-farmers (accessed 3 February 2013).

Nandy, S., Irving, M., Gordon, D., Subramanian, S.V. and Smith, G.D. (2005) Poverty, child nutrition and morbidity: new evidence from India, *Bulletin of World Health Organization*, 83 (3): 210–16

National Advisory Council (2010) Press Release (untitled), 14 July, online, http://nac.nic.in/press_releases/14_july_2010.pdf (accessed 2 January 2013).

National Commission for Enterprises in the Unorganised Sector (2007) *Report on Conditions of work and Promotion of Livelihoods in the Unorganised Sector*, NCEUS, New Delhi.

National Commission for Enterprises in the Unorganised Sector (2009) *The Challenge of Employment in India: An Informal Economy Perspective: Volume 1 Main Report*, NCEUS, New Delhi.

National Sample Survey Organisation (NSSO) (2006a) Household Ownership Holdings in India, *NSSO Report*, 491, Government of India, New Delhi.

National Sample Survey Organisation (NSSO) (2006b) Income, Expenditure and Productive Assets of Farmer Households, *NSSO Report*, 497, Government of India, New Delhi.

National Sample Survey Organisation (NSSO) (2010) Migration in India, *NSSO Report 533*, Government of India, New Delhi.

National Sample Survey Organisation (NSSO) (2012) Informal Sector and Conditions of Employment in India, *NSSO Report*, 539, Government of India, New Delhi.

Navdanya (2012) Introduction to Navdanya, online, http://www.navdanya.org/about-us (accessed 24 September 2012).

Neilson, J. and Pritchard, B. (2007) The final frontier? The global roll-out of the retail revolution in India, in Burch, D. and Lawrence, G. (eds) *Supermarkets and Agri-Food Supply Chains: Transformations in the Production and Consumption of Foods*, Edward Elgar, Melbourne: 219–42.

Neilson, J. and Pritchard, B. (2009) *Value Chain Struggles: Institutions and Governance in the Plantation Districts of South India*, Blackwell, Oxford.

Nicholson, N.K. (1984) Agricultural modernization, and local institutions in India, *Economic Development and Cultural Change*, 32 (3): 569–92.

Nin, A., Arndt, C., Hertel, T.W. and Preckel, P.V. (2003) Bridging the gap between partial and total factor productivity measures using directional distance functions, *American Journal of Agricultural Economics*, 85 (4): 928–42.

Nussbaum, M.C. (2011) *Creating Capabilities*, The Belknap Press of Harvard University Press, Cambridge MA.

Nussbaum, M.C. (2001) Symposium on Amartya Sen's philosophy: 5 Adaptive preferences and women's options, *Economics and Philosophy*, 17 (1): 67–88.

Nussbaum, M.C. (2003) Capabilities as fundamental entitlements: Sen and social justice, *Feminist Economics*, 9 (2–3): 33–59

OECD (2006) *Promoting Pro-Poor Growth: Agriculture*, OECD, Paris.

Office of the Economic Advisor (2013) Wholesale Price Index data, online, http://eaindustry.nic.in/ (accessed 14 January 2013).

Panagariya, A. (2008) *India: The Emerging Giant*, Oxford University Press, Oxford.

Pande, R. and Yazbeck, A.S. (2003) What's in a country average? Wealth, gender, and regional inequalities in immunization in India, *Social Science and Medicine*, 57: 2075–88

Pandey, S. (2013) Fighting challenges to transform banking in rural India, *Reuters India Insight*, 22 January, online, http://blogs.reuters.com/india/2013/01/22/fighting-challenges-to-transform-banking-in-rural-india/ (accessed 24 January 2013).

Pankaj, A. and Tankha, R. (2010) Empowerment effects of the NREGS on women workers: A study in four states, *Economic and Political Weekly*, 45 (30): 45–55.

Panwar, B. and Punia, D. (1998) Nutrient intake of rural pregnant women of Haryana State, Northern India: Relationship between income and education, *International Journal of Food Sciences and Nutrition*, 49 (5): 391–95.

Papola, T.S. (2008) Employment challenge and strategies in India, *ILO Working Paper Series* (not numbered), International Labour Organisation Subregional Office for South Asia, New Delhi.

Parikh, K. S. (1994) Who gets how much from PDS: How effectively does it reach the poor?, *Sarvekshana*, XVII (3): 1–34

Paris, T., Singh, A., Luis, J., and Hossain, M. (2005) Labour outmigration, livelihood of rice farming households and women left behind: A case study in eastern Uttar Pradesh, *Economic and Political Weekly*, 40 (25): 2522–29.

Parulkar, A. (2012) Starving in India, *Wall Street Journal*, 10, 11, 12 April, online, http://blogs.wsj.com/indiarealtime/2012/04/14/starving-in-india-legislating-food-security/ (accessed 24 May 2012).

Patel, R. (2007) *Stuffed and Starved: The Hidden Battle for the World Food System*, Melville House, New York and London.

Pathak, P. and Singh, A. (2011) Trends in malnutrition among children in India: Growing inequalities across different economic groups, *Social Science and Medicine*, 65: 1–10.

Patnaik, U. (2004) The republic of hunger, *Social Scientist*, 32 (9/10): 9–35.

Patnaik, U. (2007) *The Republic of Hunger and Other Essays*, Three Essays Collective, New Delhi.

Patnaik, U. (2010) A critical look at some propositions on consumption and poverty, *Economic and Political Weekly*, 45 (6): 74–80.

Patnaik, U. (2011) Wages for a quick fix, *The Indian Express*, 21 July.

Paul, S. (2007) A case study of e-Governance initiatives in India, *International Information and Library Review*, 39 (3): 176–84.

Pelletier, D.L. (1998) The potentiating effects of malnutrition on child mortality: Epidemiologic evidence and Policy Implications, *Nutrition Review*, 52 (12): 409–15.

Pelletier, D.L., Frongillo Jr, E.A., Schroeder, D.G. and Habicht J.P. (1994) A methodology for estimating the contribution of malnutrition to child mortality in developing countries, *Journal of Nutrition*, 124 (10-S): 2106S–2122S

Perkins, J.H. (1997) *Geopolitics and the Green Revolution: Wheat, Genes and the Cold War*, Oxford University Press, Oxford Press.

Piesse, J. and Thirtle, C. (2010) Agricultural R&D, technology and productivity, *Philosophical Transactions of the Royal Society*, 365: 3035–47.

Pingali, P.L., Hossain, M. and Gerpacio, R.V. (1997) *Asian Rice Bowls: The Returning Crisis*, CABI, Wallingford.

Pinstrup-Andersen, P. and Hazell, G. (1985) The impacts of the Green Revolution and prospects for the future, *Food Reviews International*, 1 (1): 1–25.

Pinstrup-Andersen, P. (1979) The market price effect and the distribution of economic benefits from new technology, *European Review of Agricultural Economics*, 6 (1): 17–46.

Planning Commission of India (2005) *Performance Evaluation of Targeted Public Distribution System*, Planning Commission, New Delhi.

Planning Commission of India (2008) *Eleventh Five-Year Plan*, Volume II, GOI, New Delhi.

Planning Commission of India (2009) *Report of the Expert Group to review the Methodology for Estimation of Poverty*, GOI, New Delhi.

Planning Commission of India (2012a) Percentage and number of poor, online, http://planningcommission.nic.in/data/datatable/0512/databook_54.pdf (accessed 1 November 2012).

Planning Commission of India (2012b) State specific poverty lines, online, http://planningcommission.nic.in/data/datatable/0512/databook_55.pdf (accessed 1 November 2012).

Planning Commission of India Expert Group (2008) *Development Challenges in Extremist Affected Areas*, Planning Commission, New Delhi.

Poorest Areas Civil Society (PACS) Program (PACS) (2007) *Status of NREGA Implementation 2006–07: Second Monitoring Report of PACS*, Development Alternatives, New Delhi.

Popli, G., Parikh, A. and Palmer-Jones, R. (2005) Are the 2000 poverty estimates for India a myth, artefact or real?, *Economic and Political Weekly*, 40 (43): 4619–24.

Prabakaran, R. and Serma Saravarana Pandian, A. (2006) Private sector partnerships in poultry production and marketing in India: Case Tamil Nadu, in Rajmanohar, T.P. and Kumaravel, K.S. (eds) *Contract Farming in India: An Introduction*, Icfai University Press, Hyderabad: 194–204.

Premchander, S., Chidambaranathan, M. and Prameela, V. (2008)Policy: Pathways to sustainable livelihoods, in Datta, S. and Sharma, V. (eds) *State of India's Livelihoods: The 4P Report*, Access Development Services, New Delhi: 59–79.

Pretty, J., Sutherland, W.J., Ashby, J., Auburn, J., Baulcombe, D., Bell, M. Bentley, J., Bickersteth, S., Brown, K., Burke, J., Campbell, H., Chen, K., Crowley, E., Crute, I., Dobbelaere, D., Edwards-Jones, G., Funes-Monzote, F., Godfray H.C.J., Griffon, M., Gypmantisiri, P., Haddad, L., Halavatau, S., Herren, H., Holderness, M., Izac, A-M., Jones, M., Koohafkan, P., Lal, R., Lang, T., McNeely, J., Mueller, A., Nisbett, N., Noble, A., Pingali, P., Pinto, Y., Rabbinge, R., Ravindranath, N.H., Rola, A., Roling, N., Sage, C., Settle, W., Sha, J.M., Shiming, L., Simons, L., Smith, P., Strzepeck, K., Swaine, H., Terry, E., Tomich, T.P., Toulmin, C., Trigo, E., Twomlow, S., Vis, J.K., Wilson, J., and Pilgrim, S. (2010) The top 100 questions of importance to the future of global agriculture, *International Journal of Agricultural Sustainability*, 8 (4): 219–36.

Pritchard, B. and Connell, J. (2011) Contract farming and the remaking of agrarian landscapes: Insights from South India's 'chilli belt', *Singapore Journal of Tropical Geography*, 32 (2): 236–52.

Pritchard, B., Gracy, C.P. and Godwin, M. (2010) The impacts of supermarket procurement on farming communities in India: Evidence from rural Karnataka, *Development Policy Review*, 28 (4): 435–56.

Pritchard, B., Rammohan, A. and Sekher, M. (2013) Food security as a lagging component of India's human development: A function of interacting entitlement failures, *South Asia: Journal of South Asian Studies*.

PRS Legislative Research (2006) *Summary – Swaminathan Committee on Farmers*, online, http://www.prsindia.org/administrator/uploads/general/1242360972~~final%20summary_pdf.pdf (accessed 7 September 2012).

Puri, R. (2012) Reforming the Public Distribution System: Lessons from Chhattisgarh, *Economic and Political Weekly*, 48 (5): 21–23.

Qadeer, I. and Priyadarshi, A.P. (2005) Nutrition policy: Shifts and logical fallacies, *Economic and Political Weekly*, 40 (5): 358–64.

Ramachandran, P. (2007) Poverty nutrition linkages, *Indian Journal of Medical Research*, 126: 249–61.

Ramakumar, R. (2010) The unsettled debate on Indian poverty, *The Hindu*, 2 January, online, http://beta.thehindu.com/opinion/lead/article74196.ece (accessed 17 March 2012).

Ramalingaswami, V., Jonson, U. and Rohde, J. (1996) Commentary: The Asian Enigma, in UNICEF, *The Progress of Nations*, New York: UNICEF, online, http://www.unicef.org/pon96/nuenigma.htm (accessed 10 September 2012).

Ramamurthy, P. (2011) Rearticulating caste: the global cottonseed commodity chain and the paradox of smallholder capitalism in south India, *Environment and Planning A*, 43: 1035–56.

Ramaswami, B. and Pray, C. (2007) India: confronting the challenge: the potential of genetically modified crops for the poor. In S. Fukuda-Parr (ed.), *The Gene Revolution: GM Crops and Unequal Development*, Earthscan, London: 156–74.

Ramaswami, B., Kotwal, A. and Murugkar, M. (2012) Some issues in the cash vs kind debate, unpublished presentation to Growth Week Conference, London School of Economics, London, 24–26 September, online, http://www.theigc.org/events/growth-week-2012 (accessed 25 January 2013).

Ramchandran, V.K., Rawal, V. and Swaminathan, M. (2010) *Socio-Economic Surveys of Three Villages in Andhra Pradesh*, Tulika Books, New Delhi.

Ramesh, T. and Gracy, C.P. (2006) Contract farming experiences of gherkin cultivators in Tamil Nadu, in Rajmanohar, T.P. and Kumaravel, K.S. (eds) *Contract Farming in India: An Introduction*, Icfai University Press, Hyderabad: 166–93.

Ravallion, M. (2011) A comparative perspective on poverty reduction in Brazil, China, and India, *The World Bank Research Observer*, 26 (1): 71–104.

Ray, R. and Lancaster, G. (2005) On setting the poverty line based on estimated nutrient prices: Condition of socially disadvantaged groups during the reform period, *Economic and Political Weekly*, 40 (1): 46–56.

Reardon, T. and Minten, B. (2011) The quiet revolution in India's food supply chains, *IFPRI Discussion Paper*, 01115, IFPRI, Washington DC.

Reardon, T. (1997) Using evidence of household income diversification to inform study of the rural nonfarm labor market in Africa, *World Development*, 25 (5): 735–48

Reardon, T. Chen, K., Minten, B. and Adriano, L. (2012) *The Quiet Revolution in Staple Food Value Chains: Enter the Dragon, the Elephant and the Tiger*, Asian Development Bank and International Food Policy Research Institute, Manila.

Rickson, R.E. and Burch, D.F. (1996) Contract farming in organizational agriculture: The effects upon farmers and the environment, in Burch, D., Rickson, R.E. and Lawrence, G. (eds) *Globalization and Agri-Food Restructuring: Perspectives from the Australasia Region*, Avebury, Aldershot: 173–202.

Rigg, J. (2006) Land, farming, livelihoods, and poverty: Rethinking the links in the rural South, *World Development*, 34 (1): 180–202.

Right to Food Campaign (2010) *National Food Security Act: An Introductory Primer on the Legal Guarantees Demanded by the Right to Food Campaign*, Capital Printers, New Delhi, online, http://www.righttofoodindia.org/data/national_food_security_act_primer.pdf (accessed 11 November 2012).

Right to Food Campaign (2011a) Right to Food Campaign's take on the Budget 2011–12, *Media Release*, 7 March, Right to Food Campaign Secretariat, E 39, First Floor, Lajpat Nagar III, New Delhi.

Right to Food Campaign (2011b) Right to Food Campaign's critique of the National Advisory Council's Note on the draft National Food Security Bill, *Media Release*, 7 March, Right to Food Campaign Secretariat, E 39, First Floor, Lajpat Nagar III, New Delhi.

Right to Food Campaign (2013) Right to Food Campaign's response to the Standing Committee's report on the National Food Security Bill, 23 January, Right to Food Campaign Secretariat, E 39, First Floor, Lajpat Nagar III, New Delhi,.

Ripley, C. (2012) E-Governance reform of the Public Distribution System in Karnataka, India, unpublished BA (Hons) thesis in Geography, School of Geosciences, University of Sydney.

Robeyn, I. (2005) The Capability Approach: a theoretical survey, *Journal of Human Development*, 6 (1): 93–117.

Rodell, M., Velicogna, I. and Famiglietti, J.S. (2009) Satellite-based estimates of groundwater depletion in India, *Nature*, 460: 999–1003.

Rose, E. (1999) Consumption smoothing and excess female mortality in Rural India, *The Review of Economics and Statistics*, 81 (1): 41–49.

Rosin, C., Stock, P. and Campbell, H. (eds) (2012) *Food Systems Failure: The Global Food Crisis and the Future of Agriculture*, Earthscan, London.

Roy, B.C., Chattopadhyay, G.N. and Tirado, R. (2009) *Subsidising Food Crisis: Synthetic Fertilisers Lead to Poor Soil and Less Food*, Greenpeace India, Bangalore.

Roy, D. and Thorat, A. (2008) Success in high value horticultural export markets for the small farmers: The case of Mahagrapes in India, *World Development*, 36 (10): 1874–90.

Saeed, M., Jugal, B. and Amalesh, B. (2012) e-Governance service delivery: An assessment of community information centre model in India, *Interdisciplinary Journal of Contemporary Research in Business*, 3 (9): 1344–59.

Sainath, P. (2008) NREGA: A fine balance, *The Hindu*, 2 June, online, http://www.hindu.com/2008/06/02/stories/2008060255151100.htm (accessed 14 August 2011).

Sainath, P. (2011) Census findings point to decade of rural distress, *The Hindu*, 25 September, online, http://www.thehindu.com/opinion/columns/sainath/article2484996.ece?homepage=true (accessed 25 October 2011).

Sánchez-Ancochea, D. and Mattei, L. (2011) Bolsa Família, poverty and inequality: Political and economic effects in the short and long run, *Global Social Policy*, 11 (2–3): 299–318.

Sarkar, A. (2012) Sustaining livelihoods in the face of groundwater depletion: A case study of Punjab, India, *Environment, Development and Sustainability*, 14: 183–95.

Saxena, N.C. and Mander, H. (2009) *Ninth Report of the Commissioners: Supreme Court Commissioners CWP 196/2001*, Office of the Commissioners, New Delhi.

Saxena, N.C. (2012) Hunger and malnutrition in India, *IDS Bulletin*, 43 (S1): 8–14.

Schischka, J., Dalziel, P. and Saunders, C. (2008) Applying Sen's Capability Approach to poverty alleviation programs: Two case studies, *Journal of Human Development and Capabilities*, 9 (2): 229–46.

Scoones, I. (2005) Sustainable rural livelihoods: A framework for analysis, *IDS Working Paper*, 72.

Second Administrative Reforms Commission (2008) *Promoting e-Governance: The SMART Way Forward*, Government of India, New Delhi.

Sekhri, S. (2012) Caste-based clustering of land parcels in two villages in Uttar Pradesh, *Economic and Political Weekly*, 47S (26 and 27): 106–09.

Sen, A. (1981) *Poverty and Famines: An Essay on Entitlement and Deprivation*, Oxford University Press, Oxford.

Sen, A.K. (1992) *Inequality Reexamined*, Harvard University, Cambridge MA.

Sen, A.K. (1985) *Commodities and Capabilities*, Elsevier, Amsterdam.

Sen, A.K. (1987) The standard of living: Lecture II, lives and capabilities, in Hawthorn, G. (ed.) *The Standard of Living: The Tanner lectures on Human Values*, Cambridge University Press, Cambridge: 20–38.

Sen, A.K. (1988) The concept of development, in Chenery H. and Srinivasan, T.N. (eds) *Handbook of Development Economics*, Elsevier, Amsterdam: 9–26.

Sen, A.K. (1993) Markets and freedoms: Achievements and limitations of the market mechanism in promoting individual freedoms, *Oxford Economic Papers* 45 (4): 519–41.

Sen, A.K. (1999) *Development as Freedom*, Oxford University Press, Oxford.

Sen, A.K. (2005) Human rights and capabilities, *Journal of Human Development*, 6 (2): 151–66.

Sen, A.K. (2009) *The Idea of Justice*, Harvard University Press, Cambridge MA.

Sen, P. (2005) Of calories and things: Reflections on nutritional norms, poverty lines and consumption behaviour in India, *Economic and Political Weekly*, 40 (43): 4611–18.

Shah, M. (2008) Direct cash transfers: No magic bullet, *Economic & Political Weekly*, 43 (34).

Shanker, D. (2008) e-Governance in rural India, *Proceedings of the 2ⁿᵈ International Conference on Theory and Practice of Electronic Governance*, Cairo, 1–4 December, online, http://www. icegov2008.icegov.org/ (accessed 4 January 2012).

Sharma, A.N. (2006) Flexibility, employment and labour market reforms in India, *Economic and Political Weekly*, 41 (21): 2078–85.

Shetty, P.K. (2004) Socio-ecological impacts of pesticide use in India, *Economic and Political Weekly*, 39 (49): 5261–67.

Shiva, V. (1988) *Staying Alive: Women, Ecology and Survival in India*, Kali for Women, New Delhi.

Shiva, V. (1989) *The Violence of the Green Revolution: Ecological Degradation and Political Conflict in Punjab*, Natraj Publishers, Dehra Dun.

Shiva, V. (1991) The Green Revolution in the Punjab, *The Ecologist*, 21 (2): 57–60.

Sidhu, S.S. (1972) Economics of technical change in wheat production in Punjab (India), PhD Dissertation, University of Minnesota, University Microfilms, Ann Arbor, Michigan.

Singh Gill, S. (1988) Contradictions of Punjab Model of Growth and Search for an Alternative, *Economic and Political Weekly*, 23 (42): 2167–73.

Singh, N. and Kohli, D.S. (2005) The green revolution in Punjab, India: The economics of technological change, *Journal of Punjab Studies* 12 (2): 285–306.

Singh, R.B., Kumar, P. and Woodhead, T. (2002) *Smallholder Farmers in India: Food Security and Agricultural Policy*, FAO Regional Office for Asia and Pacific, Bangkok.

Singh, S. and Singla, N. (2010) Fresh food retail chains in India: Organisation and impacts, *CMA (Centre for Management in Agriculture) Publication*, 238, Indian Institute of Management Ahmedabad.

Singh, S. (2002) Contracting out solutions: Political economy of contract farming in the Indian Punjab, *World Development*, 30 (9): 1261–638.

Singh, S. (2005) *Contract Farming for Agricultural Development Review of Theory and Practice with Special Reference to India*, CENTAD, New Delhi.

Singh, S. (2006) Corporate farming: Is it a 'must' for agricultural development?, *Working Paper*, 2011/11/06, Indian Institute of Management, Ahmedabad.

Singh, S. (2007) Agro-processing industry and agricultural development: New vistas in Indian agribusiness, in Ballabh, V. (ed.) *Institutional Alternatives and Governance of Agriculture*, Academic Foundation, New Delhi: 259–294.

Singh, S. (2008) Marketing channels and their implications for smallholder farmers in India, in McCullough, E.B., Pingali, P.L. and Stamoulis, K.G. (eds) *The Transformation of Agri-Food Systems: Globalization, Supply Chains and Smallholder Farmers*, FAO and Earthscan, London: 279–310.

Sinha, A. (2007) Farm sector, non-farm employment and rural livelihood: A study, *Social Change*, 37 (1): 50–76.

Skoufias, E., Tiwari, S. and Zaman, H. (2011) Can we rely on cash transfers to protect dietary diversity during food crises?, *World Bank Policy Research Working Paper*, 5548.

Smith, L.M. and Seward, C. (2009) The relational ontology of Amartya Sen's Capability Approach: Incorporating social and individual causes, *Journal of Human Development and Capabilities*, 10 (2): 213–35

Soares, F.B., Ribas, R.P. and Osório, G. (2010) Evaluating the impact of Brazil's Bolsa Familia: Cash transfer programs in comparative perspective, *Latin American Research Review*, 45 (2): 173–90.

Soares, F.V. (2011) Brazil's Bolsa Familia: A review, *Economic and Political Weekly*, 46 (21): 55–60.

Solesbury, W. (2003) Sustainable livelihoods: A case study of the evolution of DFID policy, *Overseas Development Institute Working Paper* 217, London.

Special Rapporteur on the Right to Food (2006) Mission to India. Report to the United Nations Economic and Social Council, Commission on Human Rights, Sixty-Second Session, Item 10, Document E/CN.4/2006/44/Add.2, online, http://www.righttofood.org/new/PDF/India%20PDF.pdf (accessed 20 July 2012).

Special Rapporteur on the Right to Food (2009) *Mission to Brazil*, Report to the United Nations General Assembly Human Rights Council, Thirteenth Session, Item 3, Document A/HRC/13/33/Add.6.

Srinivas, G. (2011) Conundrums in Public Distribution System in India: An assessment by states and social groups, *Indian Development Review*, 9 (2): 301–10.

Sriram, M.S. (2008) Agrarian distress and rural credit: Peeling the onion, in Datta, S. and Sharma, V. (eds) *State of India's Livelihoods: The 4P Report*, Access Development Services, New Delhi: 171–88.

Srivastava, N. and Srivastava, R. (2010) Women, work, and employment outcomes in rural India. *Economic and Political Weekly*, 45 (28): 49–63.

Standing Committee on Finance (2011) *National Identification Development Authority of India Bill 2010*, 42nd Report, Lok Sabha Secretariat, New Delhi.

Standing Committee on Food, Consumer Affairs and Public Distribution (2013) *The National Food Security Bill 2011*, 27th Report, Lok Sabha Secretariat, New Delhi.

Stark, O. (1991) *The Migration of Labour*, Basil Blackwell, Oxford.

Subbarao, D. (2010) Financial crisis: some old questions and maybe some new answers, Tenth C.D. Deshmukh Memorial Lecture delivered at *Council for Social Development*, Southern Regional Centre, Hyderabad, 5 August 2010, online, http://www.rbi.org.in/scripts/BS_SpeechesView.aspx?Id=515 (accessed 18 January 2013).

Sukhatme, P.V. (1965) *Feeding India's Growing Millions*, Asia Publishing House, London.

Supreme Court Commissioners (2011) About us, online, http://sccommissioners.org/About/thecommissioners.html (accessed 19 January 2013).

Svedberg, P. (2012) Reforming or replacing the Public Distribution System with cash transfers?, *Economic and Political Weekly*, 47 (7): 53–62.

Swain, B. and Kumaran, M. (2012) Who do ICDS and PDS exclude and what can be done to change this?, *IDS Bulletin*, 43 (S1): 32–39.

Swaminathan, M.S. (2000a) Freedom from hunger, *The Hindu*, 15 October (accessed online).

Swaminathan, M.S. (2000b) *Weakening Welfare: The Public Distribution of Food in India*, Left Word, New Delhi.

Swaminathan, M.S., Wilson, B., Sinha, S., Shatrugna, V., Roy, A., Mody, G., Drèze, J., Agarwal, B., Patnaik, A., Bagchi, A.K. and 198 others (2013) Cash transfers and UID, *Economic and Political Weekly*, 48 (1): 4–5.

Takagi, M. (2011) Implementation of the Zero Hunger Program in 2003, in da Silva, J.G., del Grossi, M.E. and de França, C.G. (eds), *The Fome Zero (Zero Hunger) Programme: The Brazilian Experience*, Ministry of Agrarian Development, Brasília, Brazil: 55–85.

Tandon, H. (2005) e-Governance: An Indian perspective, Policy and Society, 24 (3): 142–69.

Tankha, A., Srinivasan, G. and Arunachalam, R.S. (2008) Public systems: Major central government and donor-supported programmes for livelihood promotion, in Datta, S. and Sharma, V. (eds) *State of India's Livelihoods: The 4P Report*, Access Development Services, New Delhi: 103–30.

Tarozzi, A. and Mahajan A. (2007) Child nutrition in India in the nineties, *Economic Development and Cultural Change*, 55 (3): 441–86.

Task Force on Direct Transfer of Subsidies (2011) *Interim Report of Task Force on Direct Transfer of Subsidies for Kerosene, LPG and Fertiliser*, Government of India, New Delhi.

Thielemans, R. (2012) Not just waiting for the next floodunpublished BA (Hons) thesis in Geography, School of Geosciences, University of Sydney.

Times of India (2011) Food security bill cleared by Cabinet, 19 December, online, http://articles.timesofindia.indiatimes.com/2011–12–19/india/30533923_1_cabinet-meeting-national-food-security-bill-urban-population (accessed 22 December 2011).

Times of India (2012) Maharashtra food scam: Private companies eat up Rs 1,000cr meant for poor, 3 November, online, http://timesofindia.indiatimes.com/india/Maharashtra-food-scam-Private-companies-eat-up-Rs-1000cr-meant-for-poor/articleshow/17068958.cms (accessed 7 November 2012).

Tomkins, A. and Watson, F. (1989) Malnutrition and infection: A Review, Nutrition Policy Discussion Paper no. 5, United Nations Administrative Committee on Coordination/Subcommittee on Nutrition, New York.

Tripathy, T. (2009) Changing pattern of rural livelihood opportunities and constraints: A case of Orissa, India, *The IUP Journal of Applied Economics*, 8 (3 and 4): 116–39.

Udry, C. (1997) Recent advances in empirical microeconomic research in poor countries: an annotated bibliography, *Journal of Economic Education*, 28 (1): 58–75.

United Nations (1975) *Report of the World Food Conference*, UN, New York

United Nations (2008) *Response to 2008 Bihar Floods*, online, www.un.org.in/_layouts/CMS/undmt_biharfloods2008.aspx (accessed 17 January 2012).

United Nations (2010) *The Millennium Development Goals Report*, UN, New York.

United Nations Children's Fund (UNICEF) (2012) Nutrition special – comprehensive nutrition survey in Maharashtra, online, http://www.unicef.org/india/reallives_7973.htm (accessed 29 January 2013).

United Nations Committee on Economic, Social and Cultural rights (UNCESCR) (1999) Substantive Issues Arising in the Implementation of the International Covenant on Economic, Social and Cultural Rights: General Comment 12, Twentieth session, The right to adequate food (art. 11), online, http://daccess-dds-ny.un.org/doc/UNDOC/GEN/G99/420/12/PDF/G9942012.pdf (accessed 15 March 2012).

United Nations Development Program (UNDP) (2010) Origins of the Human Development Approach, online, http://hdr.undp.org/en/humandev/origins/ (accessed 17

March 2011).

United Nations Development Program (UNDP) (2012) *Towards a Human Rights Based Approach to Food Security: A Self-Assessment Tool to Achieve Balanced Plant Regimes*, UNDP, Geneva.

United Nations Educational, Scientific and Cultural Organisation (UNESCO) (2010) *Global Education Digest 2010*, UNESCO Institute of Statistics, Quebec.

United Nations Population Program (2012) Population by Age Groups and Sex, online, http://esa.un.org/wpp/population-pyramids/population-pyramids_absolute.htm (accessed 18 September 2012).

United States Department of Agriculture (2012) India: Grain and feed, *USDA-GAIN Report*, IN2026.

Uphoff, N. (2002) *Agroecological Innovations: Increasing Food Production with Participatory Development*, Earthscan, London.

Uphoff, N. (2007) Agroecological alternatives: capitalising on existing genetic potentials, *Journal of Development Studies*, 43 (1): 218–36.

Vaidyanathan, A. (2006) Depletion of groundwater: some issues, in Mujumdar, N.A. and Kapila, U. (eds) *Indian Agriculture in the New Millennium: Changing Perceptions and Development Policy*, Academic Foundation, New Delhi: 61–74.

Venugopal, K.R. (2010) National food security bill 2010, *Social Change*, 40 (4): 577–600.

Vijay, R. (2012) Structural retrogression and rise of 'new landlords' in Indian agriculture: An empirical exercise, *Economic and Political Weekly*, 48 (5): 37–45.

von Braun, J. (2008) *Food and Financial Crises: Implications for Agriculture and the Poor*, IFPRI, Washington DC, online, http://www.ifpri.org/sites/default/files/publications/pr20.pdf (accessed 1 October 2012).

von Braun, J., and Kennedy, E. (1986) Commercialization of subsistence agriculture: Income and nutritional effects in developing countries, *Working Papers on Commercialization of Agriculture and Nutrition*, 1, IFPRI, Washington DC.

von Braun, J., Achter, A., Asenso-Okyere, K. Fan, S., Gulati, A., Hoddinott, J., Pandya-Lorch, R., Rosengrant, M.W., Ruel, M., Torero, M., van Rheenan, T. and von Grabmer, K. (2008) High food prices: The what, who, and how of proposed policy actions, *IFPRI Policy Brief* (not numbered), May, 2008.

von Grebmer, K., Fritschel, H., Nestorova, B., Olofinbiyi, T., Pandya-Lorch, R. and Yohannes, Y. (2008) The challenge of hunger: The 2008 Global Hunger Index, *IFPRI Issue Briefs*, 54.

Vorley, B., Kotula, L. and Chan, M-K. (2012) *Tipping the Balance: Policies to Shape Agricultural Investments and Markets in Favour of Small-scale Farmers*, IIED and Oxfam, London.

Walton, M. (2009) The political economy of India's malnutrition puzzle, *IDS Bulletin* 40 (4): 16–24.

Weiss, T. (2010) The accelerating biophysical contradictions of industrial capitalist agriculture, *Journal of Agrarian Change*, 10 (3): 315–41.

Whitfield, L. (2012) How countries become rich and reduce poverty: A review of heterodox explanations of economic development, *Development Policy Review*, 30 (3): 239–60.

WHO (2008) *Worldwide Prevalence of Anaemia, 1993 to 2005*, Geneva: WHO.

Wolff, J. and de-Shalit, A. (2007) *Disadvantage*, Oxford University Press, New York.

World Bank (2004) *Inequality and Economic Development in Brazil*, World Bank, Washington DC.

World Bank (2008a) *World Development Report: Agriculture for Development*, World Bank, Washington DC.

World Bank (2008b) *Double Jeopardy: Responding to High Food and Fuel Prices*, Paper for G8 Summit, Hokkaido, June.

World Bank (2010) Brazil's Landmark Bolsa Família Program Receives US$200 Million Loan, *World Bank Press Release*, 2011/093/LAC, September 17, online, http://web. worldbank.org/WBSITE/EXTERNAL/NEWS/0,,contentMDK:22706087~pagePK: 64257043~piPK:437376~theSitePK:4607,00.html, (accessed 11 November 2012).

World Bank (2010) PovcalNet: the on-line tool for poverty measurement developed by the Development Research Group of the World Bank, online, http://web.worldbank.org/ WBSITE/EXTERNAL/EXTDEC/EXTRESEARCH/EXTPROGRAMS/ EXTPOVRES/EXTPOVCALNET/0,,contentMDK:22716987~pagePK:64168427~ piPK:64168435~theSitePK:5280443~isCURL:Y,00.html (accessed 22 October 2011).

World Bank (2012) GDP growth, online, http://data.worldbank.org/indicator/NY.GDP. MKTP.KD.ZG?cid=GPD_30 (accessed 22 December 2012).

World Economic Forum (2013) *Achieving the New Vision for Agriculture: New Models for Action*, online, www3.weforum.org/docs/IP/2013/NVA/WEF_IP_NVA_New_Models_for_Action_report.pdf (accessed 2 February 2013).

World Food Programme and Institute for Human Development (2008a) *Food Security Atlas of Rural Bihar*, WFP and IHD, New Delhi.

World Food Programme and Institute for Human Development (2008b) *Food Security Atlas of Rural Chhattisgarh*, WFP and IHD, New Delhi.

World Food Programme and Institute for Human Development (2008c) *Food Security Atlas of Rural Jharkhand*, WFP and IHD, New Delhi.

World Food Programme and Institute for Human Development (2008d) *Food Security Atlas of Rural Orissa*, WFP and IHD, New Delhi.

World Food Programme and Institute for Human Development (2008e) *Food Security Atlas of Rural Madhya Pradesh*, WFP and IHD, New Delhi.

World Health Organization (2001) *Iron Deficiency Anaemia: Assessment, Prevention and Control – A Guide for Programme Managers*, WHO, Geneva.

World Trade Organisation (WTO) (2005) Why trade matters for improving food security, DG Speeches, High-level Roundtable on Agricultural Trade Reform and Food Security, Rome, 13 April, online, http://www.wto.org/english/news_e/spsp_e/spsp37_e.htm (accessed 10 April 2010).

Zezza A., Davis, B., Azzarri, C., Covarrubias, K., Tasciotti, L. and Anríquez, G. (2008) The impact of rising food prices on the poor. *ESA Working Paper 08–07*, FAO, Rome, online, ftp://ftp.fao.org/docrep/ fao/011/aj284e/aj284e00.pdf (accessed 11 July 2012).

Zezza A., Winters, P., Davis, B., Carletto, G., Covarrubias, K., Tasciotti, L. and Quiñones, E. (2011) Rural household access to assets and markets: A cross-country comparison, *European Journal of Development Research*, 23: 569–97.

Zheng, Y. (2009) Different spaces for e-development: What can we learn from the capability approach?, *Information Technology for Development*, 15 (2): 66–82

Ziegler, J. (2012) Right to Food, online, www.righttofood.org/new/html/WhatRighttofood.html (accessed 20 February 2012).

Court cases

People's Union for Civil Liberties vs. Union of India and Others (PUCL), *Writ Petition (Civil) No. 196 of 2001 (India)*.

Raghbir Singh Serhrawat v. State of Haryana and Others, *Civil Appeal Nos 10080–81 of 2011*, *Supreme Court Reports: 1113–40*.

INDEX